TRUMP'S WHITE RIGHT

JOHN M. DELEHANTY

Isbn-13: 978-1719175494

Isbn-10: 1719175497

Libraryof Congress Control Number: TX 8-576-063

This book is dedicated to my wife Michele who has been my Muse for the past 50 years.

CONTENTS

PREFACE — 10

1 TRUMP TOWER ESCALATOR — 15

2 TRUMP/PUTIN LOVE AFFAIR — 17

3 TRUMP CAMPAIGN, "A THREE RING CIRCUS" — 18

School ground potty mouth! — 18

Jerry! Jerry! Jerry! Tabloid politics — 21

The Artist of the Deal or Just "Bullshit Artist" — 25

"Blood coming out her what ever" and Sexism — 29

4 WHEN REPUBLICANS LOOK IN THE MIRROR THEY SEE "ARCHIE BUNKER!" — 31

Trump's "Chief Strategist" Steve Bannon and the "Alt-Right" — 33

Trump and White Supremacists — 35

"The Wall", "The Ban" and Racism — 38

"I could shoot somebody on 5th avenue" — 40

Trump's Evangelicals ("Is Trump Born Again?") — 44

Trump's White Male Billionaires — 46

Trump Makes Other Countries Great — 48

5 TRUMP'S "REPUBLICAN CIVIL WAR"   51

   Speaker of the House "So What!"   52

   Anti-establishment President? Look Out Republicans! 55

   Republican's Fear of Being Linked to Trump   56

   Anti-Trump Republican Leaders   57

   Death to the Republican Party?   61

6 CAMPAIGN VIOLENCE   66

7 TRUMP WINS REPUBLICAN NOMINATION   74

8 TRUMP: "THE PUSSY GRABBING PREDATOR"   75

9 ANTI-TRUMP REPUBLICANS   81

   World Leaders are "Shocked!"   100

10 VICE PRESIDENT MIKE PENCE?

   (ALT-RIGHT LOVE HIM)   103

11 THE REPUBLICAN CONVENTION   108

12 THE DEMOCRATIC CONVENTION   117

13 REPUBLICANS CONCEDE "TRUMP NOT SO BAD,"

   AFTER THE SHOTGUN WEDDING!   121

14 TRUMP'S GENERAL ELECTION RALLIES

   ["WINNING" THE "RED BLUE" GAME]   124

   Trump Said "What" (Trump's Election Team)   126

   Trump's Charitable Giving "Right"   130

Trump's Flip-Flops 132

"Bullshit Artist" 135

15 HILLARY VS TRUMP IN THE GENERAL ELECTION 143

Hillary's Endorsements and Trump's Rejections 149

"Basket of Deplorables" and "Alt-Right" 158

Trump self-funding his campaign "HA HA" 167

Trump's Campaign Team Shake-ups 169

The General Election Debates 173

16 VOTER TURN OUT WILL DETERMINE THE RACE 178

Why a Shortage of Trump Black Voters? 182

Obama and the 2016 Election 187

Twitter Bots and Trolls 193

17 PUTIN TO TRUMP: "WE FOUND THE EMAILS

YOU REQUESTED AND MORE" 197

FBI and Clinton's emails 203

18 "PANIC IS SETTING IN!" TRUMP CATCHING UP

IN THE POLLS 209

19 "OH GOD" TRUMP WINS PRESIDENCY! 218

"Not My President" Protests 221

Trump won the electoral vote "bigly" but Clinton

Won the Popular vote "bigly" 227

Why pollsters got it wrong 228

Electoral College? Mobocracy?   236

Trump Said, the Popular Vote was Wrong (No Mandate)   238

20 TRUMP SHOULDN'T BE PRESIDENT

"INTERVENTION NEEDED"   243

Trump Holds Up In His Tower after Surprised Win   244

Racism Escalates So Does "The Wall"   248

Trump Perfecting his Con-Artist Skills   255

One President at a Time! "Why?"   258

Trump Still Loves Putin   259

21 TRUMP'S CABINET "ADDING ALLIGATORS TO THE

SWAMP"   262

Trump's Cabinet "Is The Top 1%"   271

Trump's White House Advisors, Staff and

Ambassadors   273

22 TRUMP'S ADMINISTRATION "BULL IN A CHINA

CLOSET"   279

Kellyanne Conway said, "Don't Believe What's Coming

Out Of His Mouth"   284

"No Press Allowed I'm On the Toilet Tweeting"   286

Trump's War on the Intelligence Agencies   290

23 "CONFLICT OF INTEREST" "ANTI-NEPOTISM"
"SHOW ME THE LAW"   294

The Fake News Continues "Spicer Stressed Out"   300

24 RUSSIAN ELECTION INVOLVEMENT   304

The Dossier and "The Golden Shower Gate"   309

25 THE INAUGURATION   311

"Pussy Hats" Record Protest at D.C.

Women's March (up to 1,000,000)   317

"Ego Maniac" Thank You Tours   320

26 TRUMP AND THE REPUBLICAN'S PRIORITIES   323

Repealing "Obamacare" and Creating "Richcare"   323

The Anti-environment President   328

Republicans Stole Supreme Court Seat   330

27 REVENGE OF THE DEMOCRATS   333

28 NOTES   340

ABOUT THIS BOOK

My book contains information from 392 News articles from major news organizations. The articles are paraphrased for "TO THE POINT" incredible historical facts, from the time Trump came down the escalator at Trump Towers to launch his campaign, to his inauguration, all chapter subjects are in chronological order and referenced to be researched further. No ramblings of descriptive adjectives. No side stories to fill up an article "just the facts".

PREFACE

WHAT POLITICAL LEADERS SAY ABOUT DONALD TRUMP:

BERNIE SANDERS: "Donald Trump is a pathological liar" (12-20-15)

JIMMY CARTER: Trump's campaign has "tapped a waiting reservoir of racism" contrary to "basic human rights." (05-24-16)

BARACK OBAMA: "Donald Trump unfit and woefully unprepared to be president" (08-02-16)

HILLARY CLINTON: "half" of Donald Trump's supporters fit into a "basket of deplorables" (09-10-16)

HILLARY CLINTON: "Donald Trump would be Putin's puppet" (10-20-16)

GEORGE W. BUSH: "Donald Trump's inaugural speech was some weird shit." (01-21-17)

NOAM CHOMSKY: "Republican Party is the most dangerous organization in the world's history" (Book TV CSPAN II 4-24-17)

Who would ever believe the USA would chose "ARCHIE BUNKER" for President?

Trump knows one thing for sure, he is going to make a lot more money selling his name and his products.

The only positive result of electing Donald Trump was exposing what most (not all) Republicans stand for. The conservative party wants to "conserve": racism, sexism, xenophobia, prejudice, bigotry and perpetuate white male dominance. What country in the world would have the same values as the Republicans?

The Electoral College was suppose to protect the Nation from Mobocracy. "IT FAILED".

To be sure politicians from both controlling parties want to keep their jobs (pays pretty good). They manipulate their constituency with their chosen issues to get their votes. A football game "red team" vs "blue team".

There is no doubt the Democratic Party has proven it's definitely more progressive then the Republicans.

The Democratic Party has several "FIRSTS". First Catholic President (John F. Kennedy), first women Vice Presidential candidate (Geraldine Ferraro), first Jewish vice Presidential candidate (Joseph Lieberman), first black President with a Muslim middle name (Barack "Hussein" Obama) and Eric Holder Jr. first African American U.S. Attorney General.

The "Party of Reagan" has evolved into the "Party of Trump" taking the country "backwards".

The Republican Party has proven by their constituency (White supremacist, NRA, Tea Party, and the duck hunter clan), that they want to go back to the good old days and "MAKE AMERICA GREAT AGAIN".

The Washington Post asked Trump a question: "how are people going to know America is great again"? Trump said "because I'm going to tell them".

To further their personal gains, these prejudicial issues were used by white males of corporate America, some Evangelical Churches and some radio/TV talk shows.

It isn't "FAKE NEWS" that 24 Million People will be taken off Medicaid, "if" Obamacare (ACA) is repealed.

It isn't "FAKE NEWS" that Rich Americans and corporations will be getting back billions of dollars used to pay for Obamacare.

Thanks to Obamacare we are closer then ever to having a "SINGLE PAYER SYSTEM" that's paid for by the "TOP 1%".

Medicare's administration costs are 2%, medical insurance companies is 12-18%. It is estimated tax payers could save 600 "Billion" dollars by cutting out the middle man!

With the help of Republicans the rich have hoarded trillions of dollars over the past several decades so it's time to pay their fair share. The trickle down theory has been tried for over 60 years and it doesn't work. All the money trickled to other countries and to the rich.

We have a President sitting on the toilet in the wee hours of the morning tweeting Presidential statements in 140 characters or less!

Steve Bannon was the President's "Chief Strategist". Bannon was the chief editor of Brietbart an "alt-right" news organization.

It takes two things to make a political lie work: A powerful person or institution to utter it, and another set of powerful institutions to amplify it (FAKE NEWS).

. er the 2010 census 33% of the U.S. population (about 102 million) were here since the 1965 civil rights movement. That means there are a lot of people living today with prejudices handed down from their parents.

The last racist whites in the U.S. are holdouts wrapped in the Confederate flag.

All men and women will be free in our country when the poison of the "prejudice generation" is drained out of our children's children!

WHAT ABOUT TRUMP ?

Narcissistic Personality Disorder

From the Diagnostic And Statistical Manual Of Mental Disorders (American Psychiatric Association). If a person has five or more of the following they have narcissistic personality disorder.

1. Has a grandiose sense of self (e.g., exaggerates achievements and talents, expects to be recognize as a superior without commensurate achievements)

2. Is preoccupied with fantasies of unlimited success, power brilliance, beauty, or ideal love.

3. Believes he or she is special " and unique and can only be understood by, or should associate with , other special or high-status people(or institutions)

4. Requires excessive admiration

5. Has a sense of entitlement, i.e., unreasonable

expectations of especially favorable treatment or automatically compliance with his or her expectations.

6. Is interpersonally exploitative, i.e., takes advantage of others to achieve his or her own ends.

7. Lacks empathy: is unwilling to recognize or identify with the feelings and needs of others.

8. Is often envious of others or believes that others are envious of him or her.

9. Shows arrogant, haughty behaviors or attitudes.

NEED I SAY ANYMORE!

1   TRUMP TOWER ESCALATOR

06-17-15

The casting company Extra Mile offered actors $50 to attend the announcement of "Donald Trump for President" at Trump Towers. The actors were to pose as Trump supporters and cheer him as he came down the escalator.

Extra Mile said "We are looking to cast people for the event to wear T-shirts and carry signs and help cheer him in support of his announcement .We understand this is not a traditional 'background job' but we believe acting comes in all forms and this is inclusive of that school of thought"

Gold Finger

He's the man, the man with the Midas touch

A spider's touch

Such a cold finger

Beckons you to enter his web of sin

But don't go in

Golden words he will pour in your ear

But his lies can't disguise what you fear

For a golden girl knows when he's kissed her

It's the kiss of death from

Mister Goldfinger

Pretty girl beware of this heart of gold

This heart is cold

Golden words he will pour in your ear

But his lies can't disguise what you fear

For a golden girl knows when he's kissed her

It's the kiss of death from

Mister Goldfinger

Pretty girl beware of this heart of gold

This heart is cold

He loves only gold

Only gold

He loves gold

He loves only gold

Only gold

He loves gold

2 TRUMP/PUTIN LOVE AFFAIR

02-20-15

Bill Browder, former fund manager in Russia wrote in his book "I believe that (Putin is worth) $200 billion. After 14 years in power of Russia, and the amount of money that the country has made, and the amount of money that hasn't been spent on schools and roads and hospitals and so on, all that money is in property, bank accounts, shares, hedge funds, managed for Putin and his cronies." This might make Putin the richest person in the world!

05-03-16

At a Bill O'Reilly interview Donald Trump said "I think he (Russian President Vladimir Putin) said some really nice things. He called me a genius. He said 'Trump's a genius'. Okay. So, you know, that's nice."

At a campaign event Trump said again "I'm not disavowing that (Putin) called me a genius. Are you crazy? Wouldn't it be good if we actually got along with countries, wouldn't it be a positive thing? Do we always have to fight?"

A couple of Russian translations say different:

"He's a very lively man, talented without a doubt." "He is very flamboyant man, very talented, no doubt about that."

I don't see genius in these translations. More important why is Trump so concern about "Putin's" opinion? Could it be because of Putin's wealth?

3 TRUMP CAMPAIGN, "A THREE RING CIRCUS"

School Ground Potty Mouth!

12-22-15

What Trump said about Hillary Clinton:

"Even a race to Obama, she was going to beat Obama. I don't know who would be worst, I don't know, how could it be worse? But he was going to beat - she was favored to win - and she got schlonged, she lost, I mean she lost."

Trump was using a Yiddish word "schlonged" a word for a man's penis.

02-26-16

During the campaign Marco Rubio (Republican candidate) was jabbing Trump for misspelling words in tweets and for applying makeup backstage to get rid of a "sweat mustache".

At a rally Trump said "you ought to see Rubio backstage, he was using a trowel to put on makeup. I will not say he was trying to cover up his ears, I won't say that."

Trump also said "he is a nasty guy, I call him a nasty little guy, but I wouldn't say that. He's a nasty guy, and we don't need nasty…..Honestly, there's no place for it.

After a debate Trump jabbed Rubio again: "I thought he was going to die, he was so scared, like a little frightened puppy". "Rubio is a choker and a lightweight".

02-29-16

Rubio's attacks on Trump:

> "Donald is not going to make America great, he's going to make America orange."

> "Now the other thing he says, he's always calling me Little Marco. And I'll admit he's taller than me. He's like 6"2, which why I don't understand why his hands are the size of someone who is 5'2. Have you seen his hands? They're like this. And you know what they say about men with small hands? You can't trust them."

> "The billionaire was worried about "wet" pants at the debate."

> "He put out a picture of having makeup put on me at the debate. Which is amazing to me that the guy with the worst spray tan in America is attacking me for putting on makeup. Donald Trump likes to sue people. He should sue whoever did that to his face."

> Rubio referred to Trump's private plane as "Hair Force One"!

04-26-16

At a rally in Warwick, Rhode Island, Trump said about John Kasich (Republican candidate):

"He has a news conference all the time when he's eating. I have never seen a human being eat in a disgusting fashion. This guy takes a pancake, and he's shoving it in his mouth. It's disgusting! Do you want that for your president? I don't think so.

05-26-16

Trump called Elizabeth Warren (D-MASS.) "Pocahontas" because she claims she was of Native American descent.

Trump also said "I don't know if you would call it a fraud or not, but she was able to get into various schools because of the fact she applied as a Native American and probably able to get other things. I think she's as Native American as I am. Okay? That I will tell you.

She's a woman that has been very ineffective other than she's got a big mouth," Trump said.

Trump tweeted, "I find it offensive "Goofy" Elizabeth Warren, sometimes referred to as "Pocahontas," pretended to be Native American to get into Harvard."

Warren tweeted, Trump needs to get his facts straight I did not attend Harvard!

A source close to the Enquirer said "Trump and Enquirer CEO David Pecker have been close for years". This is why The National Enquirer constantly attacked Trump's Republican opponents during the Primary.

One headline said "Bungling Surgeon Ben Carson Left Sponge in Patient's Brain!" The article called Carson a "White House wannabe" and claimed he "brandished a scalpel like a meat cleaver!" The Enquirer said "His presidential campaign should be dead on arrival!"

The Enquirer reported that Jeb Bush was "involved in the drug trade in Florida" in the '80s and that, as governor, he was plagued by "sleazy cheating scandals…[with a] Playboy Bunny turned lawyer."

"Home wrecker Carly Fiorina Lied About Druggie Daughter." Also "The National Enquirer has exclusively learned that Lori Ann Fiorina, who died in October 2009, was in fact Carly's stepdaughter,"

"Clinton is on her deathbed and is "engaging in a massive cover-up about her health." The Enquirer claims she is suffering from strokes, brain cancer, depression, alcoholism, multiple sclerosis, endometriosis, and paranoia, among other dire conditions.

Finally two Enquirer headlines:

"Trump's the One!" leading in the polls.

"The Man Behind the Legend!"

01-21-16

Senator Lindsey Graham was ask which Republican
Candidate he preferred between Donald Trump and
Senator Ted Cruz? He answered, "It's like being shot
or poisoned, what does it really matter?"

02-26-16

What Marco Rubio said about Trump at the debates:

Trump is a "con artist"

"Trump would be the oldest president ever elected. And it's
like an eight-year term, so you start to worry,"

Rubio pulled out his smartphone and read aloud some of
trump's misspelled attack tweets. Rubio said "Number one:
That's how they spell those words at the Wharton School of
Business, where he went. Or number two, just like Trump
Tower, he must have hired a foreign worker to do his tweets,"

Rubio: Trump requested a full-length mirror during a break in
the debate, "maybe to make sure his pants weren't wet." Also
he questioned Trump's toughness by charging that he was
"the first that begged for security protection."

"Trump would be selling watches in Manhattan if did not
receive a generous inheritance, Rubio said.

Trump kept using the names, "Lying Ted Cruz" and
"Lightweight choker Marco Rubio."

03-24-16

A Super PAC that supports Ted Cruz put an ad on Facebook that shows Trump's wife Melania in a photo shoot posing nude for GQ Magazine.

Trump responded by sharing a tweet with Ted Cruz's wife, Heidi in a picture side by side with a picture of Melania. The tweet read "A picture is worth a thousand words."

Also Fox News reporting said that Trump needs to stop attacking Megan Kelly (Fox News), calling it a "sick obsession…beneath the dignity of a presidential candidate who wants to occupy the highest office in the land."

06-30-15

Past statements by Trump:

"I have a great relationship with the Blacks. I've always had a great relationship with the Blacks."

"Laziness is a trait in blacks."

"Black guys counting my money! I hate it. The only kind of people I want counting my money are little short guys that wear yarmulkes every day."

"I think the only difference between me and the other candidates is that I'm more honest and my women are more beautiful."

"You know, it doesn't really matter what [the media] write as long as you've got a young and beautiful piece of ass."

On Rosie O'Donnell: "You take a look at her, she's a slob. She talks like a, like a truck driver."

"She is unattractive both inside and out. I fully understand why her former husband left her for a man-he made a good decision."

"If Hillary Clinton can't satisfy her husband what makes her think she can satisfy America?'

"There is something on that birth certificate—maybe religion, maybe it says he's a Muslim, I don't know. Maybe he doesn't want that. Or. he may not have one.

"It's freezing and snowing in New York. We need global warming!"

"I rented him a piece of land," he told Fox News about his relationship with Muammar Qaddafi. "He paid me more for one night than the land was worth for two years, and then I didn't let him use the land. That's what we should be doing. I don't want to use the word 'screwed', but I screwed him."

"To the victor belong the spoils," he said to Bill O'Reilly, about his stance of staying in Iraq after the war. Therefore he would "stay and we keep the oil."

"Sorry losers and haters, but my I.Q. is one of the highest—and you all know it! Please don't feel so stupid or insecure. It's not your fault."

The Artist of the Deal or Just "Bullshit Artist!"

03-13-16

Trump has called some Mexican immigrants "racist", urged banning Muslims from entering the country and declared that "Islam hates us."

Former Labor Secretary Robert Reich said "Donald Trump is a bully who's stirring up other bullies to rage against Latinos, blacks, Muslims, and other convenient scapegoats – channeling the fears and resentments of the white working class into hatefulness and violence.

"He deserves to be condemned by every decent American."

03-13-16

Trump said "We need somebody that can take our jobs back from China, our country's going to hell. Last year Chinese laborers are "paid a lot less and the standards are worse when it comes to the environment and health care and worker safety."

Sen. Marco Rubio (R-Fla.) confronted Trump's idea saying "all the Donald Trump clothing will no longer be made in China and in Mexico but will be made here in the United States." Trump dismissed the idea.

Robert Lawrence, a professor of trade and investment at Harvard's John F. Kennedy School of Government, found that the website selling Ivanka Trump's merchandise line links to

838 products — 628 of them imported. Of those, 354 are from China.

Lawrence commented about Trump, "for him to claim that this is somehow immoral and go after companies that have relocated manufacturing when he has done the same puts him in conflict with his own rhetoric."

03-31-16

Former CIA Director Michael Hayden said:

> "Trump is a bigger threat to national security than Hillary Clinton."

> "Trump's "current statements are erratic. I just don't know what he's going to do."

> About Trump's national security talk "It's not so much wrong or overly certain. It's incoherent"

> "His call to ban Muslims from entering the U.S. has made the United States less safe than it has to be."

04-01-16

Trump's "Bullshit Artistry":

Trump said, "Women should face some form of punishment for getting an abortion if the procedure were outlawed."

Trump later said, "Those who perform abortions, and not the women who undergo them, should be punished."

Trump said, "Biggest problem, to me, in the world, is nuclear, and proliferation,"

Trump later said, "He would like to see South Korea and Japan obtain nuclear weapons."

Trump said, "I said, 'Don't hit Iraq' because you're going to totally destabilize the Middle East."

Trump later said, "The invasion looks like a tremendous success from a military standpoint."

Trump commented on Israeli-Palestinian conflict: "I want to be very neutral and see if I can get both sides together."

Trump later said, "When I become president, the days of treating Israel like a second-class citizen will end on day one."

04-02-16

In his first 100 days, Trump said that he would cut taxes, "renegotiate trade deals and renegotiate military deals," including altering the U.S. role in the North Atlantic Treaty Organization.

Trump said that "he would be able to get rid of the nation's more than $19 trillion national debt "over a period of eight years."

Trump said, "I'm renegotiating all of our deals, the big trade deals that we're doing so badly on. With China, $505 billion this year in trade." He said that economic growth he foresees as a consequence of renegotiated deals would enable the United States to pay down the debt."

Economists have said that a trade war would be crippling to the U.S. economy.

Were he to be elected president, Trump said he would want high-level employees of the federal government to sign legally binding nondisclosure agreements so that staffers couldn't write insider accounts of what it's like inside a Trump White House.

Trump also said that the United States has lost its standing in the world and that he would make people respect our country. I want them to respect our leader." Asked how he would do so, Trump cited an "aura of personality."

04-07-16

Trump Institute was comprised of a series of seminars teaching "the way to wealth."

The institute was being sued by the state of New York and the students for fraud.

Ads for Trump University promised to make people "millionaires."

Trump Institute promised to make people into savvy real estate investors, thanks to advice from "The Donald" himself.

06-03-16

Gonzalo Curiel was the presiding judge in a lawsuit filed by former students of Trump University. He was born in East Chicago, Il., to parents who had emigrated from Mexico.

Trump said "I'm building the wall, I'm building the wall, I have a Mexican judge. He's of Mexican heritage. He should have recused himself, not only for that, for other things." Also "he's a hater."

TRUMP ZAP! Trump said, "I came up with Christmas!"

"Blood coming out her what ever" and Sexism

08-08-15

Trump said his M.O. (Method of Operation) when it came to women was "you have to treat 'em like shit."

Ivana in a sworn deposition accused Trump of "violating" her during sex.

Megan Kelly (FOX anchor and moderator) at a Republican debate stated to Trump that he has called women "fat pigs, dogs, slobs, and disgusting animals."

The next day Trump said of Kelly "She had blood coming out of her eyes. Or blood coming out of her what ever,"

03-17-16

According to Reuters/Ipsos polling, half of U.S. women say they have a "very unfavorable" view of the front-runner for the Republican presidential nomination.

Trump said "If Hillary Clinton were a man, I don't think she would get 5 percent of the vote." Also "She is a woman, she is playing the woman card left and right. Frankly, if she didn't, she would do very poorly. If she were a man and she was the way she is, she would get virtually no votes."

TRUMP ZAP! Trump can live without friends but he can't live without enemies!

4   WHEN REPUBLICANS LOOK IN THE MIRRIOR THEY SEE "ARCHIE BUNKER!"

09-02-15

Trump knows how to manipulate the demographic changes in our country in the last 50 years:

From 1970 to 2010, the Hispanic population of the United States grew fivefold, from 9.6 million to 50.5 million. From 2000 to 2010, the number of white children under 18 declined by 4.3 million while the number of Hispanic children grew by 4.8 million. In 2013, white children became a minority, 47.7 percent of students age 3 to 6.

Conservative constituencies, including Tea Party supporters and white evangelicals, believe "discrimination against whites has become as big a problem as discrimination against blacks and other minorities"

Trump said, "I Love the Mexican people. I do business with the Mexican people, but you have people coming through the border that are from all over. And they're bad. They're really bad. Bringing drugs, bringing crime and as rapists."

Trump also said, "You know a lot of the gangs that you see in Baltimore and in St. Louis and Ferguson and Chicago, do you know they're illegal immigrants?" Trump vows that after the election, "They're going to be gone so fast, if I win, that your head will spin."

03-03-16

Ted Cruz said, "We will do what we can to help them fight this scourge, and redouble our efforts to make sure it does not happen here. We need to immediately halt the flow of refugees from countries with a significant al Qaida or ISIS presence. We need to empower law enforcement to patrol and secure Muslim neighborhoods before they become radicalized."

05-05-16

Trump tweeted, "Happy #CincoDeMayo!" "The best taco bowls are made in Trump Tower Grill. I love Hispanics!"

The nightly news showed a photo of Trump eating one.

Trump said that "if he won the Republican nomination, one of my first pictures is going to be to get all of my Hispanic employees and take a picture in some area"… "People will be amazed. I have thousands. Thousands. I'm going to take a picture and we're going to get them all together and we're going to have a picture. They love me. I take great care of them."

Gallup poll from March, 77% of Hispanics in the United States view him unfavorably.

05-12-16

In "A King in His Castle: How Donald Trump Lives, From His Longtime Butler," New York Times reporter Jason Horowitz describes Senecal's relationship to Trump, writing "few people here can anticipate Mr. Trump's demands and desires better than Mr. Senecal, 74.

Anthony Senecal has worked at Mar-a-Lago for nearly 60 years, and for Mr. Trump for nearly 30 of them. He stopped working there in 2009. He wrote on Facebook, "Obama should have been taken out by our military and shot as an enemy agent in his first term."

Trumps "Chief Strategist" Steve Bannon, and the "Alt-Right"

12-29-15

Milo Yiannopoulos wrote in a Brietbart article, "Twitter has hired a new head of "diversity" and already some uber-progressive types are whining because he is white and male. Preposterous! They cry. But they are wrong. Actually, only rich, straight white men should have anything to do with running diversity initiatives."

02-10-16

While alt-right media met his expectations,Donald Trump shredded the New York Daily News after the paper depicted him as an evil clown and his supporters as brain-dead "mindless zombies." This came after his win in New Hampshire primary. The cover included the headline: "Dawn of the Brain Dead." A sub-title read: "Clown comes back to life with N.H. win as mindless zombies turn out in droves."

02-16-16

When Paul Rieckhoff, the CEO of Iraq and Afghanistan Veterans of America refused to take money from Trump's "Veteran's fund raising," the legions of pro-Trump trolls was unleashed.

Rieckhoff was called a "fucking scumbag" by one commenter, then told by another to "get off your ass and get the funding or get fired."

 "Keep your mouth shut and take the money," another Trump fan said.

 A tax-conscious individual commented, "I hope your asses get audited."

Phone lines and inboxes were slammed the next day with malicious fans.

05-02-16

 The Pentagon planned a normal military exercise called "Jade Helm 15" in Texas, "meanwhile," websites like Alex Jones's InfoWars created a lot of "Fake News" about Jade Helm 15. They said it was a cover-up for mass seizure of firearms and American "death squads."

Texas Governor Greg Abbott channeled the concerns of voters in the Southwest, asking the "Texas state guard" to monitor the exercise for any violations of freedom. "It is important that Texans know their safety, constitutional rights, private property rights and civil liberties will not be infringed," said the governor.

Republican presidential candidate Ted Cruz said "My office has reached out to the Pentagon to inquire about this exercise. We are assured it is a military training exercise.

I have no reason to doubt those assurances, but I understand the reason for concern and uncertainty, because when the federal government has not demonstrated itself to be trustworthy in this administration (Obama's), the natural consequence is that many citizens don't trust what it is saying. I have a great deal of faith and confidence in Governor Abbott (Rep. Texas), He is a long-time friend and mentor of mine. You know, I understand a lot of the concerns raised by a lot of citizens about Jade Helm. It's a question I'm getting a lot. And I think part of the reason is we have seen, for six years, a federal government disrespecting the liberty of the citizens. That produces fear, when you see a government that is attacking our free speech rights, or Second Amendment rights, or religious liberty rights. That produces distrust."

Trump and White Supremacists

08-26-16

David Duke (former Ku Klux Klan leader R-La.) robo-call, "It's time to stand up and vote for Donald Trump for president and vote for me, David Duke for the US Senate." Duke said "A candidate has no control over other people's opinions and support, we should vote for Donald Trump."

02-24-16

American National Super PAC founder William Daniel Johnson robo-call:

> "I am William Johnson, a farmer and white nationalist. The white race is dying out in America and Europe because we are afraid to be called "racist."

This is our mindset: Its okay that our government destroys our children's future, but don't call me racist. I am afraid to be called racist.

Its okay to give away our country through immigration, but don't call me racist.

It's okay that few schools any more have beautiful white children as the majority, but don't call me racist.

Gradual genocide against the white race is okay, but don't call me racist.

I am afraid to be called racist. Donald Trump is not a racist, but Donald Trump is not afraid."

Don't vote for a Cuban. Vote for Donald Trump. (213) 718-3908. This call is not authorized by Donald Trump.

Johnson a real estate mogul said "Trump's leading rivals, Sen. Ted Cruz (R-TX) and Sen. Marco Rubio (R-FL), may not be eligible to serve as president. Cruz was born in Calgary, Alberta to a Cuban father and an American mother, while Rubio was born in Miami to Cuban immigrants.

02-28-16

In the year 2000 Trump also wrote in the New York Times, "Although I am totally comfortable with the people in the New York Independence Party, I leave the Reform Party to David Duke, Pat Buchanan and Lenora Fulani. That is not company I wish to keep."

But during the Presidential campaign Trump said:

"Well, just so you understand, I don't know anything about David Duke, OK?"

...on't even know anything about what you're talking about with white supremacy or white supremacists."

"Did he endorse me, or what's going on? I know nothing about David Duke. I know nothing about white supremacists."

04-04-16

Mary Minshall an American Freedom Party supporter made a robo call for William Johnson. He is lawyer and self-proclaimed white nationalist who runs The American National Super PAC. She said on the PAC's Wisconsin robo call, "I am voting for Donald Trump because he will not only be presidential, he will put America first."... "Furthermore, he will respect all women and will help preserve Western Civilization."

05-10-16

Trump Selects a White Nationalist Leader as a Delegate in California, to be on a list of delegates for the upcoming Republican presidential primary in the state. He is the same William Johnson, one of the country's most prominent white nationalists.

"I can be a white nationalist and be a strong supporter of Donald Trump and be a good example to everybody," Johnson says.

The Trump campaign blamed Johnson's selection on a "database error," later Johnson told Mother Jones he would resign.

TRUMP ZAP! Trump is the "white right" pied piper!

12-08-15

America has experienced fear and racism before, legislation was passed in 1988 apologizing to the more than 100,000 people of Japanese ancestry, including many Americans, who were placed in U.S. detention camps during World War II. The law also authorized reparations for survivors of the detention.

The legislation read: "The internment of the individuals of Japanese ancestry was caused by racial prejudice, war hysteria and a failure of political leadership."

What Trump said about the internment of Japanese Americans during World War II:

"I would have had to be there at the time to tell you, to give you a proper answer," he said during a recent interview in his office in New York City. "I certainly hate the concept of it. But I would have had to be there at the time to give you a proper answer."

"It's a tough thing. It's tough," he said. "But you know war is tough. And winning is tough. We don't win anymore. We don't win wars anymore. We don't win wars anymore. We're not a strong country anymore. We're just so off."

02-29-16

Trump's racist rhetoric spilled over into student rivalry.

Fans at Andrean High School in Merrillville, Ind. Friday held a cutout showing Trump's face and chanted "Build a wall! Build a wall!" during a basketball game against Bishop Noll Institute, which has many Latino students.

Andrean administrators and the Diocese of Gary, which operates the schools, are investigating the shameful situation.

During a basketball game against Perry High School, which has a more diverse student population, students at the predominantly-white Dallas Center-Grimes High School in Iowa chanted "Trump! Trump!" during a basketball game.

Joe Enriquez Henry Vice President of the Midwest Region for the League of United Latin American Citizens said "People who have racist viewpoints have been able to successfully use 'Trump' as a code-phrase for derogatory, racist statements,"

05-11-16

Trump said about himself, "Donald J. Trump is calling for a total and complete shutdown of Muslims entering the United States until our country's representatives can figure out what the hell is going on. We have no choice… we have no choice."

London Mayor Sadiq Khan, a Muslim, said Trump's view of Islam is "ignorant… it risks alienating mainstream Muslims around the world and plays into the hands of extremists."

Trump suggested there'd be "exceptions" to his Muslim ban "so PEOPLE LIKE KHAN could still travel to the country."

What former President Jimmy Carter said about Trump:

"The presumptive GOP presidential nominee, had tapped a waiting reservoir there of inherent racism."

"When you single out any particular group of people for secondary citizenship status, that's a violation of basic human rights,"

"I don't feel good, except for one thing: I think the country has been reawakened the last two or three years to the fact that we haven't resolved the race issue adequately,"

"I think there's a heavy reaction among some of the racially conscious Republicans against an African-American being president."

"I could shoot somebody on 5th avenue"

01-14-15

The issue of gun control has been a hot button in America.

In 1996 the Republican controlled Congress stripped $2.6 million from CDC budget for a gun study. Wording was inserted into the CDC's appropriations bill that, "None of the funds made available for injury prevention and control at the Centers for Disease Control and Prevention may be used to advocate or promote gun control."

After the December 2012 mass shooting at Sandy Hook
Elementary in Newtown, Conn. Obama signed an executive
order to have the CDC to research the gun issue.

CDC spokeswoman Courtney Lenard wrote "It is possible for
us to conduct firearm-related research within the context of
our efforts to address youth violence, domestic violence,
sexual violence, and suicide, but our resources are very
limited." (The Republicans still control the Congress and their
budget)

10-25-15

Rep. Matt Salmon (R-Ariz.) introduced the Hearing
Protection Act which provides "hunters" with easier access to
gun silencers.

Gun Owners of America (GOA) executive director Larry Pratt
said "Silencers are not used in crime, nor would they be if
more widely available,"

Dan Gross, president of the Brady Campaign to Prevent Gun
Violence said "We believe that the level of background checks
currently in place for suppressors is appropriate to keep them
out of the wrong hands. The problem here is that our current
laws don't do enough to keep guns themselves from falling
into dangerous hands."

Ladd Everitt, spokesman for the Coalition to Stop Gun
Violence said "It's only a matter of time until a silenced round
injures or kills an innocent person who had no opportunity to
hear the report of gunfire and find cover."

Trump had no problem getting laughs and cheers at a rally in Sioux Center, Iowa. Trump pointed his finger at the crowd like he was shooting a handgun and said, "I could stand in the middle of Fifth Avenue and shoot people and I wouldn't lose voters."

After Trump's statement Glen Beck said "If Donald Trump wins (Iowa), it's going to be a snowball to hell."

03-28-16

A petition posted on Change.org received 44,000 signatures. The petition wanted to allow the open carry of firearms at the Quicken Loans Arena during the GOP convention in Cleveland in July. Given that Ohio is an open carry state, supporters said a ban is an infringement upon their Second Amendment rights.

Trump said"I have -- I have not seen the petition. I want to see what it says. I want to read the fine print. I have to see what it says. I'm a very, very strong person for the Second Amendment. I like very few people are stronger. And I have to see the petition."

Secret Service spokesman Robert Hoback replied "Individuals determined to be carrying firearms will not be allowed past a predetermined outer perimeter checkpoint, regardless of whether they possess a ticket to the event."

Trump said in a meandering speech to the National Rifle Association's annual gathering in Louisville, Ky.:

> "We will unsign lots of different things, including some of those terrible executive orders. Believe me, they're going to be unsigned so fast, they'll be unsigned the first hour that I'm in office."

> "Hillary's pledged to issue new anti-gun executive orders, you know that? This is the behavior, I mean you could say, of a dictator. This is the behavior of somebody, frankly I think, that doesn't know what she's doing. She's not equipped to be President in so many ways."

> "We're getting rid of gun-free zones, I can tell you," he promised after saying if "we had guns on the other side" the San Bernardino, Calif., massacre wouldn't have been as bad.

Clinton wrote, "You're wrong, @realDonaldTrump. We can uphold Second Amendment rights while preventing senseless gun violence." The tweet was accompanied by a graphic that read: "America simply cannot accept 33,000 gun deaths in a year as normal."

06-20-16

Along party lines the Republicans voted down four measures to control gun sales. It was only eight days after the massacre of 49 people in an Orlando, Fla. Nightclub.

Senator Chuck Schumer, Democrat of New York said "We will keep pushing, until they see the light."

TRUMP ZAP: If you want gun control just tell Trump "Obama wrote the 2nd Amendment!"

Trump's Evangelicals ("Is Trump Born Again?")

05-12-15

The evangelical political machine kicked in early.

Franklin Graham (Son of Billy Graham) announced:

"In 2016, I plan to hold prayer rallies in all 50 states."

"I believe God has called us to this. We're naming it the Decision America Tour. I want to challenge Christians across our land to boldly live out their faith and to pray fervently and faithfully for our nation and all its leaders."

"I want to encourage Christians to get out and vote in the coming election year. We will not be endorsing any political candidates, but I will urge people to vote for those on the ballot who uphold biblical principles, and I will be sharing the life-changing truth of God's Gospel in every state."

"LGBT activists, abortion rights advocates, aggressive atheist groups, and others who ignore God's Word are trying to shove their agenda down our throats," said Graham.

Graham kept his word and before the November 2016 election he had been to every state.

01-29-16

As of 2014, Pew survey has found that the share of Evangelicals identifying as Republican or Republican-leaning has never been higher, at 68 percent. In fact, Evangelicals comprise the single largest religious constituency inside the GOP, making up 38 percent of Republicans, with Catholics trailing them at 21 percent.

02-24-16

After Trump easily won the Nevada Republican caucuses he said "We won the evangelicals. We won with young. We won with old. We won with highly educated. We won with poorly educated. I love the POORLY EDUCATED."

05-06-16

Trump's rhetorical divide spread to bold actions.

Cassandra McWade, suffers from chronic conditions, including psoriatic arthritis, fibromyalgia, and Crohn's Disease.

She has a handicap placard hanging from her rear-view mirror and several Bernie Sanders-related bumper stickers and signs on the rear of her car.

She was driving near Asheville, NC when she was involved in a minor fender-bender with a truck that left her Toyota Camry with a little damage, but unable to start.

She called for a tow from Shupee Max Towing.

Ken Shupe, the owner (Who identifies as a Trump supporter) refused to tow her, said:

"He was unable to tow her car because she was "obviously a socialist," and helpfully suggested that she "call the government" for a tow.

"Every business dealing in recent history that I've had with a socialist-minded person, I haven't got paid," Shupe told the station. He added: "Every time I've dealt with these people in recent history, I get 'Berned.'

"I think the Lord came to me, and he just said 'Get in the truck and leave.' And when I got in my truck, you know, I was so proud."

Trump's White Male Billionaires

04-22-16

Harold Hamm, the billionaire chief executive officer of oil producer Continental Resources endorsed Donald Trump. What Hamm said about Trump:

"He is not my last choice, he is the best choice."

"He has tapped into the basic beliefs of the American people."
"He is the business leader's candidate."
"He is someone who is not beholden to special interests and has the fortitude to make tough decisions."

"With a slew of onerous regulations now threatening to cripple American business, the next President of the United States must have the courage, determination and intelligence to disrupt politics as usual."

05-11-16

Oil tycoon T. Boone Pickens to host event for pro-Trump super PAC at his Texas ranch next month. The event will be sponsored by Great America PAC.

Stanley Hubbard, a Minnesota broadcasting executive, will serve on the board of Great America PAC and Anthony Scaramucci, a New York investor.

Pickens said "he's tired of having politicians as president of the U.S."

05-17-16

Billionaire Sheldon G. Adelson endorses Trump.

Aldelson said that electing former secretary of state Hillary Clinton, the probable Democratic nominee, would be akin to granting President Obama an unconstitutional third term.

Trump Makes Other Countries Great

03-07-16

 What Mexican leaders said about Trump's "Wall" along the
Mexican boarder:

> President Enrique Peña Nieto said Trump's "strident
> expressions" put forth "very simple solutions." That
> kind of rhetoric has led to "very fateful scenes in the
> history of humanity." 'That's the way Mussolini arrived
> and the way Hitler arrived. It appears to me that
> (Trump's comments) hurt the relationship we have
> sought with the United States."
>
> Former President Felipe Calderon said "we are not
> going to pay any single cent for such a stupid wall."
>
> Former President Vicente Fox said, "Mexico will not
> pay for that f---ing wall!"

04-27-16

 Donald Trump promised in a speech to a Washington foreign
policy audience that as president, he would restore a coherent
vision to America's role in the world.

> "The U.S. would finally have a coherent foreign policy
> based on narrow self-interest, economic gain and global
> stability."

Trump focused on the alleged "disasters" created by past presidents and a foreign policy establishment who "frankly don't know what they're doing, even though they may look awfully good writing for The New York Times or talking on television."

"Moscow — I believe an easing of tensions and improved relations with Russia, from a position of strength, is possible. Common sense says this cycle of hostility must end."

"The U.S. had left Christians subject to intense persecution and even genocide."

Doug Bandow, a foreign policy scholar at the libertarian Cato Institute, who shares many of Trump's beliefs said about the speech: "He called for a new foreign policy strategy, but you don't really get the sense he gave one." … "It struck me as a very odd mishmash."

Robert "Bud" McFarlane, a former national security adviser to President Ronald Reagan said, "Trump's speech was lacking in policy prescriptions, and its strident rhetoric masked a lack of depth."

 Republican Senator Lindsey Graham of South Carolina, a former 2016 presidential rival to Trump tweeted, "the speech was full of disconnected thought and demonstrated a lack of understanding of threats we face. Ronald Reagan must be rolling over in his grave."

What Trump said about The U.S. Chamber of Commerce at a rally in a Pittsburgh suburb:

> "It was totally controlled by the special interest groups."

> "They're a special interest that wants to have the deals that they want to have."

> "They want to have T.P.P., the Trans-Pacific Partnership, one of the worst deals, and it'll be the worst deal since Nafta."

The U.S. Chamber of Commerce is a strong supporter of republican candidates, spending more than $35 million in the 2014 midterms.

A spokeswoman for the Chamber, Blair Latoff Holmes, defended its position on trade.

"The U.S. Chamber represents American businesses of all sizes from across the country, who recognize that free trade agreements, like the T.P.P., are an important way to accelerate economic growth and spur job creation in the U.S.," she said.

TRUMP ZAP: You can't make this shit up!

5 TRUMP'S "REPUBLICAN CIVIL WAR"

03-29-16

Republican National Committee chairman, Reince Priebus created a loyalty oath for all Republican Presidential Candidates to sign, saying they won't leave the Republican Party and run as a third-party candidate.

Mr. Trump said he would sign, so long as all of the other candidates did the same. So they all did, but Trump never signed it.

Trump said at a forum town hall on CNN by the moderator, Anderson Cooper, "I have tremendous support right now from the people. I have many more delegates than him," he added of Mr. Cruz. I don't want people to do something against their will, Anderson," he said.

Trump who has a large lead among delegates to the Republican National Convention, said at the forum that he did not believe he was being treated fairly. Less than a month later, his suspicions were confirmed.

04-25-16

John Kasich and Ted Cruz (Republican Presidential candidates) announced their intentions to coordinate campaigns in order to deny frontrunner Donald Trump a sweep of important primaries in Indiana, Oregon and New Mexico.

Lisa Boothe, president of High Noon Strategies -- a political communications firm -- told FoxNews.com, "It underscores how divided the Republican Party is that two presidential candidates would join together in such an unprecedented open fashion to stop Donald Trump from getting the nomination," She added that the move may even help Trump's narrative: "Donald Trump's message that the system is rigged has worked to his advantage and this only adds fuel to the fire."

Speaker of the House "So What!"

03-16-16

Former Speaker John Boehner said "If we don't have a nominee who can win on the first ballot, I'm for none of the above," Boehner said at the Futures Industry Association conference here. "They all had a chance to win. None of them won. So I'm for none of the above. I'm for Paul Ryan to be our nominee."

Ryan said he hadn't given "any thought" to a contested convention, and "a lot of people" are running for president."

04-28-16

A forum was hosted by Stanford in Government (SIG) and the Stanford Speakers Bureau at Stanford University. Former Republican House Speaker John Boehner told the audience Texas senator Ted Cruz (Rep. Presidential candidate) is "Lucifer in the flesh."… "I have Democrat friends and Republican friends. I get along with almost everyone, but I have never worked with a more miserable son of a bitch in my life."

Cruz responded to Boehner first on Twitter and then while addressing media ahead of a rally in Indiana, "If you're happy with John Boehner as speaker of the House and you want a president like John Boehner, Donald Trump is your man."

05-05-16

Speaker Paul Ryan, the nation's highest-ranking elected Republican, said that he was "not ready" to endorse Donald J. Trump for president.

Trump said that he was "not ready to support Speaker Ryan's agenda."…"Perhaps in the future we can work together and come to an agreement about what is best for the American people," he said. "They have been treated so badly for so long that it is about time for politicians to put them first!"

Ryan said Republicans want "a standard-bearer that bears our standards."…"I think conservatives want to know: Does he share our values and our principles on limited government, the proper role of the executive, adherence to the Constitution?" he said. "There's a lot of questions that conservatives, I think, are going to want answers to."

05-08-16

Sarah Palin a former Alaska governor and 2008 GOP vice presidential nominee said that she will support Speaker Paul Ryan's primary challenger Businessman Paul Nehlen in the Aug. 9 Republican primary. Palin said, "I think Paul Ryan is soon to be 'Cantored.'" (Eric Cantor (Va.), former House majority leader was stunningly defeated in a 2014 primary to now-Rep. Dave Brat.)

"His political career is over but for a miracle, because he has so disrespected the will of the people ... and for him to already come out and say who he will not support was not a wise decision of his," Palin added of Ryan.

06-02-16

After taking a month to decide, House Speaker Paul D. Ryan (R-Wis.) is formally backing his party's presumptive presidential nominee: Donald Trump.

Ryan wrote "It's a question of how to move ahead on the ideas that I—and my House colleagues—have invested so much in through the years. It's not just a choice of two people, but of two visions for America," citing the "bold" policy agenda that he will begin rolling out next week and contrasting that with Democratic front-runner Hillary Clinton's platform. "Donald Trump can help us make it a reality," Ryan said.

Peter Wehner, a former policy aide to President George W. Bush and a personal and ideological compatriot of Ryan's for two decades said, "Paul Ryan in many ways is the antithesis of Donald Trump; he's everything that Donald Trump is not. He's a decent human being. He is a conservative. He is steeped in public policy. He cares about ideas. He's a person who conducts himself with civility and grace in public life. He doesn't put down his opponents."

Anti-establishment President? Look Out Republicans!

09-10-15

Dr. Fienman from "The Progressive Professor" said the summer of 2015 has witnessed a clear cut "rebellion" against the the political establishment in both political parties. The Republican Party is observing the rise of Donald Trump, who, although he is part of the "one percent" as a billionaire, is perceived as "anti Establishment".

02-24-16

Robert Reich: The establishment is dying. The rise of figures like Bernie Sanders and Donald Trump isn't the cause; it's the symptom.

A 74-year-old Jew from Vermont who describes himself as a democratic socialist, who wasn't even a Democrat until recently, beat Hillary Clinton in the New Hampshire primary.

A 69-year-old billionaire who has never held elective office or had anything to do with the Republican Party has taken a commanding lead in the Republican primaries.

04-23-16

Donald J. Trump has been a vocal critic of the Republican Party's nomination system, calling it "rigged" and accusing other candidates of stealing his delegates. In some states, some of Ted Cruz's supporters have been selected to represent Mr. Trump at the convention. Mr. Trump has called them "double agents."

02-27-16

Senate Majority Leader Mitch McConnell told senators if Trump wins the Republican nomination, they could run negative ads about Trump to create space between him and Republican senators seeking re-election if it threatens to harm them in the general election.

02-27-16

Senate Majority Leader Mitch McConnell told associates of Trump that "We'll drop him like a hot rock" in the general election if he wins the Republican Primary.

McConnell has prepared an alternate plan to run Republican Senate candidates separately from Donald Trump.

McConnell's fear is that Trump would lose a general election race badly and bring down with other Republican candidates on state ballots, threatening Republican's majority in the Senate.

05-10-16

Public Policy Polling survey on found:

>*Donald Trump the presumptive Republican nominee more stomach-churning than the even some of the most repulsive things in the world, including lice, jury duty, root canals, traffic jams, the Department of Motor Vehicles and the reviled rock band Nickelback.

>*Voters also had a higher opinion of used car salesmen

and hipsters than they did of Trump.

*The poll says that twice as many people would rather have head bugs than Trump in the White House.

*Voters would rather see more cockroaches than more of Trump's comb over.

Anti-Trump Republican Leaders

01-22-16

National Review magazine founded by William F. Buckley was first published in the 1950s, has long been a leading voice on the American right, influencing countless conservatives, including former President Ronald Reagan.

A special issue was tweeted with a headline "Against Trump" a blistering editorial that said, "Donald Trump is a menace to American conservatism who would take the work of generations and trample it underfoot on behalf of a populism as heedless and crude as The Donald himself."

03-03-16

What former Republican presidential nominee Mitt Romney said about Trump becoming the Republican nominee:

"Mr. Trump was amplifying a "brand of anger that has led other nations into the abyss."

"His domestic policies would lead to recession."

"His foreign policies would make America and the world less safe. He has neither the temperament nor the judgment to be president."

Mr. Trump is an unacceptable candidate under any circumstances: "a phony" and "a fraud" who could not be trusted with the nation's highest office.

Trump called Mr. Romney a "failed candidate" and mocked him for his politically damaging 2012 comments about the "47 percent" of Americans who do not pay taxes, and for fumbling his final debate with Mr. Obama. He described Mr. Romney as having debased himself to secure a Trump endorsement in that election. "He was begging for my endorsement," Mr. Trump said. "I could have said, 'Mitt, drop to your knees.'"

Former Republican presidential nominee John McCain said that Mr. Trump had "uninformed and indeed dangerous statements on national security issues."

David Greenberg, a historian at Rutgers University said "There probably hasn't been this level of personal invective by one Republican nominee against another leading candidate ever, perhaps not even in 1912 when Theodore Roosevelt went after Taft."

03-08-16

The GOP and tech. leaders hold secret neoconservative meeting to stop Trump. The American Enterprise Institute's annual World Forum was held on a private island resort off the coast of Georgia. Some of the attendees were: Republican strategist Karl Rove, Senate Majority Leader Mitch McConnell and Arkansas Sen. Tom Cotton.

Weekly Standard editor Bill Kristol wrote in an emailed report "The key task now … is less to understand Trump than to stop him. "In general, there's a little too much hand-wringing, brow-furrowing, and fatalism out there and not quite enough resolving to save the party from nominating or the country electing someone who simply shouldn't be president."

Karl Rove, George W. Bush advisor presented focus group findings about Trump, which indicated that the frontrunner's biggest weakness is that voters have difficulty envisioning him as "presidential" or a role model for children.

03-18-16

Lindsey Graham (Republican presidential candidate), who just last month cracked a joke about murdering Cruz on the Senate floor begrudgingly endorses Ted Cruz for President, after losing his bid for president.

Graham mocked Cruz's unpopularity in Washington. "If you killed Ted Cruz on the floor of the Senate, and the trial was in the Senate, nobody would convict you. He's certainly not my preference, but he's a reliable Republican, conservative, which I've had many differences with."

Graham said "I have doubts about Mr. Trump, I don't think he's a Republican, I don't think he's a conservative, I think his campaign's built on xenophobia, race-baiting and religious bigotry, I think he'd be a disaster for our party and as Senator Cruz would not be my first choice, I think he is a Republican conservative who I could support."

05-19-16

The 2012 Republican nominee Mitt Romney ended recruiting efforts for an independent candidate to challenge Donald Trump and Hillary Clinton. A group of conservatives led by Romney, blogger Erick Erickson and The Weekly Standard editor Bill Kristol promoted a "Never Trump" movement that didn't succeed.

06-07-16

Trump claimed that U.S. District Judge Gonzalo Curiel has been biased while presiding over a case against Trump University because he is Latino.

Sen. Lindsey Graham (R-S.C.), presidential candidate said, referring to Trump:

> "If anybody was looking for an off-ramp, this is probably it."

> "There'll come a time when the love of country will trump hatred of Hillary."

> "Trump's recent racist comments about a federal judge with Mexican-American heritage were the most un-American thing from a politician since Joe McCarthy."

> "There are a lot of people who want to be loyal to the Republican Party, including me," he said. "But there'll come a point in time where we're gonna have to understand that it's not just about the 2016 race, it's about the future of the party and I would like to support our nominee. I just can't."

Senate Majority Leader Mitch McConnell (R-Ky.) said about Trump's remark, regarding Judge Curiel, "I couldn't disagree more with a statement like that."

Sen. Susan Collins (R-Maine) said "Those kinds of comments are very serious to me," she said. "They are completely unacceptable, and what they indicate — which is why I think this is so serious — is a lack of respect for our judicial system and for the separation of powers doctrine that is enshrined in the Constitution."

House Speaker Paul Ryan (R-Wis.) said "Claiming a person can't do their job because of their race is sort of like the textbook definition of a racist comment. I think that should be absolutely disavowed. It's absolutely unacceptable."

Death to the Republican Party?

03-08-16

 Fort Lauderdale, Florida's newspaper Sun Sentinel told its readers that none of the Republican candidates for president earned its endorsement. The paper usually endorses a Republican.

> "I hate that we didn't endorse," editorial page editor Rosemary O'Hara said. "We take this very seriously, we don't take it lightly at all. We offer endorsements not because readers always agree with us but so they know what we think and why we think it."
>
> We cannot endorse businessman Donald Trump, hometown Sen. Marco Rubio or Texas Sen. Ted Cruz because they are unqualified to be president. Ohio Gov. John Kasich is the best of the bunch, but if you measure

a candidate by the caliber of his campaign, Kasich's lack of traction and organization make a vote for him count for little."

The paper said Trump is "absurdly vague on how he would 'make America great again'" and noted that "Cruz scares us."

06-04-16

The New York Daily News told Texas Sen. Ted Cruz to take the "F-U Train to get 'outta the Bronx." After Mr. Cruz's "New York" values flub, the paper told him to "Drop Dead," featuring the Statue of Liberty giving him the middle finger.

Mr. Trump, too, has been the target of the Daily News's wrath, with them dressing him up as a carnival act, running the headline "Dead clown walking."

The paper declared the death of the Republican Party after Donald Trump won the Indiana primary.

The tabloid's cover featured a dead elephant in a casket and reads: "Dearly beloved, we are gathered her today to mourn the GOP, a once-great political party, killed by the epidemic of Trump."

05-11-16

Republican candidates have been criticized for not disclosing their tax returns for years.

Mitt Romney, the 2012 Republican nominee did not want to release his tax returns but finally relented under pressure. One of the people who was encouraging him to do so that year was Mr. Trump, who said that Mr. Romney should be proud of his wealth and not hold back his financial information.

"Mitt has to get those tax returns out," Mr. Trump said in a Fox News interview at the time. "I'm a little surprised they weren't better prepared for that."

But wait! Trump, the presumptive 2016 Republican presidential nominee said that despite indicating earlier that he would disclose his filings, he does not plan on doing so before the November general election.

Trump explained that he still intended to release his tax returns once the federal audit was completed. He said he cannot release returns from previous years because the government audits him almost every year.

Joseph J. Thorndike, an adjunct college professor who tracks presidential tax returns as the director of the Tax History Project, said Mr. Trump would be the first major candidate since 1976 to not make any of his full returns public. President Gerald R. Ford released a tax summary that year.

Dr. Thorndike noted that President Richard M. Nixon released his audit, starting the tradition of candidates making theirs public.

"I think 40 years of tradition carries real moral and ethical weight," Dr. Thorndike said. "It is quite striking that a major

candidate would decide not to release their tax information —
especially someone with an admittedly complex tax
situation."

05-30-16

Bret Stephens (a Republican) of The Wall Street Journal
said, "I will vote for the least left-wing opponent to Donald
Trump, he is the biggest loser in presidential history since, I
don't know, Alf Landon or going back further.   It's important
that Donald Trump and what he represents — this kind of
ethnic quote, 'conservatism,' or populism be so decisively
rebuked that the Republican Party, the Republican voters will
forever learn their lesson that they cannot nominate a man so
manifestly unqualified to be president in any way, shape or
form. So they have to learn a lesson in the way perhaps
Democrats learned from McGovern in '72."

George Will said, "let's have him lose in 50 states. Why not
Guam, Puerto Rico and the District of Columbia, too?"

06-02-16

Senate Majority Mitch McConnell said that Donald Trump
risks alienating Hispanics as 1964 GOP presidential candidate
Goldwater did to Blacks.

Martinez, the nation's only Hispanic female governor, came
under fire from Trump last week after she snubbed him before
he spoke at a rally in Albuquerque. She also chairs the
Republican Governors Association.

"The attacks that he's routinely engaged in — for example,
going after Susana Martinez, the Republican governor of New

Mexico — I think was a big mistake," McConnell said.

"What he ought to be doing is trying to unify the party, not attacking people," McConnell said. "Once you've won, it's a time to bring the party together and be gracious."

6 CAMPAIGN VIOLENCE

03-03-16

At a Trump rally in North Carolina Rakeem Jones (black male) was removed from a rally for protesting. While being escorted out John McGraw, 78, (white male) of Linden, North Carolina, elbowed him in the head.

Jones said "After I get it, before I could even gain my thoughts, I'm on the ground getting escorted out."

What Trump said about the protester just before the attack "I'd like to punch him in the face."

The Cumberland County Sheriff's Office earlier told the Wall Street Journal it was investigating why officers   arrested the protester but not the man who punched him in the face.

03-03-16

Trump rally at the University of Illinois (Chicago Pavilion), thousands of protesters gathered outside and hundreds more demonstrated in unison inside.

"Five people were arrested as a result, and charges against them are pending early Saturday," said Officer Janel Sedovic, a Chicago police spokeswoman.

Police said that two officers were injured during the event, they were taken to area hospitals with non-life-threatening injuries.

The rally was called off, Trump said that he felt that it was just safer to cancel."Rather than having everybody get in and mix it up," Trump said, "I thought it would be a wise thing, after speaking with law enforcement, a wise thing to postpone the rally."

Prior to his arrival Friday in Chicago, Trump appeared at a rally in St. Louis where he mocked concerns over violent acts against protesters.

"They're allowed to get up and interrupt us horribly and we have to be very, very gentle," Trump said in response to one of nearly a dozen interruptions as he spoke at the regal Peabody Opera House. "They can swing and hit people, but if we hit them back, it's a terrible, terrible thing, right?"

At a northwest suburban Republican fundraising event, a rival for the GOP nomination, Texas Sen. Ted Cruz, criticized Trump, saying, "any candidate is responsible for the culture of the campaign."… "And when you have a campaign that disrespects the voters, when you have a campaign that affirmatively encourages violence, when you have a campaign that is facing allegations of physical violence against members of the press, you create an environment that only encourages this sort of nasty discourse," Cruz said.

03-14-16

Hillary Clinton said:

> Donald Trump is "trafficking in hate and fear" and claimed that foreign leaders are calling her to express their support in order to stop the Republican frontrunner from entering the White House.

"I think all Americans should be concerned. It's clear that Donald Trump is running a very cynical campaign pitting groups of Americans against one another."

"He actually incites violence in the way that he urges his audience on, you know, now talking about punching people, offering to pay legal bills, and then on the specifics, you know, we know that he has been incredibly bigoted toward so many groups, he talks about deporting eleven, twelve million immigrants-we're a nation built on immigrants-he talks about preventing Muslims from coming into our country-we believe in religious freedom."

03-14-16

What Trump said about paying his followers physical violence legal fees:

"Knock the crap out of him, okay?"

"I promise you I will pay for the legal fees, I promise, I promise."

"Get him out! Try not to hurt him,"

"If you do, I'll defend you in court."

03-14-16

What **Ben Carson, the former** GOP candidate who has endorsed Donald Trump said about violence at Trump's rallies:

"If the protestors continue with their Alinsky-ite (Legendary organizer Saul Alinsky) tactics, there is a real possibility of escalation because those who are the victims of them have two choices: they can submit to them and meekly just do whatever those protesters want them to do, or they can fight back, and if they decide to fight back, there could be an escalation."

"The problem is that there are those who are being taught that if someone disagrees with you, you have the right to interfere with their First Amendment rights, their ability to express themselves, their freedom of speech," he said. "Now when people do things wrong such as that, it causes other people to react in a way that is negative, and therefore you see that reaction."

"The real-estate mogul's public persona is not reflective of who he is in private."… "I had an opportunity to actually spend significant time talking with him in private. I found out that he actually is a person who loves America greatly, thinks deeply and does have some openness to spiritual things."

03-15-16

Thomas DiMassimo, of Fairborn Ohio jumped a barricade and rushed the stage at a Columbus Ohio Donald Trump Rally, but security officials tackled him.

DiMassimo, 22, was charged in federal court in Dayton. The misdemeanor charge carries up to a one-year prison sentence.

His attorney Jon Paul Rion said "He clearly did not mean any ill will toward any person and was simply expressing his political views."

Less than a week after an outbreak of violence last Friday at a Trump political rally in Chicago, a letter that contained white powder and a threatening message was sent to the Central Park South home of Donald Trump's son Eric Trump.The envelope with a Massachusetts postmark was addressed to Eric Trump, 32, at his apartment in the Trump Park East.The letter contained a threatening message that implied that Donald Trump's children would be hurt if the GOP candidate did not withdraw from the presidential race.Eric's wife, Lara Yunaska, opened the envelope and white powder fell out. It was not clear what the powder was.

03-19-16

Salt Lake City Trump supporters were met by hundreds of protesters chanting slogans like "Dump Trump'.

Demonstrators shut down a highway leading to the Phoenix suburb where Trump was slated to speak at a rally alongside controversial local Sheriff Joe Arpaio.

More than 5,000 people RSVP'd to a Facebook invitation for Saturday's New York protest, which stated that "Trump's policies threaten many of us in the Black, Latino, LGBTQIA+, Muslim, and other communities. These policies and type of speech has no place in this country, and certainly does not have a place in the city that Trump grew his empire in — a city known as a melting pot and home for many of the same people Trump continues to wage war on."

05-25-16

 Out side the Albuquerque Convention Center Trump rally demonstrators were rioting.Police responded by firing pepper spray and smoke grenades into the crowd.The convention center was packed with thousands of loud and cheering Trump supporters.Protesters outside overran barricades, clashed with police in riot gear and burned T-shirts and other items labeled with Trump's catchphrase, "Make America Great Again."Albuquerque attorney Doug Antoon said that rocks were flying through the convention center windows as he was leaving Tuesday night. Glass was breaking and landing near his feet."This was not a protest, this was a riot. These are hate groups," he said of the demonstrators.

Protestors inside the convention center had signs that read ""Trump is Fascist" and "We've heard enough."

Trump ask the security to remove the protestors and followed up with, "Go home to mommy." He said of one demonstrator, "How old is this kid?" Then he provided his own answer, "Still wearing diapers."

05-28-16

 Estimated 1,000 protesters showed up at a San Diego Trump rally. Plastic bottles were being thrown and a Trump "Make America Great Again" hat was burned. Several small fights broke out in the same area when anti-Trump crowds started to mix with his supporters.

TV news video showed some protesters throwing objects at a line of police officers outside the San Diego Convention Center while Trump spoke inside. At least one protester tried to climb up to where the officers were. The video showed officers using batons to push him back into the crowd. At least 18 people received medical attention. San Diego police reported no property damage during the protests.

Donald Trump praised the San Diego police on tweeter, "Fantastic job on handling the thugs who tried to disrupt our very peaceful and well attended rally. Greatly appreciated!"

06-11-16

At a Donald Trump (presumptive GOP presidential nominee) rally violence erupted again.San Jose's police chief told the San Jose Mercury News that there were not enough officers on hand during the event. He said there were about 250 officers and more than 400 protesters.

"I'm disgusted by the violent attacks yesterday that have no place in our society or our political process," said Paul Kelly, president of the San Jose Police Officers' Assn.

Anti-Trump protesters threw punches, eggs at pro-Trump supporters and car windows were broken. Pro-Trump hats grabbed from supporters were set on fire on the ground.

Mayor Sam Liccardo, a Democrat and Hillary Clinton supporter, criticized Trump for coming to cities and igniting problems that local police departments had to deal with.

"At some point, Donald Trump needs to take responsibility for the irresponsible behavior of his campaign," Liccardo told the Associated Press.

The San Jose Mercury News, in an editorial, criticized the protests."Protesters fell into Donald Trump's trap with their response to his campaign tactics Thursday. It was not one of San Jose's finer moments. Violence has no place in American politics," the paper wrote.

TRUMP ZAP: Trump, A reporter's gift that keeps on giving!

7 TRUMP WINS REPUBLICAN NOMINATION

06-17-16

 On 06-1-16 Donald J. Trump won the Republican Party nomination!

According to a survey in an ABC News/Washington Post poll this week, two-thirds of Americans don't like Trump — and a majority "can't stand" Trump!

Bloomberg Politics poll: Trump's favorable rating is just 31 percent, with 66 percent viewing him unfavorably.

Gallup's latest figures show Trump at 31 percent favorable/63 percent unfavorable – significantly worse than Clinton's 41 percent favorable/54 percent unfavorable.

At least for a major-party candidate this far out from an election, Trump is setting modern records for being unfavorable.

TRUMP ZAP! Elect a clown expect a circus!

09-30-16

Former Miss Universe Alicia Machado Claimed Trump has repeatedly attacked her for weight after winning the contest. She is an out spoken Hillary Clinton supporter.

Trump blasted her with tweets:

> "Wow, Crooked Hillary was duped and used by my worst Miss [Universe]. Hillary floated her as an 'angel' without checking her past, which is terrible!"

> "Using Alicia [Machado] in the debate as a paragon of virtue just shows that Crooked Hillary suffers from BAD JUDGMENT! Hillary was set up by a con."

> "Did Crooked Hillary help disgusting (check out sex tape and past) Alicia M become a U.S. citizen so she could use her in the debate?"

The Daily Beast said there is zero evidence of a "sex tape."

10-03-16

According to "The Apprentice," show insiders, Donald Trump repeatedly demeaned women with sexist language.

He rated female contestants by the size of their breasts and talked about which ones he'd like to have sex with.

The Associated Press interviewed more than 20 people — former crew members, editors and contestants — who described crass behavior by Trump behind the scenes of the long-running hit show.

10-08-16

Partial transcript of tape with Donald Trump and Billy Bush talking on the set of "Access Hollywood" about Arianne Zucker. The conversation began inside a large studio buss:

Trump: I moved on her, actually. You know, she was down on Palm Beach. I moved on her, and I failed. I'll admit it.

Trump: I did try and fuck her. She was married.

Unknown: That's huge news.

Trump: No, no, Nancy. No, this was [unintelligible] — and I moved on her very heavily. In fact, I took her out furniture shopping.

She wanted to get some furniture. I said, "I'll show you where they have some nice furniture." I took her out furniture — I moved on her like a bitch. But I couldn't get there. And she was married. Then all of a sudden I see her, she's now got the big phony tits and everything. She's totally changed her look.

As the women approached the buss:

Billy Bush: Sheesh, your girl's hot as shit. In the purple.

Trump: Whoa! Whoa!

Bush: Yes! The Donald has scored. Whoa, my man!

Trump: Look at you, you are a pussy.

Trump: All right, you and I will walk out.

Trump: Maybe it's a different one.

Bush: It better not be the publicist. No, it's, it's her, it's
—

Trump: Yeah, that's her. With the gold. I better use some Tic Tacs just in case I start kissing her. You know, I'm automatically attracted to beautiful — I just start kissing them. It's like a magnet. Just kiss. I don't even wait. And when you're a star, they let you do it. You can do anything.

Bush: Whatever you want.

Trump: Grab 'em by the pussy. You can do anything.

Bush: Uh, yeah, those legs, all I can see is the legs.

Trump: Oh, it looks good.

Bush: Come on shorty.

Trump: Ooh, nice legs, huh?

10-08-16

Ways Trump objectifies women, especially his daughter Ivanka:

Trump was talking to radio host Howard Stern about his daughter, who was then 23 years old, in a 2004 interview:

"By the way, your daughter," Stern said to Trump.

"She's beautiful," the brash businessman responded.

"Can I say this? A piece of ass," Stern asked.

"Yeah," Trump replied.

In a 2003 Stern interview, Trump said Ivanka has "got the best body."

Trump said on ABC's "The View" that if Ivanka weren't his daughter, he'd be dating her.

Trump said in an interview with Rolling Stone in 2015. "Yeah, she's really something, and what a beauty, that one. If I weren't happily married and, ya know, her father ..."

Trump has apologized for what he called "locker room banter," referring to his comments about groping women.

TRUMP ZAP! Trump's bar pick up line: "I'm entitled to it!"

10-13-16

Statements about Trump walking in the dressing room of Miss Teen USA beauty pageants, some were as young as 15 years old:

> Mariah Billado, the former Miss Vermont Teen USA, said Trump caused a panic in the dressing room of the 1997 pageant when he barged in unannounced as the young women were changing.

> However, she says Trump shrugged off the intrusion, saying something along the lines of: "Don't worry, ladies, I've seen it all before."

Three other former teen beauty queens corroborated Billado's account. They recalled the girls hurrying to cover themselves, with one calling Trump's behavior "shocking" and "creepy."

During a 2005 interview with Howard Stern Trump said, "Well, I'll tell you the funniest is that before a show, I'll go backstage and everyone's getting dressed, and everything else, and you know, no men are anywhere, and I'm allowed to go in because I'm the owner of the pageant and therefore I'm inspecting it," Trump said. "You know, I'm inspecting because I want to make sure that everything is good."

10-13-16

Temple Taggart McDowell, who represented Utah as a 21-year-old in the 1997 Miss USA pageant in Shreveport, La., tells about Trumps advances:

She was introduced to Trump during a rehearsal by her father, who was a fan of Trump's.

"It was at that time that he turned to me and embraced me and gave me a kiss on the lips."

"Trump offered to help get contracts with elite modeling agencies, and during a visit to Trump Tower in Manhattan at Trump's invitation, he again embraced and kissed her on the lips, this time in front of two pageant chaperones and a receptionist."

The New York encounter made one of the chaperones so "uncomfortable" that she advised McDowell not to go into any rooms with Trump alone, McDowell said. The other chaperone accompanied her into Trump's office, she said.

Almost immediately after Trump was exposed on the "Access Hollywood" tape, "my phone blew up," said McDowell, who said a friend told her, "'Well, now nobody can say that you're making this up.' I really thought, 'I just need to probably come forward and say exactly what happened,'" she said Wednesday night. "So that it's — the honest facts. ...

TRUMP ZAP! Trump only has two emotions anger and you remind me of my daughter!

10-14-16

"People Magazine" former reporter Natasha Stoynoff said she was interviewing the Trumps during a tour of the Mar-a-Lago resort in Florida in 2005, when Trump Trump pushed her against the wall and forcibly kissed her.

Trump said in response to article:

> "I've met thousands and thousands and thousands of people, know them, know them well."… "These claims defy logic, truth, reason, common sense."

> "It's not hard to find a small handful of people willing to make false smears for personal fame, who knows, maybe for financial reasons, political purposes, or the simple reason they want to stop our movement, they want to stop our campaign."

People magazine is standing by Stoynoff's account, with

editor in chief Jess Cagle on Thursday accusing Trump of "a disgusting, pathetic attempt to victimize her again."

TRUMP ZAP! Trump was groping an American flag at a campaign rally. It could be the only American flag that burns itself!

10-14-16

Kristin Anderson said in the early 1990s, she was in her early 20s, trying to make it as a model. She was paying the bills by working as a makeup artist and restaurant hostess.

At a crowded Manhattan nightspot she was deep in conversation with acquaintances and did not notice the figure to her right on a red velvet couch — until, she recalls, his fingers slid under her miniskirt, moved up her inner thigh and touched her vagina through her underwear.

Anderson said that she shoved the hand away, fled the couch and turned to take her first good look at the man who had touched her. She recognized him as Donald Trump. "He was so distinctive looking — with the hair and the eyebrows. I mean, nobody else has those eyebrows," she said.

The episode, as Anderson described it, lasted no more than 30 seconds. Anderson said she and her companions were "very grossed out and weirded out" and thought, "Okay, Donald is gross. We all know he's gross. Let's just move on."

"It wasn't a sexual come-on. I don't know why he did it. It was like just to prove that he could do it and nothing would happen," Anderson said. "There was zero conversation. We

81

didn't even really look at each other. It was very random, very nonchalant on his part."

Anderson said, "a stranger sort of groping you on the side, on the sly, like you're some kind of stuffed animal on the couch. That's really not okay, and it opens the door for much worse behavior on [his] part and for the girl, allowing worse things to happen to them because they feel that it's inconsequential."

"It's a sexual assault issue, and it's something that I've kept quiet on my own," Anderson said. "And I've always kept quiet. And why should I keep quiet? Actually, all of the women should speak up, and if you're touched inappropriately, tell somebody and speak up about it. Actually, go to the authorities and press some charges. It's not okay."

10-15-16

Statements by Trump on the Howard Stern radio show:

> In 1993 trump said "You know, if you're young, and in this era, and if you have any guilt about not having gone to Vietnam, we have our own Vietnam — it's called the dating game,"

> "Dating is like being in Vietnam. You're the equivalent of a soldier going over to Vietnam."

> In 1997 Trump said "It's amazing, I can't even believe it. I've been so lucky in terms of that whole world, it is a dangerous world out there. It's like Vietnam, sort of. It is my personal Vietnam. I feel like a great and very brave solider."

TRUMP ZAP! Trump's Presidential Library will have to have an "Adult-Section"

05-31-16

 Hedge fund manager William Oberndorf, who has contributed approximately $1.5 million in the last year to Republican candidates and causes, told CNN in a statement: "If it is Trump vs. Clinton, and there is no viable third party candidate, I will be voting for Hillary Clinton."

Doug Elmets Republican consultant and former operative who began his career as a White House staff assistant to conservative powerhouses Ed Rollins and Lee Atwater in 1981 at the dawn of the Reagan administration commented on Donald Trump:

> Elmets became a White House spokesman under long-time presidential adviser David Gergen and then moved onto the campaign trail for Reagan's 1984 re-election campaign. He later served as press secretary for the Department of Energy until he moved to California to work in public relations, policy and political consulting.

> Elmets said Hillary is more qualified than the "xenophobic and scary" Trump. Elmets joined what's being called on Twitter, #RepublicansforHillary.

> "I've never voted for a Democrat in my entire life. And I'll vote for my first Democrat when the ballots come out in November," said Elmets, who remains a registered Republican. "I could live with four years of Hillary Clinton before I could ever live with one day of

Donald Trump as president."

"I don't believe Donald Trump is a Republican. I think Donald Trump is a brand. And he's managed to hoodwink America into believing he will lead this country through the fire. I think he will thrust us into the fire," he said.

"I do think there are a lot of disenfranchised Republicans who can't believe Donald Trump will be or should be the nominee," said Elmets, adding, "Trump lacks a moral compass or the core values of the party…I believe as the campaign evolves and Donald Trump continues down this path, Hillary Clinton is going to look like a much more sympathetic character than she might today. Republicans will come along eventually. I do think they will do it publicly at some point or they'll privately do it in the polling booth in November."

Elmets said "I, like so many people throughout the world, are horrified by what we see coming alive on our TVs as we see people fighting and disrupting. The rallies are an indication of where America is going if Donald Trump gets elected President. Is that what we want?"

10-11-16

Glenn Beck a right- wing (anti-democrat) spokesman said:

Not voting for Donald Trump — even if it leads to Clinton winning the Oval Office — could be a moral, ethical choice. Demanding that Republicans blindly vote for Trump, on the other hand, would be just the opposite."

"It is not acceptable to ask a moral, dignified man to cast his vote to help elect an immoral man who is absent decency or dignity," Beck wrote on Facebook.

"The alternative does not offer a moral person the same opportunity. If one helps to elect an immoral man to the highest office, then one is merely validating his immorality, lewdness, and depravity."

Beck has been part of the "Never Trump" movement from the beginning.

06-13-16

 Roughly 300 business and GOP leaders who attended the annual three-day "Experts and Enthusiasts" summit in Park City, Utah (former Republican nominee's, Mitt Romney donor retreat) were mostly anti-Trump, said one former Romney aide, with "60 to 70 percent of people here disgusted with the state of the race."

Romney said, "Trump presidency would lead to trickle-down racism." Priebus tweeted that he "couldn't disagree more" and that "SCOTUS [Supreme Court of the United States] is too important. Stop this and unite."

Kendal Unruh (republican Colorado delegate), who called her movement 'Free the Delegates 2016', is leading a group to change GOP rules at the Republican Convention, so that delegates aren't forced to pledge their vote towards whichever candidate won their primary. Instead, she wants them to be able to vote with their 'conscience' - essentially against Trump.

Unruh said "Nobody has any idea who is going to step in and be the nominee, But we're not worried about that. We're just doing that job to make sure that he's (Trump) not the face of our party."

"This is a coalition of Kasich, Cruz and Rubio (supporters) and we are all agreeing on one goal, which is: Anybody but Trump" Unruh said.

The RNC commanded in 2013 that delegates must bind themselves to their state's will. Rules committee member Curly Haugland said "that doesn't mean anything because the rules are dissolved and remade with each new convention.

Steve Lonegan, who is advising the group and raising money through Courageous Conservatives, a super PAC, Courageous Conservatives, said: 'I've woken up every day struggling to accept that he's going to be our candidate.

Lonegan's remarks are a sign of a growing split in the GOP, with many of the old guard suspicious of Trump's motives and Republican qualifications, and worried about polls that show him performing poorly against Hillary Clinton in a presidential match-up.

Lonegan says 'This has never been done before, so there's no textbook on how to do it. So we're building an organic effort, state by state, to convince members of the Rules Committee to sign onto a rule that unbinds the delegates to vote their moral conscience.'

"I will tell you, about every two hours people contact me about how to join this effort" Lonegan said.

06-26-16

 George Will is no longer a Republican — and it's all Donald Trump's fault, the famed conservative columnist said. Will also said:

> "I left it for the same reason I joined it in 1964 when I voted for Barry Goldwater. I joined it because I was a conservative. But I leave for the same reason, that I'm a conservative."

> "To give you a time line, shortly after Trump became the presumptive nominee, he had a summit meeting with Paul Ryan where they stressed their common principles and their vast shared ground, which is much more important than their differences. I thought that was puzzling doubly so because Paul Ryan still didn't endorse him."

> "After Trump went after the Mexican judge from northern Indiana, then Paul Ryan endorsed him. And I decided that, in fact, this is not my party anymore."

"I changed my registration to unaffiliated 23 days ago. I hardly made an announcement. I just mentioned this in a meeting with the Federalist Society."

"So the long and the short of it is, as Ronald Reagan said when he changed his registration, I did not leave the Democratic Party, the Democratic Party left me,"

Trump retaliated by attacking Will this morning on Twitter. "George Will, one of the most overrated political pundits (who lost his way long ago), has left the Republican Party. He's made many bad calls," said the Republican presidential candidate.

07-19-16

Former President George W. Bush told a group of Republican operatives in Dallas "I'm worried that I will be the last Republican president."

Former first lady Barbara Bush said "Trump says "terrible things" about those in the military and women. I don't even think about him, I'm sick of him."

08-08-16

Bret Stephens (Republican Journalist) from The Wall Street Journal said:

"This is where Republicans now find themselves with their presidential nominee. Of all of Donald Trump's vile irruptions — about Sen. John McCain's military record, or reporter Serge Kovaleski's physical handicap, or Judge Gonzalo Curiel's judicial fitness — his casual smear of Ghazala Khan is perhaps the vilest."

"The central issue in this election isn't Mr. Trump's ideas, such as they are. It's his character, such as it is. The sin, in this case, is the sinner."

"It will not do for Republicans to say they denounce Mr. Trump's personal slanders; his nativism and protectionism and isolationism; his mendacity and meanness and crassness; his disdain for constitutional protections — and still campaign for his election."

08-02-16

Retiring Rep. Richard Hanna (R-N.Y.) announced he will vote for Hillary Clinton in November because Donald Trump is "unfit to serve our party and cannot lead this country."

Hanna is the first Republican member of Congress to announce he will vote for the former secretary of state Hillary Clinton, putting him among several conservative and establishment holdouts known as the #NeverTrump movement.

Hanna said:

"In his latest foray of insults, Mr. Trump has attacked the parents of a slain U.S. soldier. Where do we draw the line?" Hanna asked in an article that the news outlet Syracuse.com published Tuesday. "I thought it would have been when he alleged that U.S. Sen. John McCain was not a war hero because he was caught. Or the countless other insults he's proudly lobbed from behind the Republican presidential podium. For me, it is not enough to simply denounce his comments: He is unfit to serve our party and cannot lead this country."

"I trust she (Hillary) can lead. All Republicans may not like the direction, but they can live to win or lose another day with a real candidate," he wrote. "Our response to the public's anger and the need to rebuild requires complex solutions, experience, knowledge and balance. Not bumper sticker slogans that pander to our disappointment, fear and hate."

08-05-16

After deciding to vote for Hillary Clinton Micheal J. Morell wrote:

"During a 33-year career at the Central Intelligence Agency, I served presidents of both parties — three Republicans and three Democrats. I was at President George W. Bush's side when we were attacked on Sept. 11; as deputy director of the agency, I was with President Obama when we killed Osama bin Laden in 2011."

"Mr. Trump has no experience on national security. Even more important, the character traits he has exhibited during the primary season suggest he would be a poor, even dangerous, commander in chief."

"These traits include his obvious need for self-aggrandizement, his overreaction to perceived slights, his tendency to make decisions based on intuition, his refusal to change his views based on new information, his routine carelessness with the facts, his unwillingness to listen to others and his lack of respect for the rule of law."

"Mr. Trump has also taken policy positions consistent with Russian, not American, interests — endorsing Russian espionage against the United States, supporting Russia's annexation of Crimea and giving a green light to a possible Russian invasion of the Baltic States."

"In the intelligence business, we would say that Mr. Putin had recruited Mr. Trump as an unwitting agent of the Russian Federation."

08-08-16

GOP senator Susan Collins (republican-Maine) wrote:

"I will not be voting for Donald Trump for president."

"My conclusion about Mr. Trump's unsuitability for office is based on his disregard for the precept of treating others with respect, an idea that should transcend politics. Instead, he opts to mock the vulnerable and inflame prejudices by attacking ethnic and religious minorities."

"I am also deeply concerned that Mr. Trump's lack of self-restraint and his barrage of ill-informed comments would make an already perilous world even more so. It is reckless for a presidential candidate to publicly raise doubts about honoring treaty commitments with our allies. Mr. Trump's tendency to lash out when challenged further escalates the possibility of disputes spinning dangerously out of control."

"I had hoped that we would see a "new" Donald Trump as a general-election candidate — one who would focus on jobs and the economy, tone down his rhetoric, develop more thoughtful policies and, yes, apologize for ill-tempered rants. But the unpleasant reality that I have had to accept is that there will be no "new" Donald Trump, just the same candidate who will slash and burn and trample anything and anyone he perceives as being in his way or an easy scapegoat. Regrettably, his essential character appears to be fixed, and he seems incapable of change or growth."

08-08-16

Fifty of the nation's most senior Republican national security officials have signed a letter declaring that Donald J. Trump "lacks the character, values and experience" to be president and "would put at risk our country's national security and well-being."

"We agreed to focus on Trump's fitness to be president, not his substantive positions," said John B. Bellinger III, who was Ms. Rice's legal adviser at the National Security Council and the State Department, and who drafted the letter."… "He is unable or unwilling to separate truth from falsehood," the letter says. "He does not encourage conflicting views. He lacks self-control and acts impetuously. He cannot tolerate personal criticism. He has alarmed our closest allies with his erratic behavior. All of these are dangerous qualities in an individual who aspires to be president and commander in chief, with command of the U.S. nuclear arsenal."

08-17-16

GOP speechwriter Richard J. Cross, III may vote for Hillary Clinton. He wrote:

> "I'm a lifelong political animal and a longtime Maryland Republican. I worked on the staffs of Maryland Congresswoman Helen Bentley and Congressman/Gov. Bob Ehrlich. I also served on the GOP staff of the House Financial Services Committee."

> "I personally drafted the speech of the "Benghazi mom," Patricia Smith. In that speech, I concluded with the following line: "If Hillary Clinton can't give us the truth, why should we give her the presidency?" As a political speechwriter, that was something of a home run moment for me. The New Yorker called the speech "the weaponization of grief."

> "While I'm proud of my service to the Republican Party, I am not proud of the present state of American politics. I look around me; everything just feels awful and sad.

The divisions in our national discourse are great, and there is no political hero waiting to rescue us from ourselves. Instead, we're confronted by the awful spectacle of a "Mothra versus Godzilla" election. And, just like in the movies, no matters who wins, Tokyo suffers."

"Regardless, the reality is, I cannot vote for Donald Trump. I could never vote for Donald Trump."

08-27-16

Anti-Trump Republicans are preparing to launch a broadcast TV ad in a handful of swing-state suburbs urging Donald Trump to quit the presidential race so the party can replace him with a more electable nominee.Regina Thomson, a Colorado Republican activist and leader of Free the Delegates group is behind the ad.

The 30-second spot is marked for a limited run on broadcast networks in suburban Florida, Virginia, Ohio and Michigan. The ad, titled "Keep Your Word," features footage of Trump during the Republican primary in which he suggested he'd drop out if he saw his poll numbers decline.

"No. 1, I'm not a masochist, and if I was dropping in the polls where I saw I wasn't going to win, why would I continue?" Trump said in an October NBC interview featured in the political ad. A graphic displaying political handicappers' predictions of a landslide Trump loss accompanies his remarks. The ad ends with a plea: "Resign the nomination. Let the RNC replace you so we can beat Hillary."

Speaker of the House Paul Ryan told fellow Republicans he will no longer defend Donald Trump and will instead use the next 29 days to focus on preserving his party's hold on Congress.

"The speaker is going to spend the next month focused entirely on protecting our congressional majorities," Ryan's spokeswoman, AshLee Strong, said in a statement.

Ryan told lawmakers, "you all need to do what's best for you and your district."

Trump responded to the House speaker on Twitter Monday, saying Ryan should focus on other policy areas instead of fighting with the Republican nominee.

10-11-16

After a video surfaced from 2005 that showed Trump making lewd and sexually aggressive comments about women, republicans lined up to condemn him.

New Jersey Gov. Chris Christie, said "I was there when he found out about it and there's no question in my mind he's embarrassed by it." ... "But I think that he should have been much more direct and much more focused on saying, just saying 'I'm sorry' and only 'I'm sorry,' and that's what I would have done.'"

Trump's response to all the republican attacks:

"Our very weak and ineffective leader, Paul Ryan, had a bad conference call where his members went wild at his disloyalty."

 "Despite winning the second debate in a landslide (every poll), it is hard to do well when Paul Ryan and others give zero support."

"The very foul mouthed Sen. John McCain begged for my support during his primary (I gave, he won), then dropped me over locker room remarks!"

"Disloyal R's are far more difficult than Crooked Hillary. They come at you from all sides. They don't know how to win - I will teach them."

"With the exception of cheating Bernie out of the nom the Dems have always proven to be far more loyal to each other than the Republicans!."

"I hear these horror shows, and we have to make sure that this election is not stolen from us and is not taken away from us."

"It is so nice that the shackles have been taken off me and I can now fight for America the way I want to."

10-12-16

 More fallout after a video surfaced from 2005 that showed Trump making lewd and sexually aggressive comments about women.

Republican fundraisers, "bundlers," and donors' (all want to remain anonymous) make their responses:

"I cannot express my disappointment enough regarding the recent events surrounding Mr. Trump," one donor wrote to a Trump fundraiser in an email with the subject line "Trump support withdrawal."

"I regret coming to the Trump support event, and in particular allowing my son to be a part of it," the donor, who had given to and raised money for Trump, said. "I respectfully request that my money be refunded."

A second donor also requested his money be returned because he is "mortified" over the leaked videotape, according to another email obtained by NBC News.

"I can not (sic) support a sexist man. I have three young children and will not support a crude sexist man," the second donor wrote. "I expect a refund of my donation. Please process immediately and I thank you for your help."

A bundler, who says he has raised close to $1 million for Trump, said he, too, is fed up with the nominee and has informed the Trump Victory fundraising leaders that he's done raising money for the candidate.

"I give up. I'm totally walking out and disappointed, and the last 72 hours I have lost sleep over it," a bundler said.

The long-time Republican bundler, who has raised money in Florida, Ohio, Los Angeles and in the Northeast, said that he is ashamed of his solicitations of cash for Trump, adding that he raised money for him as recently as last week.

"We have to make America great, but he's using the wrong slogan," he said. "It should be, 'You're destroying America,'" he said.

"I'm embarrassed. I'm really embarrassed" he said. "I shook hands with him last week and now I want to wash my hand."

10-25-16

Reps. Bob Dold (R-Ill.), Mike Coffman (R-Colo.), David Jolly (R-Fla.), John Katko (R-N.Y.) and Brian Fitzpatrick, a Pennsylvania Republican don't want to be connected to Donald Trump.They say association with the republican nominee amounts to defamation. They want the Democratic Party to stop all the ads that include them with Trump.

One Jolly ad asks voters to "imagine" Trump as president with Jolly supporting him, providing some roughly manipulated pictures of the two together to help fill in the blanks. Jolly's lawyers say the commercial is "patently false," telling a local Florida station that just because the ad includes the words "dramatization" doesn't mean it can display "fraudulent images."

World Leaders Are "Shocked!"

06-30-16

Trump said in his campaign announcement speech (06-30-15) that Mexican migrants were bringing "drugs, crime, and rapists" to the United States.

He later called his comments "100 percent correct," but insisted he was a strong supporter of Mexicans. "How can I not love people who give me many millions of dollars for apartments?"

After Trump's comments about Mexico Dalton Remirez to design an extremely bashable piñata bearing Trump's visage. The candy-filled sculpture retails for about $40, and Ramirez says it has been flying off shelves. "This piñata especially is the one everyone wants to break, the piñatas bearing Trump's likeness, included a flange of blonde hair and a big mouth."

07-20-16

What Trump said about supporting NATO allies:

> He would first look at their contributions to the alliance before automatically commit to defending them.

> In regards to the Baltic States that have recently entered NATO, if Russia attacked them, he would decide whether to come to their aid only after reviewing if those nations have "fulfilled their obligations to us."

> Trump threaten to withdraw American forces from Europe and Asia if those allies fail to pay more for American protection.

"I don't think we have a right to lecture," Mr. Trump said.

"Look at what is happening in our country, how are we going to lecture when people are shooting policemen in cold blood?"

Mr. Trump re-emphasized the hard-line nationalist approach that has marked his improbable candidacy, describing how he would force allies to shoulder defense costs that the United States has borne for decades, cancel longstanding treaties he views as unfavorable, and redefine what it means to be a partner of the United States.

07-31-16

Interview with ABC's "This Week" George Stephanopoulos, Trump was asked about arming Ukraine to push back against Putin's Russian aggression. Trump said "It's — look, you know, I have my own ideas. He's not going into Ukraine, OK, just so you understand. He's not gonna go into Ukraine, all right? You can mark it down. You can put it down. You can take it anywhere you want."

Stephanopoulos: Well, he's already there, isn't he?

Trump said, "OK— well, he's there in a certain way. But I'm not there. You have Obama there. And frankly, that whole part of the world is a mess under Obama with all the strength that you're talking about and all of the power of NATO and all of this. In the meantime, he's going away. He take — takes Crimea. He's sort of, I mean —

Stephanopoulos: But you said you might recognize that.

Trump said "I'm gonna take a look at it. But you know, the people of Crimea, from what I've heard, would rather be with Russia than where they were. And you have to look at that, also. Now, that was under — just so you understand, that was done under Obama's administration."

TRUMP ZAP! On global relationships, U.S.A. is suppose to be the grown up at the table not the crazy aunt in the attack!

10 VICE PRESIDENT MIKE PENCE ?

(ALT-RIGHT LOVE HIM)

Donald Trump choose Governor Mike Pence to balance his ticket, this pleased both Conservatives and Evangelicals of the Republican Party.

07-12-16

Trump's running mate Mike Pence, describes himself as "a Christian, a conservative and a Republican, in that order."

In 2015 as Governor of Indiana he signed a law that critics said would have allowed businesses to deny service to gay people for religious reasons.

When Pence was a Congressman he opposed President George W. Bush's Medicare expansion and the No Child Left Behind education overhaul.

Pence clashed with the local Catholic archdiocese by opposing the settlement of Syrian refugees in Indianapolis.

Pence has close ties to billionaire industrialists David and Charles Koch and their network of wealthy donors.

Pence described himself as "Rush Limbaugh on decaf, "When he was a conservative talk-radio host in the 1990s.

07-14-16

Information you need to know about Trump's presumptive VP pick:

Pence said in 2000 in his agenda for the 107th Congress. "Homosexuality is incompatible with military service because the presence of homosexuals in the ranks weakens unit cohesion."

According to the pro-LGBT organization's archives, the Human Rights Campaign gave him a "0" on his Congressional Scorecard for not supporting its position on any issue for at least three years.

Pence signed a bill that prohibits Indiana from doing business with companies that boycott Israel.

Pence expand health insurance coverage for low-income families in Indiana through Obama care. Later he had participants pay a monthly premium to offset costs.

Pence compared the upholding of President Barack Obama's health care law to the 9/11 terrorist attacks, in a closed-door House GOP meeting in 2012.

In 2001, Pence said "global warming is a myth" and that the "environmental movement has found [in climate change] a new chant for their latest 'chicken little' attempt to raise taxes and grow centralized governmental power."

Pence barred Syrian refugees from entry into Indiana "to ensure the safety and security of all Hoosiers." He later admitted that he could not block Syrians who have been admitted to America – many after months of screening – into the state.

Pence wanted to institute a state-run, taxpayer-funded news service in Indiana called JustIN. He shut down the operation due to the backlash, stressing that it was "well intentioned."

Pence said in April 2016, "I'm not against anybody, but I will be voting for Ted Cruz in the upcoming primary."

07-15-16

1998 statements from Mike Pence's website:

"Time for a quick reality check. Despite the hysteria from the political class and the media, smoking doesn't kill."

The Food and Drug Administration's tobacco regulation is an action of "big government," and that a government large "enough to go after smokers is big enough to go after you."

"Global warming is a myth," "[Bill] Clinton must be impeached" for a sexual relationship with Monica Lewinsky and "George Washington was a Republican."

Leslie Lenkowsky (Buzzfeed), who has known the governor for two decades said "Mike sees himself as a champion of a very culturally conservative set of values that represent small-town Middle America. He sees his role as protecting them."

07-16-16

More Info. You need to know about Mike Pence:

In congress Pence voted in favor of building a fence on the Mexico border.

Pence has tried to defund Planned Parenthood.

The NRA rated him "A" for his pro-gun record.

In Congress, he voted to ban product misuse lawsuits against gun manufacturers, and to loose restrictions on interstate gun purchases.

07-18-16

What Mike Pence said in 1999, about Disney's movie "Mulan":

"I suspect that some mischievous liberal at Disney assumes that Mulan's story will cause a quiet change in the next generation's attitude about women in combat and they just might be right."

"Despite her delicate features and voice, Disney expects us to believe that Mulan's ingenuity and courage were enough to carry her to military success on an equal basis with her cloddish cohorts."

"Obviously, this is Walt Disney's attempt to add childhood expectation to the cultural debate over the role of women in the military."

"The hard truth of our experiment with gender integration is that it has been an almost complete disaster for the military and for many of the individual women involved."

"Many young women find many young men to be attractive sexually. Put them together, in close quarters, for long periods of time, and things will get interesting. Just like they eventually did for young Mulan. Moral of story: women in military, bad idea."

According to Buzzfeed: After leaving his job as president of the Indiana Policy Review Foundation, Pence launched his career in talk radio. First, he hosted "The Mike Pence Show," which aired on 18 stations throughout the state for a few hours each morning. Before his stint in Congress, he hosted a weekend political talk show in Indianapolis.

07-20-16

In 2000 Mike Pence proposed that Ryan White Act money intended for organizations providing HIV/AIDS care be redirected from organizations that support LGBT rights to "those institutions which provide assistance to those seeking to change their sexual behavior."

The GOP adopted CONVERSION THERAPY into its 2016 "national platform".

After a big uproar the amendment to the platform was changed to: "We support the right of parents to determine the proper treatment or therapy, for their minor children."

11 THE REPUBLICAN CONVENTION

Many republicans headed to Cleveland Ohio with anxious reservation, not only did they anticipate a large group of protesters outside the convention hall but also inside.

06-06-16

Telly Lovelace is the national director for African American initiatives and urban media for the Republican National Committee."So far, only 18 of the 2,472 delegates headed to the Cleveland convention next month will be black. Just 18! Now, we won't know the final tally for a few more weeks but it is pretty safe to say Cleveland likely won't have as many African Americans as at other conventions," he said in email sent to an undisclosed list of recipients.

06-27-16

POLITICO contacted more than 50 prominent governors, senators and House members to gauge their interest in speaking at the Republican Convention.

Only a few said they were open to it, and everyone else said they weren't planning on it, didn't want to or weren't going to Cleveland at all — or simply didn't respond.

Here are some response:

> "I'm not," said South Carolina Rep. Mark Sanford, a former two-term governor. "But hope you have a good Thursday!"

"Don't know," said Sean Duffy, a reality-TV star-turned-Wisconsin congressman. "I haven't thought about it."

Florida Rep. Carlos Curbelo: "I won't be there."

"Everyone has to make their own choice, but at this point, 70 percent of the American public doesn't like Donald Trump. That's as toxic as we've seen in American politics," said Stuart Stevens, a longtime Republican strategist who helped to craft the party's 2012 convention. "Normally, people want to speak at national conventions. It launched Barack Obama's political career."

07-12-16

Republicans platform proposals:

Bars military women from combat.

Describes coal as a "clean" energy source.

Stipulating "that man-made law must be consistent with God-given, natural rights."

An amendment encourages the teaching of the Bible in public schools. A good understanding of its contents is "indispensable for the development of an educated citizenry."

Overturn the Supreme Court gay marriage decision with a constitutional amendment.

Appoint judges "who respect traditional family values."

Promoted state laws to limit which restrooms transgender people could use.

Proposed "conversion therapy" for gays by saying that parents should be free to make medical decisions about their children without interference and stated that "natural marriage" between a man and a woman is most likely to result in offspring who do not become drug-addicted or otherwise damaged.

Build a wall along the United States border with Mexico.

Conservative activists like Tony Perkins, the president of the Family Research Council, help with dozens of amendments on issues like gun control, religious expression and bathroom use.

Perkins said "He is going to be the nominee for the party. He has his own ideas," Mr. Perkins told reporters on Monday. "But this is a statement of not Donald Trump's campaign, but of the Republican Party."

07-18-16

Donald Trump upstaged his own Republican Convention.

Trump called Fox News for an interview on the Bill O'Reilly's show to trash Ohio Gov. John Kasich, a fellow Republican with whom he competed in the GOP primary, while previewing his Thursday speech.

New York Times reporter Maggie Haberman called the move "unusual."

CNN senior media correspondent Brian Stelter found it "fascinating."

During Trump's call Fox News did not air the impassioned speech of Patricia Smith, the mother of a victim of the 2012 terror attack in Benghazi, Libya.

07-18-16

 At the Republican Convention Anti- Trump forces lost their attempt to demand for a state-by-state roll call vote on the party rules. Hundreds of socially conservative delegates opposed to nominating Trump protested noisily after the convention's presiding officer, Arkansas GOP Rep. Steve Womack, abruptly put the rules to a vote and declared them approved by voice.

Carol Hanson, an Iowa delegate, said some members of the state delegation left just before the vote and others walked out as soon as the roll call was denied. "Some of them were disgusted," she said.

Iowa Governor Terry Branstad said in a brief interview he was glad that most of his state's delegation did not walk out because it was critical to avoid anything that would jeopardize the State's first in the nation status.

Colorado State Rep. Justin Everett, a Cruz supporter, said some of the state's delegation briefly walked out, but returned in time for the motion to reconsider.

A two-paragraph section of Melania's Trump's speech about family values bears nearly identical phrasing to Michele Obama's 2008 address."My parents impressed on me the values that you work hard for what you want in life. That your word is your bond, and you do what you say and keep your promise. That you treat people with respect," Melania told delegates about halfway through her speech Monday night.

Compare that to Michele's, which said: "Barack and I were raised with so many of the same values: that you work hard for what you want in life; that your word is your bond and you do what you say you're going to do; that you treat people with dignity and respect, even if you don't know them, and even if you don't agree with them."

Melania went on to emphasize the need to "pass those lessons on to the many generations to follow, because we want our children in this nation to know that the only limit to your achievements is the strength of your dreams and the willingness to work for them."

It's a near mirror of the next line in Michele's speech: "We want our children — and all children in this nation — to know that the only limit to the height of your achievements is the reach of your dreams and your willingness to work for them."

"In writing her beautiful speech, Melania's team of writers took notes on her life's inspirations, and in some instances included fragments that reflected her own thinking," Trump senior communications advisor Jason Miller said in the statement. "Melania's immigrant experience and love for

America shone through in her speech, which made it such a success."

The media was immediately citing the nearly verbatim text from Obama's speech.

Trump slips up?

Trump said on the TODAY Show that she wrote the speech largely on her own, telling host Matt Lauer that: "I read once over it, and that's all. Because I wrote it…with as little help as possible."

07-19-16

At the Republican Convention Sajid Tarar, founder of American Muslims for Trump, prayed for peace and an end to terrorism, a man stood up in the upper part of the arena and tried to shout him down.

The Trump supporter repeatedly chanting "No Islam." He refused to give his name to reporters, but he had a badge signifying he was an alternate delegate and was wearing a blue "Make America Great Again" hat."My obligation is to God. This is an abomination to God," the man said.

07-20-16

Queen's longtime guitarist Brian May complained about "We Are the Champions" being played at a Trump event, reported Rolling Stone magazine.

"This is not an official Queen statement, but I can confirm that permission to use the track was neither sought nor given," May said on his website on June 8. "We are taking advice on what steps we can take to ensure this use does not continue.

"Regardless of our views on Mr. Trump's platform, it has always been against our policy to allow Queen's music to be used as a political campaigning tool. Our music embodies our own dreams and beliefs, but it is for all who care to listen and enjoy."

(Queen's Song "We Are the Champions" was played at the Republican Convention on Monday. It was not authorized, the British band said on social media, charging that the song was played against its wishes.)

Queen's label Sony/ATV Music also issued its own statement after the song was played when Donald Trump, now the official Republican Party presidential nominee, appeared at the convention Monday night to introduce his wife Melania Trump, noted People magazine.

Sony/ATV's said it was never asked by Trump, his campaign or company to use "We Are the Champions."

"On behalf of the band, we are frustrated by the repeated unauthorized use of the song after a previous request to desist, which has obviously been ignored by Mr. Trump and his campaign," said a Sony/ATV statement, per People Magazine.

"Queen does not want its music associated with any mainstream or political debate in any country. Nor does Queen want 'We Are the Champions' to be used as an endorsement of Mr. Trump and the political views of the Republican Party. We trust, hope and expect that Mr. Trump and his campaign will respect these wishes moving forward."

07-22-16

Comments by Ted Cruz (Republican presidential candidate) after he was booed at the Republican Convention for not endorsing Trump during his speech:

> Cruz said that he's not "in the habit" of backing politicians who attack his family.
>
> "I congratulate Donald Trump on winning the nomination last night," Cruz said. "And like each of you, I want to see the principles that our party believes prevail in November" Cruz said.
>
> "Don't stay home in November," Cruz said toward the end of his otherwise very well-received speech. "Stand and speak and vote your conscience."

Andy Abboud, a senior aide to the Las Vegas casino magnate GOP mega donor Sheldon Adelson, said "When he didn't endorse, they were stunned and disappointed, "We could not allow Ted Cruz to use the Adelsons as a prop against Donald Trump."

New Jersey Gov. Chris Christie -- a former presidential candidate said "I think it was awful, "And quite frankly, I think it was something selfish. And he signed a pledge. And it's his job to keep his word."

Trump said "Wow, Ted Cruz got booed off the stage, didn't honor the pledge! I saw his speech two hours early but let him speak anyway. No big deal!"

TRUMP ZAP! Thanks to Trump the official new language of the U.S.A. is "Bullshit!"

12 THE DEMOCRATIC CONVENTION

The Democratic National Convention was also met with protestors outside its doors and on the floor. Philadelphia was not the "City of Brotherly Love" this week.

07-22-16

Presumptive Democratic presidential nominee Hillary Clinton has named Virginia Sen. Tim Kaine as her running mate for the 2016 election.

Hillary tweeted "I'm thrilled to announce my running mate, Tim Kaine, a man who's devoted his life to fighting for others."

During his time at Harvard Law School, Kaine taught vocational school along side Jesuit missionaries (he speaks fluent Spanish). He worked as a housing rights lawyer and part-time law school professor in Richmond for more than 15 years before running for city council. He was mayor of Richmond, then served as lieutenant governor to Mark Warner in 2002 and later as Virginia governor and chairman of the Democratic National Committee.

07-25-16

Some statements by Senator Elizabeth Warren at the Democratic Convention:

> "On one side is a man (Trump) who inherited a fortune from his father and kept it going by cheating people, by skipping out on debts. A man who has never sacrificed

anything for anyone. A man who cares only for himself, every minute of every day."

"There is lots of wealth in America but it isn't trickling down to hard-working families like yours."

"Not once did he (Trump) lift a finger to help working people. And why would he? His whole life has been about taking advantage of that rigged system. Time after time, he preyed on working people, people in debt, people who had fallen on hard times… Donald Trump goes on and on and on about being a successful businessman but he filed business bankruptcy six times."

"Donald Trump wants to get rid of the federal minimum wage… Donald Trump has a tax plan to give multimillionaires and billionaires like himself an average tax cut of $1.3 million a year."

"Trump thinks he can win votes by fanning the flames of fear and hatred. By turning neighbor against neighbor. By persuading you that the real problem in America is your fellow Americans – people who don't look like you, or don't talk like you, or don't worship like you."

"Donald Trump's America, an America of fear and hate. An America where we all break apart. Whites against blacks and Latinos. Christians against Muslims and Jews. Straight against gay. Everyone against immigrants."

07-25-16

Some statements at the Democratic Convention by Bernie Sanders, runner-up in the race to become the Democratic nominee:

> "While Donald Trump is busy insulting one group after another, Hillary Clinton understands that our diversity is one of our greatest traits."

> "We need leadership in this country which will improve the lives of working people, the children, the elderly, the sick and the poor. We need leadership that brings our people together and makes us stronger, not leadership that insults Latinos and Mexicans, insults Muslims and women and African-Americans and veterans and seeks to divide us up."

> "Brothers and sisters," Sanders said, his "revolution" was built – universal health care, raising the minimum wage, rebuilding infrastructure, limiting the influence of big-money campaign donations, tackling climate change and protecting abortion rights, LGBT rights and more – and he insisted for each one: "Hillary Clinton understands."

07-27-16

Former New York City Mayor Michael Bloomberg, the self-made media mogul and one of the wealthiest men in the world Comments at the Democratic Convention:

> "Trump says he wants to run the nation like he's running his business? God help us, I'm a New Yorker,

and I know a con when I see one."

"I am asking you to join with me, not out of party loyalty, but out of love of country, and together, let's elect a sane, competent person (Hillary Clinton)."

TRUMP ZAP! Trump's new sign at the Statue of Liberty says "Don't let the door hit you where the good lord split you!

13 REPUBLICANS CONCEDE "TRUMP NOT SO BAD," AFTER THE SHOTGUN WEDDING!

06-17-16

Duncan Hunter (R-Calif.), who co-chairs Trump's House Leadership Committee, comments after Trump wins Republican Party nomination:

"Trump's going to do what Trump's going to do."

"What I'm done with is trying to articulate or explain or answer for what Donald Trump says," Hunter said. "I think he'll be a great president. I think he'll make good decisions on the economy, on the border, on national security, but it doesn't mean we endorse what he says. I think what he says and what he'll do are two different things."

"But you just said you don't necessarily believe what he says is what he's going to do," said a Washington Post reporter.

"Right," Hunter said. "True. But him talking about things and saying things about things is different than him saying what he's going to do. I think he'll do what he says he's going to do. I'm not trying to parse words; I think he'll do what he says he's going to do. But he says things about things that I don't endorse, and I'm not going to try to articulate for him."

07-12-16

House Speaker Paul Ryan comments after endorsing Trump:

> "In the balance of things, the good clearly outweighs the things I don't agree with," Ryan said. "We don't have people who run for office who 100% reflect all of our views. It doesn't work like that."

> "It is a binary choice, it is either Donald Trump or Hillary Clinton. You don't get a third option."

08-08-16

Former Florida governor's eldest son, George P. Bush, 40, is a Texas Land Commissioner. He said to members of the State Republican Executive Committee, "From Team Bush, it's a bitter pill to swallow, but you know what? You get back up and you help the man that won and you make sure that we stop Hillary Clinton."

09-23-16

What Republican Presidential Candidate Senator Ted Cruz had to say about voting for Trump:

> "After many months of careful consideration, of prayer and searching my own conscience, I have decided that on Election Day, I will vote for the Republican nominee, Donald Trump."

> "First, last year, I promised to support the Republican

nominee. And I intend to keep my word. Second, even though I have had areas of significant disagreement with our nominee, by any measure Hillary Clinton is wholly unacceptable — that's why I have always been #NeverHillary."

"Donald Trump is the only thing standing in her way, and if you don't want to see a Hillary Clinton presidency, I encourage you to vote for him."

Conservative talk show host Steve Deace, who backed Cruz during the primaries, called the move the "worst political calculation I've ever witnessed."

TRUMP ZAP! Trump doesn't have a closet full of skeletons he has a warehouse!

14 TRUMP'S GENERAL ELECTION RALLIES

["WINNING" THE "RED BLUE" GAME]

08-02-16

What Trump said at a campaign rally in Ashburn, Virginia about a baby crying in the audience:

"I love babies. I hear that baby cry, I like it, ... What a baby. What a beautiful baby. Don't worry, don't worry. The mom's running around, like, don't worry about it, you know. It's young and beautiful and healthy, and that's what we want."

Later the baby kept crying:

"I think she really believed me that I love having a baby crying while I'm speaking. That's OK. People don't understand. That's OK."

08-06-16

What Trump said at a rally about Hillary Clinton:

"Unstable Hillary, she lacks the judgment, temperament and moral character to lead this country," Trump said at his rally. "She is a totally unhinged person."

"Her greatest achievement is getting out of trouble, it's true," Trump said, prompting chants of "lock her up."

"She is a horrible, horrible human being," Trump said. "She's incompetent, and I don't think that you can even

think of allowing this woman to become the president
of the United States."

"She took a little short-circuit in the brain, she has
problems," the GOP nominee said at a rally in
Windham, New Hampshire. "I think the people of this
country don't want somebody who's going to short-
circuit up here."

10-06-16

What Trump said at a rally in Henderson, Nevada about
Terminally ill people getting out to vote:

> "I don't care how sick you are, I don't care if you just
> came back from the doctor and he gave you the worst
> possible prognosis, meaning it's over, you won't be
> around in two weeks. Doesn't matter. Hang out till
> Nov. 8. Get out and vote."

> "All we're going to say is, 'We love you and we will
> remember you always.'"

> "I say kiddingly, but I mean it."

10-14-16

After winning the GOP nomination, Trump's campaign
decided teleprompters were necessary to keep the famously
impatient and rambling Trump on topic and on message.

What Trump said at North Carolina rally after the
teleprompters and speakers malfunctioned:

> "These teleprompters haven't been working for the last

125

20 minutes," Trump complained. "And I actually like my speech better without teleprompters."

"You know what? I like it better without the teleprompter. Get this thing outta here, will you."

"So, here's the story, Here's the way I work. Here's the way government works. So, the teleprompter's a bummer. It doesn't work. That means the company doing the teleprompter is in the back. That means they didn't do a good job. So I won't pay them."

"You know whoever runs this place is not doing very well," Trump said. "Do you hear me over there? Great job fellas! So now we don't have to pay for this and now we don't have to pay for that. Man! Who the hell runs this place?"

"And tomorrow I'll have a story in the newspaper: 'Donald Trump did not pay a contractor who put up the teleprompters.' Well why should I? They don't work. And they'll make me like I'm a bad guy like I'm a bad person."

Trump Said "What" (Trump's Election Team)

Much of what Trump said on the road was off the written speech. He continued to challenge his campaign team.

06-06-16

Priorities USA Action, a super PAC backing Clinton, aired a TV ad showing Trump mocking a reporter's disability.

Trump says of New York Times reporter Serge Kovaleski, whose arthrogryposis impairs his arm movements, "You ought to see this guy," The Republican presidential hopeful waving his arms, widening his eyes and speaking in a weird voice.

Parents of disabled children resisted Trump's crude actions.

Chris and Lauren Glaros, talking about raising a toddler with spina bifida:

> "The children at Grace's school all know never to mock her, and so for an adult to mock a person with a disability is shocking."

> "The incident exposed Trump's soul. "It showed me his heart, and I didn't like what I saw," said Chris.

06-17-16

What Donald Trump the presumptive Republican presidential nominee said about the Orlando shooting inside the Pulse nightclub, at a rally in the Woodlands Waterway Marriott Hotel and Convention Center near Houston:

> "If we had people with bullets going the opposite direction right smack between the eyes of this maniac — if some of those wonderful people had guns strapped right here, right to their waist or right to their ankle, and this son of a bitch comes out and starts shooting — and one of the people in that room happened to have it and goes 'boom, boom,' you know what, that would have been a beautiful, beautiful sight, folks. That would have been a beautiful, beautiful sight."

> "So don't let them take your guns away — and, believe me, you put me in there, we're going to save that

Second Amendment."

"We're gonna save your guns. They're not going to take away your bullets. They're not going to shorten up your magazines. They're not going to do anything."

08-02-16

 At a rally in Ashburn, Virginia a man walked up to Trump and gave him his Purple Heart, Afterwards Trump said, "He said, 'That's my real Purple Heart. I have such confidence in you.' And I said, 'Man, that's, like, that's, like, big stuff.' I always wanted to get the Purple Heart. This was much easier."

In an interview with ABC News' Martha Raddatz on "This Week" in July 2015, his answers to a questions about when he received a lottery number for the draft:

> "I was then entered into the draft, because if I would've gotten a different number, I could've been drafted. I was fortunate, in a sense, because I was not a believer in the Vietnam War," Trump said. "I got a very, very high draft number."

> Raddatz said that the lottery didn't start until 1969. Trump said, "I was entered, excuse me, excuse me. I was entered into the lottery, the draft lottery," he said. "If I would've gotten a low number, I would've been drafted. I would have proudly served. But I got a number, I think it was 356, that's right at the very end. And they didn't get, I don't believe, past even 300."

Trump received five draft deferments, four for education and another for a medical injury. Trump said his medical injury was for bone spurs. Trump claimed to have received a doctor's note. When asked for a copy of the report, he could not provide the doctor's name or documents to prove it.

08-11-16

 US Secret Service official spoke to Trump about his second amendment comment at a rally. What Trump said, "Hillary wants to abolish -- essentially abolish the Second Amendment. By the way, if she gets to pick, if she gets to pick her judges, nothing you can do, folks. Although the Second Amendment people, maybe there is, I don't know," Trump said. "But I tell you what, that will be a horrible day, if Hillary gets to put her judges in, right now we're tied."

Hillary Clinton responded at an Iowa rally. "Words matter my friends, and if you are running to be president or you are president of the United States, words can have tremendous consequences," Clinton said. "Yesterday we witnessed the latest in a long line of casual comments from Donald Trump that cross the line."

08-11-16

 At a rally in Fort Lauderdale Trump accused President Barack Obama of founding the Islamic State terror group. "He is the founder of ISIS," Trump said, repeating, "He's the founder of ISIS, OK?... He's the founder! He founded ISIS."

"And I would say, the co-founder would be crooked Hillary Clinton," Trump added.

09-09-16

 What Trump said at a rally in Pensacola, Florida about

Hillary:

> "being so protected she could walk into this arena right now and shoot somebody with 20,000 people watching right smack in the middle of the heart and she wouldn't be prosecuted, OK."

> "That's what's happening. That is what's happened to our country. I never thought I'd see the day where this has happened to our country."

What Trump said at 2016 Values Voters Summit:

> "A Trump administration, our Christian heritage will be cherished, protected, defended like you have never seen before. Believe me, and that includes religious liberty."

TRUMP ZAP! Trump has such a short attention span he needs a bookmark for greeting cards!

Trump's Charitable Giving "Right"

Trump continually claimed charitable contributions, but he had problems providing proof of his claims.

07-03-16

In 2004 Trump told radio personality Howard Stern that he was giving his royalties from the reality television show "The Apprentice," (over 1 million dollars) to AIDS research and the Police Athletic League…Yet that year Mr. Trump's foundation gave just $1,000 for AIDS research and $106,000 to the Police Athletic League.

In the late 1980s Trump promised to give royalties from his
successful book, "The Art of the Deal," to charities for the
homeless, Vietnam veterans, AIDS and multiple sclerosis.

 Only 8 percent of his charitable giving in those years went to
those causes. Much more went to society galas, his alma
maters and the exclusive schools his children attended.

10-29-16

The Trump foundation gifts:

Largest ever gift $264,631 - was used to renovate a
fountain outside the windows of Trump's Plaza Hotel.

The smallest gift $7 was paid to the Boy Scouts in 1989,
at a time when it cost $7 to register a new Scout.
Trump's oldest son was 11 at the time. Trump did not
respond to a question about whether the money paid to
register him.

Funds to settle legal disputes involving Trump's for-
profit companies and to buy two large portraits of
himself, including one that wound up hanging on the
wall of the sports bar at a Trump-owned golf resort.
Were claimed under charitable contributions.

"All of this is completely consistent with who Trump is.
He's a man who operates inside a tiny bubble that
never extends beyond what he believes is his self-
interest," said Tony Schwartz, Trump's co-author on his
1987 book "The Art of the Deal."

"If your worldview is only you - if all you're seeing is a
mirror - then there's nobody to give money to,"

Schwartz said. "Except yourself."

Trump has declined to supply details about his giving, saying that if charities knew what Trump had donated they would badger him to give more.

"I give mostly to a lot of different groups," Trump said in one interview.

"Can you give us any names?" asked The Washington Post's Drew Harwell in May.

"No, I don't want to. No, I don't want to," Trump responded. "I'd like to keep it private."

New York Attorney General Eric Schneiderman office is also investigating the Trump Foundation, examining its acts of possible self-dealing.

Trump's Flip-Flops

The number of contradictory statements added up rapidly through the campaign. Trump made no effort to be consistent.

06-22-16

Lies Trump said in a speech at his Soho New York Hotel:

The lie: "It all started with her (Hillary) bad judgment in supporting the war in Iraq in the first place. Though I was not in government service, I was among the earliest to criticize the rush to war, and yes, even before the war ever started. But Hillary Clinton learned nothing from Iraq, because when she got into power, she couldn't wait to rush us off to war in Libya."

The truth: while Clinton certainly voted to authorize

the war in Iraq, there is no evidence that Trump criticized it "before the war ever started."

The lie: The United States is "the highest taxed nation in the world."

> The truth: Comparing taxation as a percentage of GDP (26 percent in the U.S.), the Organization for Economic Cooperation ranked us 27th out of 30 countries considered to be our economic peers.

The lie: "Under [Clinton's] plan, we would admit hundreds of thousands of refugees from the most dangerous countries on Earth — with no way to screen who they are or what they believe."

> The truth: The process to get a refugee to the United States takes about two years, and involves running names, biographical information and fingerprints through federal terrorism databases.

The lie: Clinton "has spent her entire life making money for special interests — and I will tell you, she has made plenty of money for them, and she has been taking plenty of money out for herself."

> The truth: "Early in her career, Mrs. Clinton worked for the Children's Defense Fund and as a lawyer for the House impeachment inquiry against President Richard Nixon, and later worked at the private Rose Law Firm in Arkansas, focusing on intellectual property and other cases. Much of her career has been devoted to government service, as first lady, United States senator and Secretary of State.

But Mrs. Clinton did receive millions of dollars in paid speeches to banks and others and has served on the boards of corporations like Walmart. Mr. Trump argues that she also made money for big donors through her activities at the State Department and her family foundation, but he has not offered clear, convincing proof."

07-27-16

The Democratic Party candidates had raised issue with the minimum wage, Trump responded, "The minimum wage has to go up," Trump said at a tumultuous news conference, saying it should go up to $10 from $7.25. He did say that "states should really call the shot," but "at the same time, people have to be taken care of."

Asked if he meant the federal minimum wage has to go up to $10 in a follow-up question, Trump indicated yes. "Federal," he clarified.

In May, Trump told Fox News that states should choose the wage. "In some states, where it's more expensive, maybe they do have to lift the minimum wage, and in others, they don't have to do it. And those people live very well," Trump said then.

During a Republican primary debate in November, he also said that wages were "too high" and that the U.S. was becoming a "non-competitive country."

"I would leave it and raise it somewhat," Trump told Bill O'Reilly on the Fox News Channel Tuesday. Asked again, he said, "I would say 10. I would say 10." He added, "But the thing is, Bill, let the states make the deal."

Speaker Paul Ryan, like most Republicans, has opposed raising the minimum wage for years, contending a higher minimum wage would hurt the economy.

"Its bad economics," the Wisconsin Republican told CNBC in 2014, opposing a $10 minimum wage. "We don't want to make it more expensive for employers to be able to hire people."

"Bullshit Artist"

The media and candidates attacked Trump for his lack of honesty through out campaign.

08-04-16

Harry Frankfurt, an eminent moral philosopher and former professor at Princeton, said the difference between a lie and "bullshit" is:

> "Telling a lie is an act with a sharp focus. It is designed to insert a particular falsehood at a specific point. . . . In order to invent a lie at all, [the teller of a lie] must think he knows what is true."

> Harry Frankfurt concludes that liars and truth-tellers are both acutely aware of facts and truths. They are just choosing to play on opposite sides of the same game to serve their own ends.

> But someone engaging in B.S., Frankfurt says, "is neither on the side of the true nor on the side of the false. His eye is not on the facts at all . . . except insofar as they may be pertinent to his interest in getting away

with what he says." Frankfurt writes that the B.S.-er's "focus is panoramic rather than particular" and that he has "more spacious opportunities for improvisation, color, and imaginative play. This is less a matter of craft than of art. Hence the familiar notion of the 'bullshit artist.' "

The B.S. artist, however, has lost all connection with reality. He pays no attention to the truth. "By virtue of this," Frankfurt writes, "bullshit is a greater enemy of truth than lies are."

Fareed Zakaria (CNN) called Trump a "Bullshit Artist" and said, "We see the consequences. As the crazy talk continues, standard rules of fact, truth and reality have disappeared in this campaign. Donald Trump has piled such vast quantities of his trademark product into the political arena that the stench is now overwhelming and unbearable."

08-22-16

Fox News host Ainsley Earhardt asked Vice-presidential nominee why "Donald Trump is telling the African-American community 'I am the guy for you,' and he says by 2020 he's going to have 95 percent of the African-American support."

Pence chuckled in response, prompting Earhardt to ask, "Why are you laughing?"

Pence then immediately deflected, "Well, that's Donald
Trump. Look, he has a heart for every American. And also
he's a truth teller. He speaks the truth. It's been the failed
policies of Democratic politicians that have harmed people
living in the cities in this country now for generations... [A]nd
his optimistic view about the 2020 when he's running for re-
election, that's pure Donald Trump."

08-29-16

   Trump's doctor Harold N. Bornstein of New York wrote a
note about Trump's health that he later admitted was dictated
by Trump.

Bornstein told NBC News in an interview broadcast last week
that he wrote the letter in about five minutes while a
limousine waited outside. He said he didn't proofread it.
Bornstein said in writing the letter that he "picked up"
Trump's "kind of language and then just interpreted it to my
own."

 He said that Trump would be "unequivocally" the "healthiest
individual ever elected to the presidency."

The Clinton's blog post said:

"Dr. Bornstein describes Trump's lab test results as
'astonishingly excellent,' which isn't a real medical
description. And while we're at it: Why would a doctor ever
be astonished by good test results?" the post says. "Dr.
Bornstein doesn't explain what tests he conducted to know
that Trump's 'physical strength and stamina are
extraordinary,' so we'll just have to take his word for it."

Leonard E. Burman from The Tax Policy Center said that Trump's initial tax plan would increase budget deficits by 2.8 percent to 5.5 percent of GDP between 2017 and 2026. That would raise the trade deficit by 1.7 percent to 3.3 percent of GDP. Thus, by 2026, trade deficits could be roughly double their recent levels (2.7 percent to 3.0 percent of GDP between 2011 and 2015).

Trump has since withdrawn his original tax proposal and now suggests he may adopt some version of the plan House Speaker Paul Ryan proposed last June.

Trump Tax Plan II, as we understand it, would still add trillions to the deficit because it would cut tax rates dramatically, especially on business income, without significantly broadening the tax base or cutting spending.

08-30-16

Speaking to supporters in Iowa on Saturday, Trump said he would crack down on visitors to the United States who overstay their visas and declared that when any American citizen "loses their job to an illegal immigrant, the rights of that American citizen have been violated."

Trump's New York modeling agency, Trump Model Management, has profited from using foreign models who came to the United States on tourist visas that did not permit them to work here, according to three former Trump models, all noncitizens.

Canadian-born Rachel Blais spent nearly three years working for Trump Model Management said, "Honestly, they are the most crooked agency I've ever worked for, and I've worked for quite a few."

Anastasia Tonello, global head of the US immigration team at Laura Devine Attorneys in New York said "Even unpaid employment is against the law for foreign nationals who do not have a work visa. "If the US company is benefiting from that person, that's work."

These rules for immigrants are in place to "protect them from being exploited," she said. "That U.S. Company shouldn't be making money off you."

09-01-16

Where some of Trump's Republican donors money went:

> $430,000 dollars went to pay his own Mar-a-Lago resort for two parties and a news conference in March — and what's more, he could have saved several thousand dollars if he had booked a different venue instead.

> The Huffington Post reports: "Had Trump instead chosen to hold those events at the nearby West Palm Beach Marriott, he likely would have spent no more than $45,000 for [all three events], based on its estimates for catering the number of people who attended his parties."

> Instead of spending $48,000 at his club in Westchester County, New York, Trump could have used a ballroom at the Westchester Marriott 9 miles away. The likely

cost there: approximately $20,000, said that hotel's
director of catering. [The Huffington Post]

Florida strategist Rick Wilson told The Huffington Post he didn't think Republican donors understood the extent of Trump's self-indulgent splurges. "I think they're only vaguely aware. It's Putinesque," he said.

09-06-16

The children's dance troupe "The USA Freedom Kids" said in a newly filed lawsuit the Trump campaign broke verbal agreements for performances at two events and refused to pay even a $2,500 stipend for the group's travel expenses.

After nine months of haggling with Trump staffers, the group sued the campaign in Sarasota County, Florida, for as much as $15,000 in damages.

Founder Jeff Popick said "This is not an opportunistic thing where we're suing Donald Trump. We're not suing for emotional distress and all that other stuff that people do when they trump up—no pun intended—when they trump up a lawsuit. That's not what this is. This is tangible dollars I spent under false pretenses."

TRUMP ZAP! Trump knows a con-job because he is the "Chancellor of Trump University."

09-20-16

Martin Greenberg won the $1 million hole-in-one contest at the 2010 golf tournament. Trump's Golf Club said the shot had to travel at least 150 yards. The hole was made short on purpose by Trump's Golf Club.

Greenberg's attorney William Fried said the claim was ultimately denied because "the markers at the tee were not set at the right yardage" and that "the course" — owned by Trump in this case — "traditionally sets those markers."

Trump's club and Greenberg settled the case, with the company agreeing to donate $158,000 to a charity chosen by Greenberg, which he later decided would be the Martin Greenberg Foundation.

The money given to Greenberg's charity, however, came from the Donald J. Trump Foundation which is illegal.

"Clearly the Trump Foundation is as much a charitable organization as Trump University is an institute of higher education," the Hillary Clinton campaign said in a statement. "Once again, Trump has proven himself a fraud who believes the rules don't apply to him."

"Trump cannot be trusted with his own charity, but we are supposed to believe he can manage the nation's treasury?" Senator Minority Leader Harry Reid (D-Nev.) tweeted.

09-21-16

"After spending 5 years championing a conspiracy theory to undermine our first African American President, Donald Trump hasn't actually changed his mind. He only gave his 36 second press statement last week to try to change the subject," said Clinton spokesman Jesse Ferguson in a statement.

Trump said that Obama "was" born in the United States and falsely blamed Hillary Clinton for starting the "birther" conspiracy he clung to for years.

"Well, I just want to get on with, you know, we want to get on with the campaign," Trump told ABC 6 of Columbus on Wednesday, when asked what had changed. "And a lot of people were asking me questions. And you know, we want to talk about jobs. We want to talk about the military. We want to talk about ISIS and how to get rid of ISIS. We want to really talk about bringing jobs back to this area because you've been decimated. So we really want to get just back on to the subject of jobs, military, taking care of our vets, et cetera."

10-03-16

What the blue-collar voters that support Trump don't know is that Trump has been stiffing American steel workers on his own construction projects for years.

At least two of Trump's last three construction projects, Trump purchase his steel and aluminum from Chinese manufacturers rather than United States corporations based in states like Pennsylvania, Ohio, Michigan and Wisconsin.

Depriving untold millions of dollars from four key electoral swing states and instead directing it to China. These trade practices have helped decimate the once-powerful industrial center of the United States.

TRUMP ZAP! Trump is like a Magic 8 Ball every time you shack it you get a different answer!

06-02-16

What Hillary Clinton said at a San Diego rally:

"Making Donald Trump our commander in chief would be a historic mistake."

"This is not someone who should ever have the nuclear codes. Because it's not hard to imagine Donald Trump leading us into a war just because somebody got under his very thin skin."

"There's no risk of people losing their lives if you blow up a golf course deal."

"He is not just unprepared, he is temperamentally unfit to hold an office that requires knowledge, stability and immense responsibility."

"His proposal to ban 1 1/2 billion Muslims from even coming to our country doesn't just violate the religious freedom our country was founded on, it's a huge propaganda victory for ISIS," she said.

"We all know the tools Donald Trump brings to the table, "Bragging, mocking, composing nasty tweets. I'm willing to bet he's writing a few right now."

06-13-16

Hillary Clinton's response to Trump complaining she won't say "radical Islam":

> "From my perspective, it matters what we do, not what we say … To me, radical Jihadism, radical Islamism, I think they mean the same thing. I'm happy to say either, Clinton told "Today" co-host Savannah Guthrie.

> Trump's term is like declaring "war on an entire religion."

> "All of his talk and demagoguery and rhetoric is not going to solve the problem. I'm not going to demonize and demagogue and declare war on an entire religion."

> "I think Trump, as usual, is obsessed with name calling and from my perspective it matters what we do, not what we say. It matters that we got [Osama] bin Laden, not what name we called him."

06-27-16

In Cincinnati Ohio Hillary Clinton and Massachusetts Sen. Elizabeth Warren campaign together.

Hillary Clinton push back against Trump's claim to putting "America First" by addressing how his actions invested in other countries instead of Ohio industries.

Clinton said, "IIe rails against other countries, doesn't he? IIe says he's for our workers, but Trump's own products are made in a lot of countries that aren't named America, Trump Suits were made in Mexico. He could have had them made in Brooklyn, Ohio. Trump Furniture is made in Turkey instead of Cleveland. Trump Barware is made in Slovenia instead of Toledo. So how does that all fit into his talk about America first? But that's just the start."

Elizabeth Warren hit hard at Trump:

> "Donald Trump says he'll make America great again, It's right there. It's stamped on the front of his goofy hat. You want to see goofy? Look at him in that hat," Warren said.

> "What kind of a man does that? What kind of a man roots for people to lose their jobs, to lose their homes, to lose their life's savings?" Warren asked. "I'll tell you what kind of a man: A small, insecure, money grubber who fights for no one but himself. What kind of a man? A nasty man who will never become president of the United States."

> But Clinton, Warren said, knows how to beat a "thin-skinned bully who is driven by greed and hate."

> Clinton has the brains, guts, thick skin, steady hands and a good heart that America needs, Warren stressed, adding that those qualities are why she's backing the former secretary of state.

07-25-16

A Trump event was held in Virginia the home state of Clinton's new running mate, Sen. Tim Kaine, whom Trump derided as a "weird little dude" and a political "hack."

Trump spoke in a ballroom in Roanoke. He made fun of Clinton not using her maiden name

"Why did she get rid of it? Hillary Rotten Clinton, Rotten Clinton. Hillary Rotten Clinton, right?" Trump told the crowd. "Maybe that's why, it's too close."

08-08-16

Clinton spoke at St. Petersburg campaign rally:

> "He's got -- I don't know -- a dozen or so economic advisors he just named, hedge fund guys, billionaire guys, six guys named Steve. Now, they tried to make his old, tired ideas sound new."

> "Americans "all know" that Trump's proposals "will give super big tax breaks to large corporations and the really wealthy."

> "Just like him and the guys who wrote the speech, right? We're going to turn that upside down -- we're going to make the wealthy pay their fair share in taxes for a change!"

"There is no other Donald Trump, what you see is what you get, who takes apparent pleasure in tormenting protesters... a reporter with a tough question, even a crying baby and a Gold Star family."

"Here's the other thing I want you to know, because I want you to tell your friends," she said. "Don't let a friend vote Trump."

08-25-16

Trump never stopped his demeaning attacks by stereotyping African Americans, Trump said, "Poverty. Rejection. Horrible education. No housing. No homes. No ownership" … "Crime at levels nobody has seen. Right now … you walk down the street, you get shot."

Clinton's response:

> "From the start, Donald Trump has built his campaign on prejudice and paranoia. He's taking hate groups mainstream and helping a radical fringe take over one of America's two major political parties. His disregard for the values that make our country great is profoundly dangerous."

> "He doesn't see the success of black leaders in every field. The vibrancy of black-owned businesses, the strength of the black church. He doesn't see the excellence of historically black colleges and universities or the pride of black parents watching their children thrive. … He certainly doesn't have any solutions to take on the reality of systemic racism and create more equity and opportunity in communities of color. It

takes a lot of nerve to ask people he's ignored and mistreated for decades, "What do you have to lose?" The answer is everything!"

"A man with a long history of racial discrimination, who traffics in dark conspiracy theories drawn from the pages of supermarket tabloids and the far reaches of the Internet, should never run our government or command our military. If he doesn't respect all Americans, how can he serve all Americans?"

08-26-16

Tim Kaine spoke the next day at a rally in Tallahassee, Florida said:

"Yesterday, Hillary Clinton gave a speech in Reno, Nevada, calling out Donald Trump on a lot of things on this equality idea. Calling him out on the fact that he has supporters like David Duke connected with the Ku Klux Klan who are going around and saying Donald Trump is their candidate because Donald Trump is pushing their values."

"Ku Klux Klan values, David Duke values, Donald Trump values are not American values, they're not our values. We've got to do all we can to fight to push back and win to say that we're still about heading toward that North Star that we set out so long ago."

09-16-16

As the campaign wore on Trump became more inclined to violence.

Two statements made by Donald Trump calling on the assassination of Hillary Clinton:

> "Let's see what happens to her" after the Secret Services abandons her.

> Trump called for the "Second Amendment people" to kill Clinton, in a remark so dangerous and illegal that the Secret Service was compelled to put out a statement about it.

> *Hillary's Endorsements and Trump's Rejections*

Unusual endorsements from traditionally "Republican" individuals and groups as well as non partisan ones were given to Clinton.

06-06-16

What Buzzfeed CEO Jonah Peretti wrote in an internal memo:

> "Buzzfeed had terminated an advertising agreement with the RNC that both parties signed back in April. The agreement called for the GOP to "spend a significant amount on political advertisements slated to run during the fall election cycle."

> "The Trump campaign is directly opposed to the freedoms of our employees in the United States and around the world and in some cases, such as his proposed ban on international travel for Muslims, would make it impossible for our employees to do their jobs."

While "we certainly don't like to turn away revenue that funds all the important work we do across the company," this is a "business exception" the company must make."

"We don't run cigarette ads because they are hazardous to our health, and we won't accept Trump ads for the exact same reason."

09-06-16

The Dallas Morning News editorial board labeled the New York businessman as "not qualified" and someone who "does not deserve your vote."

Under the headline "Donald Trump is no Republican," the newspaper's editorial board said:

"Donald Trump is no Republican and certainly no conservative," the board wrote, later adding, "We have no interest in a Republican nominee for whom all principles are negotiable, nor in a Republican Party that is willing to trade away principle for pursuit of electoral victory. Trump doesn't reflect Republican ideals of the past; we are certain he shouldn't reflect the GOP of the future."

The Morning News has backed every GOP nominee since Richard Nixon in 1968.

The Cincinnati Enquirer endorsed Democratic nominee Hillary Clinton in the 2016 presidential race, breaking from a nearly century-long tradition of backing Republicans:

The editorial board of the Enquirer said that they didn't take breaking their tradition of endorsing GOP candidates lightly.
"But this is not a traditional race, and these are not traditional times," they wrote.

The board called Clinton and her Republican rival, Donald Trump, "the most unpopular pair of presidential candidates in American history."

"Trump, despite all of his bluster about wanting to 'make America great again,' has exploited and expanded our internal divisions," they wrote. "Clinton's arrogance and unwillingness to admit wrongdoing have made her a divisive and distrusted figure as well."

The board called Trump "a clear and present danger to our country," citing his lack of foreign policy experience and exclusionary remarks about women and minorities as some of their "fears" about his candidacy.

"Hillary Clinton has her faults, certainly, but she has spent a lifetime working to improve the lives of Americans both inside and outside of Washington," they wrote. "It's time to elect the first female U.S. president — not because she's a woman, but because she's hands-down the most qualified choice."

09-24-16

The New York Times editorial board endorsed Hillary Clinton for president, and said:

> "Over 40 years in public life, Hillary Clinton has studied these forces and weighed responses to these problems," the editorial stated. "Our endorsement is rooted in respect for her intellect, experience, toughness and courage over a career of almost continuous public service, often as the first or only woman in the arena."

> "A comparison like that would be an empty exercise in a race where one candidate — our choice, Hillary Clinton — has a record of service and a raft of pragmatic ideas, and the other, Donald Trump, discloses nothing concrete about himself or his plans while promising the moon and offering the stars on layaway."

09-28-16

Former GOP Sen. John Warner of Virginia endorses Hillary Clinton and said:

"I will, when I go into the booth cast a vote for the Clinton-Kaine ticket, There's no question about it."

> "We have today the strongest military in the world. No one can compare with us," Warner said. "Does it need to be modified and changed and added to and modernized? You bet it has. But it is not in shambles. It

is not the admirals and the generals and the seniors and rubble in the hallways of the Pentagon...They're still as vibrant as the day I left there during the war in Vietnam."

"You do not pull up a quick text like 'National Security for Dummies,' You have to build on a foundation of experience for how you will go forward in the leadership of this country."

09-28-16

The Arizona Republic editorial board endorses Hillary and said:

> "Since The Arizona Republic began publication in 1890, we have never endorsed a Democrat over a Republican for president. Never. This reflects a deep philosophical appreciation for conservative ideals and Republican principles, this year is different."

> "The 2016 Republican candidate is not conservative and he is not qualified," the editorial board continued. "That's why, for the first time in our history, The Arizona Republic will support a Democrat for president."

09-30-16

Some statments the USA Today editorial board said about Trump:

> "In the 34-year history of USA TODAY, the Editorial

Board has never taken sides in the presidential race. Instead, we've expressed opinions about the major issues and haven't presumed to tell our readers, who have a variety of priorities and values, which choice is best for them. Because every presidential race is different, we revisit our no-endorsement policy every four years. We've never seen reason to alter our approach. Until now."

"This year, the choice isn't between two capable major party nominees who happen to have significant ideological differences. This year, one of the candidates — Republican nominee Donald Trump — is, by unanimous consensus of the Editorial Board, unfit for the presidency."

"Where does that leave us? Our bottom-line advice for voters is this: Stay true to your convictions. That might mean a vote for Clinton, the most plausible alternative to keep Trump out of the White House. Or it might mean a third-party candidate. Or a write-in. Or a focus on down-ballot candidates who will serve the nation honestly, try to heal its divisions, and work to solve its problems."

"Whatever you do, however, resist the siren song of a dangerous demagogue. By all means vote, just not for Donald Trump."

09-30-16

The San Diego Union-Tribune endorses Hillary Clinton and said:

Donald Trump is "vengeful, dishonest and impulsive."

"Terrible leaders can knock nations off course. Trump could be our Chávez," it wrote, referring to Hugo Chávez, the controversial former president of Venezuela. "We cannot take that risk."

Trump "ruins U.S. trustworthiness" and has "an open enemies list."

"Imagine that," the board implores. "Imagine President Trump."

The News paper hasn't endorsed a democrat in 148 years.

10-07-16

Some statements by the editors at The Atlantic Magazine regarding the endorsement of Hillary Clinton:

The Atlantic has endorsed only three presidential candidates in 159 years. Abraham Lincoln (1860) and Lyndon B. Johnson (1964) were the first two.

Donald Trump has no record of public service and no qualifications for public office. His affect is that of an infomercial huckster; he traffics in conspiracy theories and racist invective; he is appallingly sexist; he is erratic, secretive, and xenophobic; he expresses admiration for authoritarian rulers, and evinces authoritarian tendencies himself.

He is easily goaded, a poor quality for someone seeking control of America's nuclear arsenal. He is an enemy of fact-based discourse; he is ignorant of, and indifferent to, the Constitution; he appears not to read.

Our endorsement of Clinton, and rejection of Trump, is not a blanket dismissal of the many Trump supporters who are motivated by legitimate anxieties about their future and their place in the American economy. But Trump has seized on these anxieties and inflamed and racialized them, without proposing realistic policies to address them.

10-10-16

What the editors of Foreign Policy Magazine says about endorsing Hillary for president:

"A Donald Trump presidency is among the greatest threats facing America, and the Republican standard-bearer is the worst major-party candidate for the job in U.S. history."

"In the nearly half century history of Foreign Policy, the editors of this publication have never endorsed a candidate for political office,"

"We cherish and fiercely protect this publication's independence and its reputation for objectivity, and we deeply value our relationship with all of our readers, regardless of political orientation."

"A Donald Trump presidency is among the greatest threats facing America, and the Republican standard-

bearer is the worst major-party candidate for the job in
U.S. history."

And yes, that makes Trump the worst candidate for
president in over 200 years of American history, since
George Washington in 1789. If you want to be precise,
that is 227 years and 44 presidents.

In every key element of a president's duties, Donald
Trump is a disaster. He is, as experts warn, a danger to
not only US national security, but to global security.

11-01-16

Editors-in-chief and Variety Magazine's publisher, Michelle
Sobrino-Stearns endorsed Clinton they said:

"We didn't want to sit on the sidelines and come down
on the wrong side of history, noting the presidential
endorsement is the Magazine's first in its 111-year
history."

"As for Trump's run, the magazine blasted his bid for
president as nothing more than "a ploy to land another
TV deal or launch a new cable channel so he can
continue spewing his sexist, racist views."

"Hillary has often talked about the strength of diversity
in the American fabric, a topic that only recently has
been given meaningful attention among studio chiefs,
network heads, and industry organizations. We would
expect her to continue this conversation from the bully
pulpit of the presidency."

Not-so-subtle remarks, signs and tolerance for blatant acts of bigotry emerged in campaign.

06-13-16

What Pastor Anderson said in a YouTube video about the Orlando Fl. Massacre:

> "These homosexuals are a bunch of perverts and pedophiles, that's who was a victim here, a bunch of disgusting homosexuals at a gay bar," he said. He later added: "The good news is that at least 50 of these pedophiles are not going to be harming children anymore. The bad news is that a lot of the homos in the bar are still alive, so they're going to continue to molest children and recruit people into their filthy homosexual lifestyle."

> "These people all should have been killed anyway, but they should have been killed through the proper channels, as in, they should've been executed by a righteous government."

> "Gun owners and pastors are the real victims of the tragedy, predicting that the government will use the massacre as an opportunity to confiscate firearms, demonize Christians and outlaw hateful speech."

07-15-16

What Newt Gingrich said about American Muslims:

> "Let me be as blunt and direct as I can be. Western

civilization is in a war. We should frankly test every person here who is of a Muslim background, and if they believe in sharia, they should be deported," Gingrich said. "Sharia is incompatible with Western civilization. Modern Muslims who have given up sharia — glad to have them as citizens. Perfectly happy to have them next door."

08-29-16

A prominent white nationalist, David Duke said on a robo-call pitching both his and Trump's campaigns as a way to halt increases in immigration and cure what he calls racial aggression, "It's time to stand up and vote for Donald Trump for president and vote for me, David Duke for the US Senate."

In an interview with CNN, Duke said "A candidate has no control over other people's opinions and support, we should vote for Donald Trump."

09-09-16

The man who coined the term "alt-right" Richard Spencer had a news conference at the Peacock Lounge in Washington D.C.. Statements he made:

"Race is real, race matters, and race is the foundation of identity." The ultimate ideal is that the world be divided into ethno-states so that white people could have a "homeland."

"I don't think our support of Trump is really about policy at the end of the day, I think it's really about Trump's style, the fact that he doesn't back down, the fact that he's willing to confront his enemies…You look at that and you think, 'This is what a leader looks like.'"

"It really is about him and it's about, in a way, projecting onto him our hopes and dreams. There's something called 'meme magic,'* and that is a self-fulfilling prophecy…We want to make Trump; we want to imagine him in our image. And that is maybe—you can see that in a meme of Trump as a Napoleon or Trump as some figure out of the Dune novels in an arcade of the future in a robotic suit of armor fighting enemies. All of that stuff is silly, all of that stuff is ridiculous, but it actually gets at something real and that is that we want something more, we want something heroic, we want something that is not defined by liberalism or individual rights or bourgeois norms. We want something that is truly European and truly heroic."

Rather than a multicultural America, his ideal is a white empire. He described his "dream…ethno-state" as "a homeland for all Europeans," which would take an "imperial form."

. "If the alt-right were in power, we would all have arrived here via magnetic levitation trains," he said. "We would have passed by great forests and beautiful images of blond women in a wheat field with their hands, running them through the wheat."

The once-fringe movement has suddenly found a prominent place in the Trump campaign and among its most loyal backers. Stephen Bannon, the Trump campaign CEO, was until recently the head of the conservative website Breitbart News, which he called "the platform for the alt-right."

09-15-16

Excerpts from Breitbart News Daily, SiriusXM show hosted by Trump's new campaign CEO Stephen Bannon from fall 2015:

What Roger Stone , Trump surrogate and former campaign adviser said On the danger facing America:

"The rise of Trump is a repudiation of 30 years of bipartisan treason and failure. Bush equals Clinton equals Bush equals Obama equals Clinton. It's the same policies…immigration policies that may turn us into Europe, where hordes of Islamic madmen are raping, killing, pillaging, defecating in public fountains, harassing private citizens, elderly people — that's what's coming. That wave is coming this way. Only one guy can stop it."

On Hillary Clinton adviser Huma Abedin: "Look, I also think now that Islamic terrorism is going to be front and center, there is going to be a new focus on whether this administration, the administration of Hillary Clinton at State, was permeated at the highest levels by Saudi intelligence and others who are not loyal Americans. I speak specifically of Huma Abedin."

Praise from Bannon: "One of the top political thinkers, strategists, practitioners of the dark arts of politics…a gentleman who, as we've gotten to know him over the last couple of years, has been so right on so many topics time and time again."

Frank Gaffney , president and founder of the Center for Security Policy said On President Obama's alleged sympathies: "I'm afraid that Donald Trump is right, that the president has exhibited sympathy, if not for the terrorists, then certainly for the Islamic supremacists."

Praise from Bannon: "He is one of the senior thought leaders and men of action in this whole war against Islamic radical jihad…doing amazing work, doing God's work, sir. Just fantastic."

Pamela Geller, president of Stop Islamization of America said on radical Muslim "infiltration" of the US government:

"There was some of this under Bush, but nothing like with President Obama. The infiltration of the Department of State, the Department of Defense, you know, even 1600 [Pennsylvania Avenue, i.e., the White House]. It's been a drip, drip, drip. We've reached critical mass now…you know, Obama has stacked these agencies. And that's why the next president, it's not enough for us to elect the right guy, I mean we need someone who is going to do a major purge…The Department of Justice has become a de-facto legal arm for Muslim Brotherhood groups. I mean, they are suing towns, they are suing schools, they are suing prisons, really to impose the Shariah."

Praise from Bannon: "Pamela Geller is one of the top

word experts in radical Islam and Shariah law and Islamic supremacism…the top leading expert in this field…one of the great American patriots. She has been a voice in the wilderness, and now her time has come."

09-20-16

Donald Trump Jr. tweeted a picture of a bowl of Skittles and a statement that said "said it all":

"If I had a bowl of skittles and I told you just three would kill you. Would you take a handful?" "That's our Syrian refu-gee problem." Trump Jr. added: "Let's end the politically correct agenda that doesn't put America first. #trump2016"

"Skittles are candy. Refugees are people. We don't feel it's an appropriate analogy," Wrigley, the parent company of Skittles, said in a statement sent by its vice president of corporate affairs, Denise Young. "We will respectfully refrain from further commentary as anything we say could be misinterpreted as marketing."

The Cato Institute, a libertarian think tank, published a report last week finding that, each year, the risk to an American of being killed by a refugee in a terrorist attack is 1 in 3.64 billion.

09-22-16

Omarosa Manigault was on the first season of Trump's "Apprentice" reality TV series. Trump made her director of African-American outreach.

After hearing President Obama cracking jokes about Trump Omarosa said "It just kept going and going and he just kept hammering him," Manigault said. "And I thought, 'Ohhhh, Barack Obama is starting something that I don't know if he'll be able to finish."

Omarosa said "Every critic, every detractor, will have to bow down to President Trump. It's everyone who's ever doubted Donald, who ever disagreed, who ever challenged him. It is the ultimate revenge to become the most powerful man in the universe."

09-24-16

 Kathy Miller, former chair of Trump's campaign in Mahoning County, Ohio said:

> "Growing up as a kid, there was no racism, believe me."

> "I don't think there was any racism until Obama got elected. We never had problems like this," Miller said. "Now, with the people with the guns, and shooting up neighborhoods, and not being responsible citizens, that's a big change, and I think that's the philosophy that Obama has perpetuated on America."

> "If you're black and you haven't been successful in the last 50 years, it's your own fault. You've had every opportunity, it was given to you." Miller said.

Mark Munroe, the GOP chair for the county, heard the comments, he told the Guardian that he contacted the Trump campaign in Ohio to have Miller dismissed.

In Aurora, Indiana the "Annual Aurora Farmers Fair Parade" had a float made by Frank Linkmeyer.

The description was a morbid execution scene showing Hillary Clinton strapped into an electric chair, flanked by the Grim Reaper, a pastor and a familiar-looking executioner Republican presidential candidate Donald Trump.

It also had on the front a miniature Easter Island head, spray-painted black and labeled "Obama."

Linkmeyer said "It's all in fun, Laughter is the best medicine in life and this country needs more laughter — and the people that are offended by it, I'm sorry. Don't come to the parade next time."
Penny Britton, a mother of five who has lived in Aurora with her husband for more than a decade said "I know a half-dozen minority children that were marching in that parade and even more sitting on the sidewalk watching it go by, and this is the message we are sending to our children?" she added. "I don't see how anyone could look at the statue on the float and not say it was racist."

Britton posted a photo of the float and spoke about it to local media:

> "People have been sending me hateful messages for several days now," she said. "They're telling me I don't belong here, and that if I don't like it I can leave. People have told me this is why they don't like it when outsiders move to their town, and I've been here 10 years."

"The KKK marched in the parade until the '80s,"
Britton noted. "This town has history that goes back for
generations of racism and bigotry. It's something that
nobody likes to talk about."

Mayor Hastings said "We are disappointed that the actions of
a few individuals have taken the focus away from what was
otherwise a very successful 108th Aurora Farmers Fair,"

Britton said she and her husband are now sleeping with a
shotgun beside their bed.

10-22-16

An envelope containing powder was delivered to Clinton's
office in midtown Manhattan on Friday and opened by
campaign staffers, before being taken to Clinton's campaign
headquarters in Brooklyn.

The police said it has been deemed "non-hazardous."

11-02-16

The Crusader, a quarterly journal that bills itself as "The
Premier Voice of the White Resistance," supports Trump.

"Make America Great Again!' It is a slogan that has been
repeatedly used by Donald Trump in his campaign for the
presidency," the Crusader's Pastor Thomas Robb wrote. "You
can see it on the shirts, buttons, posters and ball caps such as
the one being worn here by Trump speaking at a recent rally.
... But can it happen? Can America really be great again? This
is what we will soon find out!"

TRUMP ZAP! Trump "A bigot's hero!"

Trump self-funding his campaign "HA HA"

08-23-16

When Donald trump was still paying for his presidential run mostly out of his own pocket, his campaign spent $35,458 to rent its headquarters in Trump Tower.

Last month, however, that figure surged to $169,758, even as the number of paid campaign employees and staff dropped from 197 to 172 over the same period, the Huffington Post reports.

The sharp increase in campaign spending appears to correspond to a large infusion in cash from outside donors. According to the Huffington Post, the amount Trump Tower has charged the campaign for rent has steadily increased since May, the same month that Trump clinched the nomination and inked a deal with the Republican National Committee to fund his campaign.

At the end of May the campaign doled out $72,800, followed by $110,684 in June, and $169,758 in July.

08-24-16

Donald Trump's top donors Robert and Rebekah Mercer, the father-daughter duo spending millions to boost right-wing candidates, have substantial clout in the Trump campaign. While most Republican mega-donors have stayed away from Trump, Mercer and Co. are all in for him.

09-19-16

Trump had amassed $50 million in small contributions into his campaign, FEC records show. He has since announced he raised $90 million in August "mostly" from small donors both directly for his campaign and in joint committees shared with the Republican National Committee — suggesting at least $45 million raised last month came from small contributors. Additionally, there is some money from small contributors in those shared RNC accounts — Trump said they contained $37 million at the end of July — that he has helped raise.

Trump, a self-proclaimed billionaire who bragged during the primaries about how he didn't need anyone else's cash to run for president, would appear at first to be the unlikeliest of Republican fundraising heroes. But the combination of his celebrity, anti-establishment populism, and running against Clinton has led to a windfall, even as his skeletal campaign did little for more than a year to cultivate a donor list or build digital infrastructure to lure contributors.

10-28-16

Of late, Donald Trump has been promising to start self-funding his campaign again. "I mean, look, I'm going to be in for over $100 million," Trump told ABC's George Stephanopoulos earlier this week. Pressed by Stephanopoulos for a more specific amount, Trump demurred: "I would say a lot. I'm not going to say what. But I will be over $100 million, and it could be much more than that."

Trump gave his campaign only $31,000 in in-kind
contributions over the first 19 days of October bringing his
total investment in the campaign to $56 million. Trump, after
some controversy, wound up forgiving personal loans totaling
$50 million in mid July.

It's possible that since the filing deadline closed last week,
Trump has dropped the $44 million that would bring him up
to $100 million in personal donations to the campaign. But if
he had already done so, doesn't it seem like he would have
made sure to tell everyone? He's not exactly the kind of guy
who hides his light under a bushel, after all.

Trump's Campaign Team Shake-ups

08-17-16

 Statements about Trump choosing Breitbart News chief
Stephen Bannon to run his flailing campaign:

> "I think Donald Trump is a turd tornado, but I also
> understand that he has no capacity whatsoever to
> control himself," Ben Shapiro, who reported to the
> Breitbart News executive chairman as an editor-at-large
> before he bolted from the site earlier this year, told
> CNN.

> Shapiro further trashed his former boss Bannon as "a
> legitimately sinister figure," who is bound to send
> Trump's already soiled campaign into even darker
> territory.

> Kurt Bardella, a former media consultant and
> spokesman for Breitbart, called Bannon's hiring a
> "recipe for catastrophe."

"When you put someone in power who's as much of a bully and has as dictator-like tendencies as Steve does, that's very concerning," Bardella told The News. "Steve's management style is berating, bullying, and profanity-laced tirades at people."

Trump is turning "his campaign over to someone who's best known for running a so-called news site that peddles divisive, at times racist, anti-Muslim, anti-Semitic conspiracy theories," Clinton campaign chair Robby Mook said Wednesday.

08-19-16

Paul Manafort resigned as the chairman of Donald Trump's presidential campaign.

Trump hired Breitbart Chairman Steve Bannon to be his campaign's CEO and promoted Kellyanne Conway to campaign manager, moves that were widely seen as sidelining Manafort.

But Manafort indicated he would remain in his post, writing in a staff memo that he remained "the Campaign Chairman and Chief Strategist, providing the big-picture, long-range campaign vision and working with all of you to implement our strategy that will guide us to victory in November."

Manafort's resignation comes after multiple reports have raised questions about his work for pro-Russian forces in the Ukrainian government.

Earlier this week, The New York Times reported that Manafort's name appeared in a secret ledger used by the party of Viktor Yanukovych, the former president of Ukraine.

The Associated Press reported Thursday night that a firm run by Manafort helped orchestrate a lobbying effort on behalf of Ukraine, but Manafort did not register as a foreign agent, which is required by federal law.

Robby Mook, Hillary Clinton's campaign manager, said Paul Manafort's resignation is a clear admission that the disturbing connections between Donald Trump's team and pro-Kremlin elements in Russia and Ukraine are untenable. But this is not the end of the story. It's just the beginning. You can get rid of Manafort, but that doesn't end the odd bromance Trump has with Putin."

"This morning Paul Manafort offered, and I accepted, his resignation from the campaign," Trump said in a statement. "I am very appreciative for his great work in helping to get us where we are today, and in particular his work guiding us through the delegate and convention process. Paul is a true professional and I wish him the greatest success."

09-01-16

David N. Bossie was president of Citizens United before Trump picked him to be deputy campaign manager.

Citizens United was known for the 2010 Supreme Court decision, "Citizens United v. Federal Election Commission," a historic ruling that ended many restrictions on political spending for corporations and unions.

Bossie was central in recommending Trump's political hires ahead of the 2016 election, introducing Trump to the campaign's first manager, Corey Lewandowski, and introducing Bannon to Trump.

"He's a battle-tested warrior and a brilliant strategist," Conway said. "He's a nuts-and-bolts tactician as well, who's going to help us fully integrate our ground game and data operations, and help with overall strategy as my deputy."

Conway said Bossie would be assisting her with managing day-to-day operations and with strategic planning.

What Trump said about Bossie "A friend of mine for many years, Solid. Smart. Loves politics, knows how to win."

08-16-16

Fox News CEO Roger Ailes left Fox News in late July following allegations of sexual harassment by former anchor Gretchen Carlson, who filed suit against him.

Ailes issued a statement denying the claim saying "Gretchen Carlson's allegations are false. This is a retaliatory suit for the network's decision not to renew her contract, which was due to the fact that her disappointingly low ratings were dragging down the afternoon lineup."

"When Fox News did not commence any negotiations to renew her contract, Ms. Carlson became aware that her career with the network was likely over and conveniently began to pursue a lawsuit."

Ailes is advising Donald Trump on his debate preparation, but does not have a formal role in the campaign.

After Ailes left Fox News trump said "Well, I don't want to comment, But he's been a friend of mine for a long time."

TRUMP ZAP! Bringing coal back is like bringing back 3M Kodak film!

The General Election Debates

Hillary Clinton and Donald Trump began debating in early fall 2016. The media played it up like a prize fight between two heavy weights before, during and after every debate.

09-27-16
Hillary Clinton said "Trump was making charges and claims that were demonstrably untrue, offering opinions that I think a lot of people would find offensive and off-putting."

 Donald Trump said "I may hit her harder in certain ways." "When Clinton criticized him for his treatment of women, he resisted. "I was going to hit her with her husband's women. And I decided I shouldn't do it because her daughter was in the room."

Clinton said "He can run his campaign however he chooses."

Trump said "The debate moderator, Lester Holt of NBC News, asked him "very unfair questions" and that he was given a "very bad" microphone.

Clinton said "Anyone who complains about the microphone is not having a good night."

Clinton said "He talks down America every chance he gets. He calls us names. He calls us a Third World country. He talks in such dire and dark terms. That's not who America is, the real point is about temperament and fitness and qualification to hold the hold the most important, hardest job in the world."

"He loves beauty contests, supporting them and hanging around them and he called this one 'Miss Piggy' and then he called her 'Miss Housekeeping."

Clinton reminded the public of Trump's verbal abuse of women.
Trump defended his insults of the Venezuelan-born Alicia Machado who is now a U.S. citizen Trump said "She was the winner and she gained a massive amount of weight, and it was a real problem. We had a real problem. Not only that - her attitude - and we had a real problem with her."

Clinton said "Trump has really started his political activity based on this racist lie that our first black president was not an American citizen. There was absolutely no evidence for it. But he persisted. He persisted year after year."

Clinton suggested her opponent was refusing to release his tax returns to avoid showing Americans "he's paid nothing in federal taxes" or that "not as rich as he says he is. It must be something really important, even terrible, that he's trying to hide."

Trump said that as a businessman, paying low taxes was important. "That makes me smart."

09-27-16

During Monday night's presidential debate between Hillary

Clinton and Donald Trump the Internet's fact-checking engines were working overtime.

Trump repeatedly stretched the truth, denied making certain statements despite ample evidence to the contrary, and twisted the facts until they broke.

According to one estimate, Trump made more than 34 comments that were either lies or mis-statements of fact during the debate. Clinton, by comparison, was tagged with four. According to much of the post-debate analysis.

The biggest problem with fact-checking Trump is that he seems to have a reality-distortion field that applies to his fan base in which even if he tells what appears to be a lie, he is seen as telling some larger truth.

09-28-16

Trump says he "won the first debate."

"I won on Slate," Trump said during the same "Fox and Friends" interview. "I won Drudge in almost 90% of the vote in that poll. I won Time magazine. I won CBS. I won every single poll other than CNN."

The problem is that the "polls" on Slate, Drudge and Time were online surveys in which there was no scientifically drawn sample of people that was representative of US voters. Anyone could sign on and vote -- and one could vote as many times as they liked. Such surveys are not considered credible.

Oh, and there was no CBS post-debate poll at all.

"Preparation for the first Trump vs Clinton debate."

Both candidates prepared for the debate, but in much different ways.

"I know who I am, and it got me here," Mr. Trump said, boasting of success in his 11 primary debate appearances and in capturing the Republican nomination over veteran politicians and polished debaters. "I don't want to present a false front. I mean, it's possible we'll do a mock debate, but I don't see a real need."

Tony Schwartz, the "Art of the Deal" co-author weighed in, "Trump has severe attention problems and simply cannot take in complex information — he will be unable to practice for these debates," said Mr. Schwartz, who was the subject of a New Yorker profile last month that portrayed Mr. Trump as a charlatan. "Trump will bring nothing but his bluster to the debates. He'll use sixth-grade language, he will repeat himself many times, he won't complete sentences, and he won't say anything of substance."

"Even so," Mr. Schwartz said, "Clinton has to be careful — she could get everything right and still potentially lose the debates if she comes off as too condescending, too much of a know-it-all."

09-29-16

For all of the blowback on Trump's performance in the first presidential debate, the NBC News Survey Monkey poll found that 68 percent of Trump supporters, both men and women, said their opinion of him hadn't changed because of it.

Overall, the poll found that a majority of likely voters (52 percent) who either watched the debate or said they followed debate coverage in the news said Hillary Clinton won. Twenty-one percent thought Trump won, and 26 percent said neither had.

10-06-16

Regal Cinemas will broadcast the Second Presidential Debate debate between Hillary Clinton and Donald Trump in 206 theaters nationwide.

"While our auditoriums feature the likes of Batman V. Superman or Alien vs. Predator, we are excited to offer voters a chance to watch Clinton vs. Trump as they go head to head on the big screen," said Steve Bunnell, Chief Content and Programming Officer at Regal Entertainment Group. "As we continue to look at ways to bring alternative content to our screens, we invite you to come cheer and jeer the candidates at Regal this Sunday."

Admission is free, and attendees get a free small drink with a purchase of popcorn.

TRUMP ZAP! Trump is a centipede that keeps dropping shoes!

08-05-16

The Politico Caucus is a panel of activists and strategists from 11 swing states. What they said in a survey:

> "I'd rather take our chances with nearly anyone else than continue with this certain loser who will likely cost the Senate and much more," said a New Hampshire Republican.

> "The effect Trump is having on down-ballot races has the potential to be devastating in November," added a Florida Republican. "His negative image among Hispanics, women and independents is something that could be devastating to Republicans. Trump's divisive rhetoric to the Hispanic community at large has the potential to be devastating for years to come."

Of the 30% who want him to stay in, a number of those don't believe he'll win in November, but feel that after a devastating trouncing in November, the party can begin to heal itself.

08-08-16

According to a recent poll in Georgia by Atlanta Journal-Constitutional:

> Clinton has a 9-point advantage over the Republican nominee, 51 percent to 42 percent, well above the roughly 4.3 percent margin-of-error on immigration

issues.

Clinton has virtually the opposite view of Trump in every way on immigration. She's backed comprehensive immigration reform and a pathway to citizenship.

Evangelicals overwhelmingly selected Trump on immigration. The Republican nominee won nearly three-quarters of voters polled from that group. He also polled strongly among voters over 65 and people from northern Georgia.

08-17-16

CNN host Brianna Keilar asked Trump Organization Executive Vice President Michael Cohen about the hiring of campaign manager Kellyanne Conway and CEO Stephen Bannon, widely perceived as a shakeup intended to remedy the Republican nominee's struggling campaign.

"I think bringing on someone like Kellyanne Conway was a great move, and it was something, personally, I would have liked to see happen earlier," Cohen said. "But the campaign wasn't ready for it. Now they are. I think she is a brilliant individual. I think that she understands the data that's coming in."

09-16-16

The Two Team additions seemed to add steam to Trump's campaign.

A 50-state Washington Post-SurveyMonkey poll said:

With nine weeks until Election Day, Donald Trump is within striking distance in the Upper Midwest, but Hillary Clinton's strength in many battlegrounds and some traditional Republican strongholds gives her a big Electoral College advantage.

The state-by-state numbers are based on responses from more than 74,000 registered voters during the period of Aug. 9 to Sept. 1.

What once was a Clinton lead nationally of eight to 10 points shortly after the party conventions ended a month ago is now about four points, according to the RealClearPolitics polling average. A number of battleground states also have tightened, according to surveys released from other organizations in recent days.

Trump's strength across some of the states in the Midwest is one potential bright spot for the Republican nominee. Clinton's biggest lead among the contested states in that region is in Pennsylvania, where her margin is just four points. In Wisconsin and Michigan, she leads by a nominal two points, while Trump leads by four points in Iowa and three points in Ohio.

10-04-16

According to a new NBC News/Survey Monkey online poll:

In a four-way matchup, Clinton also leads Trump by six points, the poll, released on Tuesday, shows:

Clinton: 46 percent;

Trump, 40 percent;

Libertarian nominee Gary Johnson, 9 percent;

Green Party nominee Jill Stein, 3 percent.

In the two-way contest:

Clinton, 50 percent;

Trump, 44 percent.

The poll, conducted from Sept. 26 - Oct. 2, surveyed 26,925 likely voters and carried a margin of error of 1 point. It shows Clinton still ahead with women and Trump holding onto his lead with men:

Women overall: Clinton, 52-34 percent;

Never-married women: Clinton, 67-18 percent;

Married women: Clinton, 48-40 percent.

Women without children: Clinton, 63-23 percent;

Women with children: Clinton, 50-38 percent.

Men overall: Trump, 52-35 percent;

Married men, Trump, 52-35 percent;

Never-married men: Clinton, 51-28 percent.

Men with children: Trump, 52-35 percent;

Donald Trump continued to show his bigoted attitude to people of color. He made insensitive blunder after blunder.

06-06-16

At a recent Trump rally, Trump spotted a black man in the crowd and said "Look at my African-American over here! Look at him! Are you the greatest? You know what I'm talking about, OK?"

"I am not a Trump supporter," Gregory Cheadle told NPR News. "I went to go hear Donald Trump because I have an open mind."

Cheadle, a Republican candidate in a California congressional race, said he was using a "Veterans for Trump" sign to shield his head from the sun, and added he took no offense from Trump's comments.

"I was not offended by it because he had been speaking positively about black people prior to that statement," Cheadle told NPR News. "People around me were laughing [at the fact] that he noticed me and everybody was happy. It was a jovial thing."

06-22-16

During the campaign year everything was magnified by the media. The Republicans were appearing racist.

Harriet Tubman was an American abolitionist, humanitarian, and an armed scout and spy for the United States Army during the American Civil War. Born into slavery, Tubman escaped and subsequently made some thirteen missions to rescue approximately seventy enslaved people, family and friends, using the network of antislavery activists and safe houses.

 What Iowa Republican Representative Steve King had to say about putting Tubman on the $20 Bill:

. "It's not about Harriet Tubman, it's about keeping the picture on the $20," he said, according to Politico. "Y'know? Why would you want to change that? I am a conservative, I like to keep what we have."

"Putting Tubman on the $20 is an example of Obama "doing everything he can think of to upset this society and this civilization"

07-08-16

 What Conservative radio host Rush Limbaugh had to say about Black Lives Matter protest:

"They're a terrorist group," he said. "They're quickly becoming a terrorist group committing hate crimes."

"We have a political party that's seeking to benefit from all of this," he said. "A political party, the Democrats, that are seeking to advance their agenda with every one of these unfortunate incidents. If that's the case, this isn't going to stop."

08-19-16

 What Trump says to black voters:

"If elected I will be so good for black Americans that "at the end of four years I guarantee you I will get over 95% of the African-American vote."

"What do you lose by trying something new like Trump?"

"What the hell do you have to lose?"

"You're living in poverty, you have no jobs, 58% of your youth is unemployed, what the hell do you have to lose?"

"African-Americans are refugees in their own country."

"It's time to hold Democratic politicians accountable for what they've done for these communities."

08-24-16

At a rally in Jackson Miss. Trump Said, "Hillary Clinton is a bigot who sees people of color only as votes, not as human beings worthy of a better future."

Trump went on to say:

"She's going to do nothing for African-Americans, she's going to do nothing for the Hispanics. She's only going to take care of herself, her husband, her consultants, her donors," the billionaire said. "These are the people she cares about."

"It's time Republicans gave Democrats some "competition" for minority voters' support and pledged to rebuild inner cities and lift black and Hispanic communities up with his policies on trade and immigration."

Clinton said that Trump has already proven himself to be a monger of prejudice and paranoia and said he has taken his "hate movement mainstream."

08-29-16

The liberal-leaning firm Public Policy Poll asked African-American voters a set of questions, including whether they preferred Trump to things such as bedbugs, junk mail, carnies, and bubonic plague and middle airplane seats.

The Poll showed Republican presidential nominee Donald Trump's favorability rating among African-American voters at zero percent.

09-21-16

What Trump said about "stop-and-frisk" by police:

"One of the things I'd do," he said, "is I would do stop-and-frisk. I think you have to. We did it in New York, it worked incredibly well and you have to be proactive."

"I see what's going on here, I see what's going on in Chicago," Mr. Trump said before praising the technique again as "incredible."

"NYC politicians better stop pandering — ending stop & frisk would be a disaster," he wrote on Twitter.

185

"Stop-and-frisk is a very positive thing."

09-26-16

Trump wanted to visit the Civil Rights Museum in Greensboro, North Carolina and asked The International Civil Rights Center and Museum for exclusive treatment, requesting that the museum be closed for at least five hours to accommodate the visit.

The VIP visit request was denied, calling his team rude and demanding.

"The approach, the type of disrespect ... pretty much a demand and bullying us to use the museum in their manner and their way in their time — it was inappropriate and I think it's probably reflective of the type of insensitivity of civil rights and human rights that's reflective of Mr. Trump over the years," museum co-founder Earl Jones said.

10-02-16

What Hillary Clinton spoke in Charlotte, North Carolina in a black congregation she reffered to 9-year-old Zianna Oliphant, who garnered national attention when she tearfully spoke about the recent police killings of African-Americans:

> "I am a grandmother and like every grandmother, I worry about the safety and security of my grandchildren. But my worries are not the same as black grandmothers, who have different and deeper fears about the world that their grandchildren face," Clinton said.

> Clinton said she "wouldn't be able to stand it" if her

own grandchildren ever felt the kind of fear and worry
that Oliphant and others have expressed.

"But because my grandchildren are white, because they
are the grandchildren of a former president and
secretary of state -- let's be honest here: They won't face
the kind of fear that we heard from the young children
testifying before the city council," Clinton said.

"Can you imagine? Nine years old -- she should be
thinking about happy adventures, dreaming about all
the wonderful things that her future holds for her,"
Clinton said. "Instead, she is talking about graveyards."

With tears streaming down her face, the distressed girl
said at a heated city council meeting: "It's a shame that
our fathers and mothers are killed and we can't see
them anymore."

"It's a shame that we have to go to their graveyard and
bury them. And we have tears," she said. "We shouldn't
have tears. We need our fathers and mothers to be by
our side."

Obama and the 2016 Election

Donald Trump, who for years was a major public voice
against President Obama, used his campaign to continue his
attack.

06-13-16

Trump blamed Obama for the attack on an Orlando LGBT
nightclub. The largest mass shooting in American history, a

terrorist attack and a hate crime:

> "Truly, our president doesn't know what he's doing. He's failed us, and he's failed us badly. And under his leadership, this situation will not get any better, it will only get worse, and I've been saying that for a long time," Trump said during a speech at Saint Anselm College, which was billed as a major foreign-policy address.

> "The burden is on Hillary Clinton to tell us why she believes that immigration from these dangerous countries should be increased without any effective system ... to screen," Trump said.

The Orlando shooter was a U.S.-born citizen. Inspite, of this, Trump continued to criticize immigrants.

"Well, there are a lot of people that think maybe he doesn't want to get it," Trump said Monday on NBC about Obama. "A lot of people think maybe he doesn't want to know about it. I happen to think that he just doesn't know what he's doing, but there are many people that think maybe he doesn't want to get it."

"If you had some guns in that club the night that this took place ... you wouldn't have had the tragedy that you had," Trump said on CNN Monday morning.

08-02-16

President Obama started to speak out.

What Obama had to say about Trump:

"There has to come a point at which you say, 'Somebody who makes those kinds of statements doesn't have the judgment, the temperament, the understanding to occupy the most powerful position in the world,'" the president said at a White House news conference.

Obama said that in standing by their nominee, GOP leaders risked blurring a distinction between conservative philosophies and what he has called Trump's demagogic views. He diagnosed Trump's liabilities coolly and with lawyer-like precision; among them, that he "doesn't appear to have basic knowledge around critical issues in Europe, in the Middle East, in Asia."

"The Republican nominee is unfit to serve as president," Obama said. "I said so last week" — at the Democratic convention — "and he keeps on proving it."

Obama noted that he had serious policy differences with the two Republican presidential nominees he defeated, McCain and former Massachusetts Gov. Mitt Romney. "But I never thought that they couldn't do the job," Obama said.

"Had they won, I would have been disappointed, but I would have said to all Americans, 'This is our president, and I know they're going to abide by certain norms and rules and common sense — will observe basic decency," he said.

But with Trump, Obama said, Republican leaders need to say, "Enough."

"The alternative is that the entire party, the Republican Party, effectively endorses and validates the positions that are being articulated by Mr. Trump," he said.

08-04-16

A CNN/ORC Poll was conducted by telephone July 29-31 among a random national sample of 1,003 adults, including 894 registered voters. Results among the sample of registered voters have a margin of sampling error of plus or minus 3.5 percentage points:

> Obama's approval rating dipped to 50% after the Republican convention, but has risen to 54% in the wake of his party's convention, with 45% disapproval, according to a new CNN/ORC Poll. That's the most positive approval rating of his second term.

> Compared with other recent two-term presidents, Obama's approval rating at this stage of his presidency ranks on par with Ronald Reagan's ratings in 1988, and are approaching Bill Clinton's 57% at this point in 2000.

10-17-16

Obama started getting ready for his departure.

A new group, called the National Democratic Redistricting Committee, was developed in close consultation with the White House. President Barack Obama himself has now identified the group — which will coordinate campaign strategy, direct fundraising, organize ballot initiatives and put together legal challenges to state redistricting maps — as the main focus of his political activity once he leaves office.

 Former Attorney General Eric Holder will chair the new group.

The group will focused on redistricting reform — with the aim of taking on the gerrymandering that's left the party behind in statehouses and made winning a House majority far more difficult.

One number that's on their mind: Republicans got 52 percent of the votes in 2014 but won 57 percent of the seats.

"American voters deserve fair maps that represent our diverse communities — and we need a coordinated strategy to make that happen," Holder said. "This unprecedented new effort will ensure Democrats have a seat at the table to create fairer maps after 2020."

10-24-16

 "I ran,"Hillary Clinton said in Seattle recently, "because I really believe that we need to build on the progress that we have made under President Obama."

Obama recorded TV or radio ads for three Democrats running for governor, eight for Senate and 10 for the House. He attended 21 fundraisers for Democratic congressional and governors committees and five for individual candidates. He weighed in on behalf of 150 Democrats running for state legislatures.

"Progress is on the ballot," Obama said at a campaign rally

here last week. "Tolerance is on the ballot. Justice is on the ballot. Equality is on the ballot. Our democracy is on the ballot!"

Obama stumped for democrats in Miami:

> "Republican politicians and far-right media outlets had just been pumping out all kinds of toxic, crazy stuff," Obama said last week in Miami, barely keeping his voice from cracking into laughter. "And there were a lot of politicians, like Marco Rubio, who know better, but they just looked the other way."

> "Don't boo. Vote!" he told the crowd in Miami. "And get your friends to vote! Get Uncle Joe to vote! Get Pookie to vote! And Javier to vote!"

> "They're counting on people thinking that gridlock is the best we can do, because that plays to their basic philosophy" that government has no role in helping people, Obama said. "They're OK with gridlock. But you know what? We can do so much better than that."

Trump fired back at Obama when he was in Florida, "I'd like to see him in the White House working instead of campaigning for 'Crooked Hillary."

Late in the campaign awareness of a new computer generated influence was starting to sound alarms. The source of these computer generated influences was both foreign and malicious.

11-01-16

Political campaigns worldwide now use bots, software developed to automatically do tasks online, as a means for gaming online polls and artificially inflating social-media traffic.

Recent analysis by a research team at Oxford University reveals that more than a third of pro-Trump tweets and nearly a fifth of pro-Clinton tweets between the first and second debates came from automated accounts, which produced more than 1 million tweets in total.

This data corroborates recent reports suggesting that both candidates' social media followings are highly automated.

One pro-Trump bot, @amrightnow, has more than 33,000 followers and spams Twitter with anti-Clinton conspiracy theories. It generated 1,200 posts during the final debate. Its competitor, the recently spawned @loserDonldTrump, retweets all mentions of @realDonaldTrump that include the word loser — producing more than 2,000 tweets a day. These bots represent a tiny fraction of the millions of politicized software programs working to manipulate the democratic process behind the scenes.

The artificial-intelligence company Luka is designing intelligent bots that "you teach and grow through conversation." These digital automatons are marketed as a new form of online companion.

Currently, there is almost no regulation on the use of bots in politics. The Federal Elections Commission has shown no evidence of even recognizing that bots exist.

Bots that are used to trumpet hate speech, harass women journalists, and spread propaganda are also designed to conceal the identity of their creators. This layer of anonymity challenges the ability to hold people legally responsible.

Moreover, it challenges notions of free speech — what happens when a bot, which might do things unforeseen by its maker, is the entity committing malicious acts?

These developments foreshadow a future where bots will be intimately interwoven with everyday social interaction online. As bot awareness and usage grows, the greater pressure there will be for governments, nonprofit organizations, and research institutions to develop bots that protect and empower citizens — and don't convince people to vote for particular presidential candidates.

The conservative political commentator Scottie Nell Hughes summed up the relative value of digits in a conversation with Anderson Cooper. "The only place that we're hearing that Donald Trump honestly is losing is in the media or these polls," she said. "You're not seeing it with the crowd rallies, you're not seeing it on social media — where Donald Trump is two to three times more popular than Hillary Clinton on every social media platform."

A third of pro-Trump tweets and nearly a fifth of pro-Clinton tweets came from automated accounts.

The Clinton campaign, meanwhile, has stuck by traditional polls as evidence of her success.

11-03-16

The Macedonian town of Veles (population 45,000, 6,000 miles away) has experienced a digital gold rush as locals launched at least 140 US politics websites. These sites have American-sounding domain names such as WorldPoliticus.com, TrumpVision365.com, USConservativeToday.com, DonaldTrumpNews.co, and USADailyPolitics.com.

They almost all publish aggressively pro-Trump content aimed at conservatives and Trump supporters in the US.

This strange hub of pro-Trump sites in the former Yugoslav Republic of Macedonia is now playing a significant role in propagating the kind of false and misleading content that was identified in a recent BuzzFeed News analysis of hyper partisan Facebook pages.

"Yes, the info in the blogs is bad, false, and misleading but the rationale is that 'if it gets the people to click on it and engage, then use it,'" said a university student in Veles who started a US politics site.

"I started the site for a easy way to make money," said a 17-year-old who runs a site with four other people. "In Macedonia the economy is very weak and teenagers are not allowed to work, so we need to find creative ways to make some money. I'm a musician but I can't afford music gear. Here in Macedonia the revenue from a small site is enough to afford many things." The more people who click through from Facebook, the more money they earn from ads on their website.

The young men running these sites know the Trump traffic bonanza will soon come to an end. They expect traffic and revenue to decline significantly once the election is over. But they also hold out hope that a Trump win will keep their sites afloat.

"If Trump loses I plan to redirect my site to sports," the 16-year-old's partner said. "It means that there will be no more politics [worth covering]."

TRUMP ZAP! Mama said if you don't have anything nice to say, you must be speaking for Trump!

17 PUTIN TO TRUMP: "WE FOUND THE EMAILS YOU REQUESTED AND MORE"

06-14-16

Two separate Russian intelligence-linked cyberattack groups were both in the DNC's networks according to Dmitri Alperovitch, co-founder and chief technology officer of CrowdStrike said.

They stole opposition research on Donald Trump.

CrowdStrike names the cyberattack groups it identifies, using the term "Bear" for Russian-linked groups. The two groups involved with the DNC hack are nicknamed "Fancy Bear," the Trump files group, and "Cozy Bear," which was in the communications systems.

A Department of Homeland Security official told CNN the agency is aware of the reports and is currently looking into the matter.

Trump's candidacy has especially raised his relationship with Russia throughout the campaign. He has at times spoken admiringly of Russian President Vladimir Putin, and some of his foreign policies have drawn praise in Moscow.

"Obviously, you have the DNC engaged in communication with lots of different parties, and anything you can use to gain intelligence about what's going on in the U.S. political system and what the candidates are thinking is of high interest to Russian intelligence," Alperovitch said.

"It is troubling just as all cyberattacks against our businesses and our institutions and our government are," Clinton said in an interview with Telemundo. "So far as we know, my campaign has not been hacked into and we're obviously looking hard at that, but cybersecurity will be an issue that I will be absolutely focused on as president, because whether it's Russia or China, Iran or North Korea, more and more countries are using hacking to steal our information to use it to their advantage and we can't let that go on."

07-25-16

Suspicion of Russian influence in the Presidential Election grew.

 The FBI suspects that Russian government hackers breached the networks of the Democratic National Committee and stole emails that were posted to the anti-secrecy site WikiLeaks on Friday.

It's an operation that several U.S. officials now suspect was a deliberate attempt to influence the presidential election in favor of Donald Trump.

The theory that Moscow orchestrated the leaks to help Trump — who has repeatedly praised Russian President Vladimir Putin and practically called for the end of NATO — is fast gaining currency within the Obama administration because of the timing of the leaks and Trump's own connections to the Russian government.

About 20,000 internal DNC emails were disclosed just days before the beginning of the Democratic National Convention in Philadelphia.

"The release of emails just as the Democratic National Convention is getting underway this week has the hallmarks of a Russian active measures campaign," David Shedd, a former director of the Defense Intelligence Agency.

Officials also noted Trump's own connections to the Russian government. Putin has publicly praised the nominee, who said he was "honored" by the compliment.

Trump's campaign manager, Paul Manafort, was a consultant for Viktor Yanukovych, the former president of Ukraine who was ousted for his pro-Moscow orientation (and now lives in Russia).

One of Trump's top national security advisers, retired Army Gen. Michael Flynn, sat with Putin at a dinner celebrating the 10th anniversary of Kremlin-backed media network RT and was paid to give a speech at the event; Flynn later retweeted an anti-Semitic message that called into question any Kremlin-Trump link.

Another Trump adviser, Carter Page, recently denounced America's "often-hypocritical focus on democratization" while in Moscow. And last week, Trump said that he might not come to the aid of U.S. NATO allies in the face of Russian aggression unless they paid what he thinks they owe for Europe's common defense.

"If there is a concerted effort to undermine the campaign of the Democratic Party nominee, we can and should expect additional embarrassing emails to be released by WikiLeaks, including from candidate Hillary Clinton's personal server," Shedd, the former Defense Intelligence Agency chief, said.

"If the hack is linked to Russian actors, it would not be the first time cyber intrusions linked to the Kremlin and its supporters have sought to influence the political process in other countries," Rep. Adam Schiff said in a statement.

"Given Donald Trump's well known admiration for Putin and his belittling of NATO, the Russians have both the means and the motive to engage in a hack of the DNC and the dump of its emails prior to the Democratic Convention. That foreign actors may be trying to influence our election—let alone a powerful adversary like Russia—should concern all Americans of any party."

07-27-16

Donald Trump could not resist confronting the national norms by publicly seeking foreign support and involvement.

Trump said at a televised news conference in Doral, Fla.:

"Russia, if you're listening, I hope you'll be able to find the 30,000 emails that are missing. I think you'll probably be rewarded mightily by our press," referring to deleted emails from the private account Hillary Clinton used as secretary of State.

Trump called President Obama "the most ignorant president in our history," alleged that Russian President Vladimir Putin had disparaged Obama with "the n-word" and inaccurately paraphrased Obama speaking in a stereotype of African American dialect.

"This undoubtedly sends a message to Russia that Trump is, at best, a fan, and at worst, manipulable and a bit of a loose cannon," said Olga Oliker, director of the Russia and Eurasia program at the Center for Strategic and International Studies. "Russia will look at this, whether it's political theater or not, as [confirmation] that Trump would be better for them than Clinton, who would take a measured approach and discourage things that run counter to U.S. interests."

Trump's comments probably did not meet the standard for criminal incitement but showed poor judgment, said Susan Hennessey, a national security and governance fellow at the Brookings Institution.

"Someone who is asking to be elected to the presidency should be more respectful of this nation's institutions," said Hennessey, a former lawyer for the National Security Agency.

"If Russia or China or any other country has those emails, I've got to be honest with you, I'd love to see them," said Trump.

Trump tweaked his position further on Twitter, suggesting that any hacked emails should be shared with law enforcement rather than him or the public: "If Russia or any other country or person has Hillary Clinton's 33,000 illegally deleted emails, perhaps they should share them with the FBI!"

Rep. Adam B. Schiff (D-Burbank), the top Democrat on the House Intelligence Committee, called it "staggeringly poor judgment even for him" and "breathtakingly irresponsible" in a statement.

"What Donald Trump did today needs to be examined not through a political lens, but this is a national security issue now," Robby Mook, Clinton's campaign manager, said during a Democratic convention lunch in Philadelphia hosted by the Wall Street Journal.

07-28-16

Donald Trump says that he was being "sarcastic" when he said he hopes Russian hackers obtain deleted emails from Hillary Clinton's private server.

"They have no idea if it's Russia, if it's China, if it's somebody else," the GOP presidential nominee said in an interview aired Thursday on "Fox and Friends." "Who knows it is?"

"The real problem is what was said on those emails from the Democratic National Committee," he told host Brian Kilmeade. "They talk about religion, they talk about race, they talk about all sorts of things, including women.

"What they said on those emails is a disgrace. It's disgraceful, it's disgraceful. They're just trying to deflect from that."

Clinton gave the State Department roughly 30,000 work-related emails from the private storage device she used while serving as secretary about 30,000 more personal emails were deleted.

10-16-16

Democrats weighed in on Russian hacking:

> Vice-president Joe Biden told NBC on Friday "we are sending a message" to Putin, and said retaliation for Russia's hacking attacks "will be at the time of our choosing, and under the circumstances that will have

the greatest impact".

Hillary Clinton's running mate, senator Tim Kaine, said "There will be time for figuring what that consequence is. But you can't let it go unchallenged because if you do, you just could encourage more of it," he told CBS. "I don't think it's funny when you have a nation like Russia that has engaged in activity to destabilize elections in countries – Ukraine, Estonia, they've engaged in that activity.

"And somebody running to be president of the United States shouldn't be encouraging another nation to cyber-hack the US," Kaine added.

"Here's something that we do have to just state very plainly," Kaine said. "Not only are these emails an effort by WikiLeaks in Russia to try to destabilize our election, but second, you can't assume that they're all accurate. One of the emails that came up this week referred to me. It was completely inaccurate."

FBI and Clinton's emails

10-30-16

FBI Director James Comey uncovered more of Hillary's emails as part of the bureau's investigation into Clinton aide Huma Abedin's estranged husband, Anthony Weiner.

"It's pretty strange to put something like that out with such little information right before an election," Clinton told supporters in Daytona Beach, Florida, where the crowd booed at the mention of Comey's letter.

"In fact, it's not just strange, it's unprecedented and it's deeply troubling because voters deserve to get full and complete facts."

Clinton called on Comey to swiftly release more information, saying he must "explain everything right away, put it all right on the table."

Clinton also swiped at Republican rival Donald Trump, saying he's "doing his best to confuse, mislead and discourage the American people" over the issue.

"Of course, Donald Trump is already making up lies about this," Clinton said.

Clinton campaign chairman John Podesta accused Comey of failing to be "forthcoming with the facts." Podesta blasted both the timing and contents of the letter Comey sent to congressional leaders on Friday, summing the director's actions as "providing selective information."

"The Justice Department's longstanding practice is: Don't do anything seen as trying to influence an election," Clinton campaign manager Robby Mook said. "It's completely unfair to Secretary Clinton and it's really unfair to the voters."

Clinton press secretary Brian Fallon said, "We are taking issue with a decision to publicly surface FBI activities on the eve of an election, which is an undisputed violation of protocol that both the current Attorney General and Republicans like George Terwilliger have acknowledged."

Democrats got angry at FBI Director James Comey one sided treatment of Hillary's email investigation and not Trump's Russian connection investigation just before the election.

Senate Democratic Minority Leader Harry Reid upped the ante. He sent Comey a fiery letter saying the FBI chief may have broken the law and pointed to a potentially greater controversy: "In my communications with you and other top officials in the national security community, it has become clear that you possess explosive information about close ties and coordination between Donald Trump, his top advisors, and the Russian government...The public has a right to know this information."

In August, Reid had written to Comey and demanded an investigation of the "connections between the Russian government and Donald Trump's presidential campaign," and in that letter he indirectly referred to Carter Page, an American businessman cited by Trump as one of his foreign policy advisers, who had financial ties to Russia and had recently visited Moscow.

An FBI spokeswoman says, "Normally, we don't talk about whether we are investigating anything." But a senior US government official not involved in this case but familiar with the former spy tells Mother Jones that he has been a credible source with a proven record of providing reliable, sensitive, and important information to the US government.

In the letter Reid sent to Comey on Sunday, he pointed out that months ago he had asked the FBI director to release information on Trump's possible Russia ties. Since then, according to a Reid spokesman, Reid has been briefed several times. The spokesman adds, "He is confident that he knows enough to be extremely alarmed."

11-04-16

Does Anti-Hillary atmosphere at the FBI bias Investigations?

FBI officials outrage over director James Comey's July decision "not" to recommend an indictment over Clinton's maintenance of a private email server on which classified information transited.

An FBI agent said Clinton is "the antichrist personified to a large swath of FBI personnel," and that "the reason why they're leaking is they're pro-Trump."

The agent called the bureau "Trumplandia", with some colleagues openly discussing voting for a GOP nominee who has garnered unprecedented condemnation from the party's national security wing and who has pledged to jail Clinton if elected.

"There are lots of people who don't think Trump is qualified, but also believe Clinton is corrupt. What you hear a lot is that it's a bad choice, between an incompetent and a corrupt politician," said a former FBI official.

Senator Ron Wyden, an Oregon Democrat on the intelligence committee, said: "The continued leadership failures at the FBI are another reminder we can't let intelligence agencies say 'trust us' and then give them a blank check to probe into Americans' lives. While I've argued for years that Congress must create ironclad protections for Americans' security and privacy, we also need vigilant oversight of agencies that have the power to deprive citizens of their liberty or change the course of an election."

11-06-16

 FBI Director James Comey claimed "No charges against Hillary Clinton" two days before election.

"Based on our review, we have not changed our conclusions that we expressed in July with respect to Secretary Clinton," Comey wrote Sunday, in a letter sent to members of Congress and released by Rep. Adam Schiff (D-California).

"Since my letter, the FBI investigative team has been working around the clock to process and review a large volume of emails from a device obtained in connection with an unrelated criminal investigation," Comey wrote on Sunday. "During that process we reviewed all of the communications that were to or from Hillary Clinton while she was Secretary of State ... I am very grateful to the professionals at the FBI for doing an extraordinary amount of high-quality work in a short period of time."

Clinton communications director Jennifer Palmieri "We have seen Director Comey's latest letter to the Hill," she said. "We were glad to see that as we were -- that he has found as we were confident that he would that he has confirmed the conclusions that he really -- reached in July and we're glad this matter is resolved."

"You have to understand, it's a rigged system," Trump said. "And she's protected." And then in Sterling Heights, Michigan, he cast doubt on the FBI's ability to process the emails so quickly.

TRUMP ZAP! Trump said to Putin "I can't get the brown stain off my nose!"

IN THE POLLS

Late in game anxiety is building as FBI statement cast shadows on both campaigns.

10-11-16

 At a Mike Pence rally in Newton Iowa, a Trump voter named Rhonda said "I'm on social media all day, everyday nonstop since last June" and called for a revolution if Hillary won the election.

Rhonda told Pence, "One of the biggest things I can tell you that a lot of us are scared of is this voter fraud. There's a lot of us saying that when we go to vote, we're gonna wear red. Our lives depend on this election, our kids futures depend on this election." The room gently applauds.

She continues, "And I will tell you, just for me, I don't want this to happen but I will tell you for me, personally, if Hillary Clinton gets in, I myself, I'm ready for a revolution."

[Pence quickly responds, "No, no don't say that."]

Trump the GOP nominee went after House Speaker Paul Ryan on Twitter calling him "weak and ineffective," and slamming members of the Republican Party who have dropped their support for him as "disloyal."

Trump tweeted how he was finally free of his "shackles" and said he was going to "fight for America the way I want to."

Using polling data from RealClearPolitics and Washington Post/Survey Monkey, Business Insider found that Clinton, as of this week, would lead Trump 278 to 181 electoral votes in states that were either safe or likely bets to go in favor of either party's nominee. That alone would give Clinton more than the 270 electoral votes needed to clinch the presidency.

It's looking like a landslide win for Democratic presidential nominee Hillary Clinton.

10-25-16

Steven Law, Senate Leadership Fund's president and a close McConnell ally, acknowledged Republicans have a tough road to keep their majority — and said the spending push was designed to close a growing funding deficit. In numerous Senate battles, Democrats are outspending Republicans by millions of dollars.

"Over the last two weeks, we've seen every liberal Democratic group descend on these races," Law said. "Democrats feel like the presidential race is in the bag for them and are looking for fresh game in the Senate."

With just two weeks to go until Election Day, the Democratic cash advantage, Law said, was starting to have an effect, hurting Republican prospects across the board. He said the $25 million expenditure would narrow the GOP deficit but wouldn't erase it. He also said he expected to make additional investments in the days to come.

10-26-16

Analysis of North Carolina and Florida by CBS Battleground Tracker:

> Most early voters are female, but so are most registered voters. In both Florida and North Carolina, early voters are 56 percent female and 44 percent male. Because polls have indicated Hillary Clinton has a lead with women overall, this finding might indicate she is up in the early vote. However, most of these women are also older, and older women have been relatively less supportive of Clinton in the polling.
>
> For the Trump campaign specifically, there is not much evidence that the Trump campaign bringing out first-time Republican voters so far. The vast majority of Republican early voters have voted in the last two presidential elections -- they are not new. In North Carolina 85 percent voted in 2012, and 75 percent voted in 2008. Only 10 percent are voting for the first time this year.

11-01-16

Trump is trying to get absentee voters in Wisconsin, Pennsylvania, Michigan and Minnesota to change their vote. Because recent disclosures from WikiLeaks and emails newly uncovered by the FBI that may tie into its investigation of Clinton's private email server.

"This is a message for any Democratic voter who has already

cast their ballots for Hillary Clinton and who are having a bad case of buyer's remorse, in other words you want to change your vote: Wisconsin is one of several states where you can change your early ballot if you think you've made a mistake," Trump said Tuesday night at a rally in Eau Claire, Wis.

"A lot of stuff has come out since you voted. If you live here, or Michigan, or Pennsylvania, or Minnesota, you can change your vote to Donald Trump" he said.

11-01-16

Democrats are filing lawsuits against Republicans who are intimidating voters at the polling places.

In the Ohio lawsuit, the state Democratic Party asked a federal judge to stop the Trump campaign, state party officials and a group associated with Trump supporter Roger Stone from sending people not officially appointed as poll watchers to voting locations.

"This is nothing more than a publicity stunt from the Ohio Democratic Party," Brittany Warner, a spokeswoman for the Ohio GOP, said in a statement. "The arguments cited are not at all related to our official operations at the Ohio Republican Party. Republican leadership in Ohio has created opportunities for greater ballot access and in no way would we ever be involved in the intimidation of voters. Our attorneys are working to prepare the appropriate response."

"We are not coordinating with the Trump campaign, the Republican National Committee or the individual Republican state committees," Stone said. "We are not engaged in poll watching. We seek only to determine if the election is honestly and fairly conducted and to provide an evidentiary basis for a challenge to the election if that is not the case."

"When people call and tell us they're experiencing something they deem hostile, we take that seriously," said Kristen Clarke, president of Lawyers' Committee for Civil Rights Under Law, which has seen increased calls to their offices this election cycle.

Trump has made "an escalating series of statements, often racially tinged, suggesting that his supporters should go to particular precincts on Election Day and intimidate voters," the Ohio lawsuit states. "Trump's exhortations have grown more ominous and specific as the election draws closer."

11-04-16

At least 4 ads appearing on Twitter saying you can vote by texting. Lifting imagery directly from Hillary Clinton's campaign materials, the ads encourage supporters of the Democratic nominee to "vote early" and "vote from home" by texting their candidate's name to a random five-digit number.

"Save time. Avoid the line," one reads.

"Vote early. Text 'Hillary' to 59925," says another.

Ads began making rounds on social media this week, each containing the Clinton campaign's "H" logo and a line saying they were "paid for by Hillary for President." Some featured images of Clinton that appear to be pulled from actual campaign marketing materials, while others showed a black woman and a Hispanic woman, in what may be an attempt to dupe to minority voters.

Twitter user @TheRickyVaughn tweeted them out along with the pro-Clinton hashtag #ImWithHer. The user, who had roughly 11,000 followers before his account was suspended, has previously tweeted conspiracy theories and racial and homophobic slurs, and regularly linked to stories and polls favorable to Republican nominee Donald Trump.

Some people tried texting "Hillary" to the number listed. When they did, they got a variation of this response:

"The ad you saw was not approved by iVisionMobile OR Hillary For America in any way. To opt-in to the real HFA list, text HFA to 47246. Reply STOP to cancel."

11-05-16

At a Trump rally in Reno Nevada scenes of chaos broke out near the front of the stage after a scuffle involving a protester, when an unidentified individual yelled "gun," the Secret Service said in a statement.

Trump was stopped mid-sentence when two Secret Service agents rushed him off stage to safety behind a curtain. An announcer alerted the crowd that Trump would return soon.

A man was escorted out of the crowd by agents, but, "upon a thorough search of the subject and the surrounding area, no weapon was found," the Secret Service said. "A thorough investigation is ongoing at this time by the U.S. Secret Service and the Reno Police Department."

The Republican nominee unharmed came back on stage, finishing his speech.

"Nobody said it was going to be easy for us, but we will never be stopped. I wanna thank the Secret Service. They don't get enough credit. They're amazing. So let's get back," Trump said on his return to the stage.

Later Trump said: "I would like to thank the United States Secret Service and the law enforcement resources in Reno and the state of Nevada for their fast and professional response. I also want to thank the many thousands of people present for their unwavering and unbelievable support. Nothing will stop us - we will make America great again!"

After the incident, Donald Trump, Jr., tweeted: "As @realDonaldTrump just showed the American people, no matter what happens he will not be deterred & he will not give up fighting for you!"

11-06-16

 Several pre-emptive lawsuits filed by Democrats across the country accused Donald Trump's campaign of "conspiring to threaten and intimidate minority voters in urban neighborhoods from voting in the 2016 election."

"Although the Democrats did not prevail in these cases, they did at least force the Republican Party to state, for the record, that they will not engage in voter intimidation," said Joshua A. Douglas, an election law expert at the University of Kentucky College of Law. "That by itself is important, as it means that the Republican Party is on record saying they will comply with all state voting laws."

"Over the past several months, Donald J. Trump has warned that the 2016 election will be stolen from him unless supporters in Ohio and elsewhere swarm urban communities and "watch," "[a]nd when [I] say 'watch,' you know what I'm talking about, right?"

Marc Elias, a lawyer for the Democrats argued in briefs with the high court. "Trump has said "[t]he only way we can lose . . . and I really mean this . . . is if cheating goes on."

11-06-16

Michael Ferrara, 33 threw a rock through a window at the Donald Trump campaign office in Denver, narrowly missing a 10-year-old child. About two dozens Trump volunteers and staff were inside making calls at the time. No one was hurt. An armed security guard and a volunteer ran him down and captured him.

11-07-16

CNN'S Fareed Zakaria said:

> "Donald Trump is different, not just because he is obnoxious, tacky and vulgar, or that his business dealings show him to be a scam artist. He is different because of what he believes."

> Zakaria insisted that Trump's views on policy issues, from social security to taxes, were "insincere" and simply "reflections of what he thinks his supporters want to hear."

> Zakaria said, Trump has "contempt for many of the foundations of liberal democracy," from banning Muslims from entering America to threatening to jail his opponent if he is elected.

"Donald Trump is not a normal candidate. He is a cancer on American democracy," Zakaria concluded.

"And that is why I will vote against him next Tuesday."

TRUMP ZAP! Fox News theory: Don't let facts get in the way of a good argument!

Lyrics to theme song of Trump's TV show "Celebrity Apprentice"

"FOR THE LOVE OF MONEY" (BY THE OJAYS)

Money, money, money, money, money [6x]

Some people got to have it

Some people really need it

Listen to me y'all, do things

Do things, do bad things with it

You wanna do things, do things

Do things, good things with it

Talk about cash money, money

Talk about cash money

Dollar bills, yall

For the love of money

People will steal from their mother

For the love of money

People will rob their own brother

For the love of money

People can't even walk the street

Because they never know

Who in the world they're gonna beat

For that lean, mean, mean green

Almighty dollar, money

For the love of money

People will lie, Lord, they will cheat

For the love of money

People don't care who they hurt or beat

For the love of money

A woman will sell her precious body

For a small piece of paper

It carries a lot of weight

Call it lean, mean, mean green

Almighty dollar

I know money is the root of all evil

Do funny things to some people

Give me a nickel, brother can you spare a dime

Money can drive some people out of their minds

Got to have it, I really need it

How many things have I heard you say

Some people really need it

How many things have I heard you say

Got to have it, I really need it

How many things have I heard you say

Lay down, lay down, a woman will lay down

For the love of money

All for the love of money

Don't let, don't let, don't let money rule you

For the love of money

Money can change people sometimes

Don't let, don't let, don't let money fool you

Money can fool people sometimes

People, don't let money, don't let money change you

It will keep on changing, changing up your mind

Donald J. Trump was elected President of the United States on November 8, 2016. The next week protests erupted around the world.

11-09-16

 Thousands of people across the country marched, shut down highways, burned effigies and shouted angry slogans on Wednesday night to protest the election of Donald J. Trump as president.
In New York, crowds converged at Trump Tower, on Fifth Avenue at 56th Street in Midtown Manhattan, where the president-elect lives. They chanted "Not our president" and "New York hates Trump" and carried signs that said, among other things, "Dump Trump."

On Facebook, a page titled "Not My President" called for protesters to gather on Inauguration Day, Jan. 20, in the nation's capital.

"We refuse to recognize Donald Trump as the president of the United States, and refuse to take orders from a government that puts bigots into power," the organizers wrote.

"We have to make it clear to the public that we did not choose this man for office and that we won't stand for his ideologies."

"These proposals are not simply un-American and wrong-headed, they are unlawful and unconstitutional," Anthony Romero, executive director of the ACLU, said in a statement Wednesday. "They violate the First, Fourth, Fifth, Eight and Fourteenth Amendments. If you do not reverse course and instead endeavor to make these campaign promises a reality, you will have to contend with the full firepower of the ACLU at every step."

Margaret Huang, executive director of Amnesty International USA, said Trump's "poisonous," "xenophobic" and "sexist" rhetoric during the campaign has no place in government.

"This rhetoric cannot and must not become government policy," Huang said in a statement. "President-elect Trump must publicly commit to upholding the human rights of all without discrimination. From concentration camps to the use of torture, we have seen disastrous results when those we elect to represent us flout the United States' obligations to uphold human rights."

"Now that he has secured victory, President-elect Trump should move from the headline-grabbing rhetoric of hatred and govern with respect for all who live in the United States," Kenneth Roth, executive director at Human Rights Watch, said in a statement. "He found a path to the White House through a campaign marked by misogyny, racism and xenophobia, but that's not a route to successful governance. President-elect Trump should commit to leading the U.S. in a manner that fully respects and promotes human rights for everyone."

11-13-16

"I would tell them, don't be afraid, absolutely," Trump said in an interview with CBS News' "60 Minutes."

"Don't be afraid. We are going to bring our country back. But certainly, don't be afraid," he continued, wondering whether there would have been a "double standard" against his supporters had Hillary Clinton won the election.

"I think it's built up by the press, because, frankly, they'll take every single little incident that they can find in this country, which could've been there before," he added about concerns from some minority groups about his victory.

I think the fears, you know, while they may be there, some fabricated, some not, are totally unfounded," his son Donald Trump Jr. said in the interview.

Trump said that he was "surprised" to hear about the hate crimes, racial slurs and threats from some of his supporters after the election and told them to "stop it."

Trump stated, "I am so saddened to hear that. And I say, stop it. If it — if it helps, I will say this, and I will say right to the cameras, stop it."

Trump said that he is committed to reforming Washington, despite appointing numerous lobbyists to the transition team preparing his administration.

"They know the system right now, but we're going to phase that out. You have to phase it out," he said, adding that he will take a salary of only $1 as president.

11-14-16

Protesters hit the streets Sunday over the election of Donald Trump, marking the fifth day of demonstrations in cities such as New York, Los Angeles and San Francisco.

Over the weekend, Los Angeles saw anti-Trump protests swell to 8,000 people on Saturday. In New York, thousands peacefully marched two miles on Saturday and gathered outside Trump Tower, the President-elect's home in Manhattan, where they chanted "not my president."

11-15-16

Residents of the Trump Place apartment complex on Manhattan's Upper West Side started an online petition to have their landlord, Equity Residential, change the name of the properties. Almost 600 supporters signed the petition, and tenants should be seeing some changes soon, Bloomberg News first reported Tuesday.

"We are currently in the process of changing the name of the buildings at 140, 160 and 180 Riverside to their street addresses," a spokesperson told CNBC. "We are assuming a more neutral building identity that will appeal to all current and future residents."

Linda Gottlieb, one of the petition's authors, previously told NBC News she felt "embarrassed" to say where she lived when asking taxi drivers to take her home. She said "the straw that broke the camel's back" was when footage came out showing Trump bragging in lewd terms about trying to have sex with women.

11-23-16

The great political divide caused by the campaign spills over into holiday celebrations and family gatherings.

 Thanksgiving this year anticipate postelection combat with relatives.

Every election provokes some level of stress among voters, but mental health professionals say that the polarization of this year's presidential race appeared to have amplified the tension.

"It was a very significant stressor for people this year," said Dr. Vaile Wright, director of research and special projects at the American Psychological Association.

Vince Garcia, 48, said he heard rumblings that two relatives were planning to wear Trump gear at their Thanksgiving gathering. "Quite honestly I'm not looking forward to it at all," he wrote in an email.

TRUMP ZAP! Trump's request at Thanksgiving: Let's go around the table and say why you are thankful "FOR ME."

01-14-17

 Civil rights icon Rep. John Lewis -- an ally of Martin Luther King Jr. who was brutally beaten by police in Selma, Alabama, in 1965 while marching for civil rights said:

> "I don't see this President-elect as a legitimate president."

"I think the Russians participated in helping this man get elected. And they helped destroy the candidacy of Hillary Clinton."

Lewis said he planned to skip Trump's inauguration next week, which he said would be the first ceremony he would not attend since coming to Washington. He was elected to Congress in 1986.

"You cannot be at home with something that you feel that is wrong," Lewis said.

"Congressman John Lewis should spend more time on fixing and helping his district, which is in horrible shape and falling apart (not to mention crime infested) rather than falsely complaining about the election results. All talk, talk, talk - no action or results. Sad," Trump tweeted Saturday, which happened to fall on the weekend of the King federal holiday.

01-20-17

A protest outside of Trump International Hotel in New York City included actors Robert De Niro, Sally Field, and Alec Baldwin.

Michael Moore posted updates about the rally on his Twitter account:

"With a lot of work on our part, we will stop this man," Moore said. "He will not last four years."

Moore also called for "100 days of protest" as Trump begins his term in office.

TRUMP ZAP! Trump doesn't like to be called a "PUBLIC SERVANT!'

Trump won the electoral vote "bigly" but Clinton won

the popular vote "bigly."

11-16-16

 President-elect Donald Trump captured the threshold 270 Electoral College votes on Election Day, November 8, earning him the title of the 45th president of the United States. Trump's rival, Hillary Clinton, however, is handily winning the popular vote, and her lead is only growing.

Trump received 290 Electoral College votes, thanks to states like Florida (29) and Pennsylvania (20). The former secretary of state, meanwhile, won 232 electoral votes with the help of California (55), New York (29) and Illinois (20).

Votes are still being counted, but the Associated Press' election results show the Democratic candidate, 69, leading the Republican nominee, 70, by 797,724 votes (0.62 percent of voters). According to the AP's tally, she earned 61,324,576 votes (47.85 percent) and he garnered 60,526,852 votes (47.23 percent).

CNN reported that Trump is likely to lose the popular vote "by anywhere from 500,000 to over a million votes." Numbers tallied by the Cook Political Report suggest Clinton's lead may already be over 990,000.

Trump said "If the election were based on total popular vote I would have campaigned in N.Y. Florida and California and won even bigger and more easily. The Electoral College is actually genius in that it brings all states, including the smaller ones, into play. Campaigning is so much different!"

More than 4.3 million people, including stars such as Lady Gaga and Pink, have signed a Change.org petition to ask Republican electors to honor the popular vote and declare Clinton the next POTUS.

"We are calling on the Electors to ignore their states' votes and cast their ballots for Secretary Clinton," the petition reads. "Why? Mr. Trump is unfit to serve. His scapegoating of so many Americans, and his impulsivity, bullying, lying, admitted history of sexual assault, and utter lack of experience make him a danger to the Republic."

Ohio Northern University political science professor Robert M. Alexander wrote an op-ed for CNN stating that the petition will likely be ineffective.

TRUMP ZAP! Trump set the bar so low to be president that the drug lord "El Chapo" could be president!

Why pollsters got it wrong

11-09-16

The eletion results amounted to a repudiation, not only of Mrs. Clinton, but of President Obama, whose legacy is suddenly imperiled. And it was a decisive demonstration of power by a largely overlooked coalition of mostly blue-collar white and working-class voters who felt that the promise of the United States had slipped their grasp amid decades of globalization and multiculturalism.

From Pennsylvania to Wisconsin, industrial towns once full of union voters who for decades offered their votes to Democratic presidential candidates, even in the party's lean years, shifted to Mr. Trump's Republican Party.

One county in the Mahoning Valley of Ohio, Trumbull, went to Mr. Trump by a six-point margin. Four years ago, Mr. Obama won there by 22 points.

Hillary Clinton came closer than any other woman to the highest elected office in America. But why has the United States been so resistant to electing a female head of state?

For Mrs. Clinton, the defeat signaled an astonishing end to a political dynasty that has colored Democratic politics for a generation. Eight years after losing to President Obama in the Democratic primary — and 16 years after leaving the White House for the United States Senate, as President Bill Clinton exited office — she had seemed positioned to carry on two legacies: her husband's and the president's.

11-10-16

Who voted for whom:

Forty-three percent of people with college degrees backed the Republican, although post-graduates voted overwhelmingly for Clinton, the Democrat, at 58 percent to 35 percent.

Trump's success was rooted in profound dissatisfaction with

the status quo — felt keenly in rural areas and smaller towns far from prosperous cities that voted overwhelmingly for Clinton.

Latino turnout was at a record high.

While two-thirds voted Clinton, Trump won 29 percent of that demographic compared to Romney's 27 percent in spite of inflammatory remarks about Mexicans and his tough stance on immigration.

American women traditionally lean Democratic, and Clinton won the female vote 54 to 42 percent, about the same as Obama, according to Pew Research Center.

According to the Pew Research Center, eight in 10 white born-again, evangelical Christians say they voted for Trump compared to 16 percent for Clinton.

This shocked some observers given the twice-divorced Republican's vulgar remarks about groping women and Hillary's record as a socially liberal New Yorker who has been accepting of gay and transgender rights.

Obama was propelled into office on a wave of hope and optimism by harnessing the youth vote. But young Americans threw less weight behind the Democratic candidate this time, disappointed in Obama's administration and unenthusiastic about his anointed successor.

Clinton's long-running email scandal, perceptions that she was untrustworthy and her ties to Wall Street damaged the Democrat. Millennials had overwhelmingly favored her challenger Bernie Sanders in the primary.

Ways the Republicans suppress the minority vote:

A study from the Joint Center for Political and Economic Studies showed that black voters wait twice as long as white people to cast a ballot, with the longest wait times being in South Carolina, Florida and Maryland.

 Harvard researcher Stephen Pettigrew found that African-Americans were six times more likely than members of demographic groups to spend more than an hour in line in order to vote.

Part of the problem is the resources allotted to polling places in predominantly black communities. Those districts have fewer poll workers to assist voters and guide them through the process and have fewer voting machines on hand to process voters in a timely manner.

The Joint Center for Political and Economic Studies survey found that 730,000 Americans found the lines in 2008 to be so excessive that they didn't show up again four years later.

Following the 2012 election, the U.S. Census polled Americans who didn't vote. The No. 1 reason that low-income voters said they stayed away from the polling place (for 20.1 percent of respondents) was that a disability or illness prevented them from voting. Other popular answers included "transportation problems" (9.4 percent), "registration problems" (5.6 percent) and an "inconvenient polling place" (2.3 percent).

The absence of federal oversight of the Supreme Court's 2013 decision to nullify Section 4, related to preclearance, in the Voting Rights Act of 1965. That portion of the law, passed under the President Lyndon Johnson administration to prevent voter suppression on the basis of race, requires that states with a history of such practices gain approval from U.S. Department of Justice before making any changes to voting regulations, has allowed numerous states to restrict early voting hours, which is aimed at targeting voting among people of color. Black voters are more likely to cast ballots in the early morning than any other group.

The Leadership Conference Education Fund found that there will be 868 fewer polling places in states that had previously been covered by the law. Of the counties surveyed in Arizona, every single one had restricted voting access. Texas and Alabama also decimated the availability of polling places: A respective 53 percent and 67 percent of counties had fewer places to vote than they did during the previous election.

Three states — Colorado, Washington, and Oregon — conduct all of their polling through mail (mail-in-ballot), with appropriate paperwork automatically shipped to the addresses of registered voters. In 2012, those three states had some of the highest turnout in the nation, ranking among the top 15 of U.S. states. Although Minnesota led the U.S. with a 76 percent turnout rate, Colorado wasn't too far behind; 69.9

percent of eligible voters cast a ballot in the 2012 race. The national average was 57.5 percent.

11-13-16

Email from Navin Nayak, Clinton's head of opinion research said:

"We believe that we lost this election in the last week."

"Comey's letter in the last 11 days of the election both helped depress our turnout and also drove away some of our critical support among college-educated white voters – particularly in the suburbs.

"We also think Comey's [second] letter, which was intended to absolve [Secretary] Clinton, actually helped to bolster Trump's turnout."

The New York Times quoted a donor as saying:

"Clinton said: "There are lots of reasons why an election like this is not successful … our analysis is that Comey's letter raising doubts that were groundless, baseless, proven to be, stopped our momentum."

Comey's second letter was sent last Sunday, two days before the election. In it, he said a review of the newly discovered emails had been completed, and that it found no evidence to merit reopening the investigation of Clinton.

Trump discussed the call he took from his Democratic opponent in the small hours of that morning.

"So Hillary called and it was a lovely call," he said,

adding: "She couldn't have been nicer. She just said, 'Congratulations, Donald, well done.' And I said, 'I want to thank you very much, you were a great competitor.'"

11-13-16

Fareed Zakaria said on CNN:

We have all managed to ignore rural America and the pain of economic hardship and social dislocation it has faced over the last few decades. The big divide in America today is urban versus rural.

Over the last three or four decades, America has sorted itself into a highly efficient meritocracy where people from all walks of life can move up the ladder of achievement and income, usually ending up in cities. It's a better way than using race or gender or blood lines as a path to wealth and power but it does create its own problems. As with any system, there will be people who don't ascend to the top. And because it's a meritocracy, it's easy to believe that this is justified, that they deserve it.

The Republicans' great success in rural communities has been that even though they often advocate economic policies that would not these help people, indeed, policies that often hurt them, they demonstrate respect by identifying with them culturally, religiously, emotionally.

The Republicans' great success in rural communities

has been that even though they often advocate economic policies that would not these help people, indeed, policies that often hurt them, they demonstrate respect by identifying with them culturally, religiously, emotionally.

And here is the key point. Trump is not unusual. Right wing populism is on the rise across a vary variety of western countries. It is rising in countries in northern Europe where economic growth has been robust. It is rising in countries like Germany where manufacturing jobs have stayed very strong. In France, where the state provides many protections for the working class. The one common trait in all these places is that a white majority population faces a recent influx of immigrants.

Perhaps the phenomenon might be better described as a reaction to cultural change but it often expresses itself simply as hostility to people who are different and are usually brown and black.

Consider, for example, that 72 percent of registered Republican voters still doubt that Barack Obama was born in the United States. This is according to an August NBC poll.

12-09-16

"Pizzagate," was a false report spread online that erroneously accused Clinton and her campaign of running a child sex ring at a pizza shop. A fake news story that lead to a man with an assault rifle firing a shot in Comet Ping Pong, the Washington shop that has been falsely accused in the fake news stories.

Hillary Clinton said that the spread of fake news, which has "flooded social media over the past year," is a trend that "can have real world consequences."

"This is not about politics or partisanship. Lives are at risk, lives of ordinary people just trying to go about their days to do their jobs, contribute to their communities," Clinton said. "It is a danger that must be addressed and addressed quickly."

Clinton backed "bipartisan legislation" that looks to give Congress more power to respond to "foreign propaganda." an apparent reference to Russia's role in funding some of the fake news, according to two studies, with the goal of influencing US politics.

"It is imperative that leaders in both the private and pubic sector step up to protect our democracy and innocent lives,"

TRUMP ZAP! Trump's archenemy "The Popular Vote!"

Electoral College? Mobocracy?

The Electoral College was created for two reasons. The first purpose was to create a buffer between the population and the selection of a President. The second as part of the structure of the government that gave extra power to the smaller states.

The first reason that the founders created the Electoral College is hard to understand today. The founding fathers were afraid of direct election to the Presidency. They feared a tyrant could manipulate public opinion and come to power.

Hamilton and the other founders believed that the electors would be able to insure that only a qualified person becomes President. They believed that with the Electoral College no one would be able to manipulate the citizenry. It would act as check on an electorate that might be duped. Hamilton and the other founders did not trust the population to make the right choice. The founders also believed that the Electoral College had the advantage of being a group that met only once and thus could not be manipulated over time by foreign governments or others.

We all know it didn't work in the 2016 Presidential election!

11-15-16

 Four years ago, when President Obama won reelection, Trump called for a march on Washington and decried the system of electors (Electoral College).

After winning the 2016 election Trump said the Electoral College is a "Genius".

Trump, despite trailing by nearly 1 million ballots in the popular vote, with 94 percent of the count in, won an Electoral College victory 290-232, with Michigan outstanding.

Rust Belt states that were considered largely safe for Democrats, such as Pennsylvania and Wisconsin -- a move that stunned observers. Trump won by narrow margins in both states.

This is the second time in five presidential elections that the winner was projected to lose the popular vote. The other was in 2000 when George W. Bush won.

Wisconsin Green Party co-chairman George Martin said the party is seeking a "reconciliation of paper records" -- a request that could go further than a simple recount, possibly spurring an investigation into the integrity of Wisconsin's voting system. "This is a process, a first step to examine whether our electoral democracy is working," Martin said.

Trump tweeted, "The Green Party scam to fill up their coffers by asking for impossible recounts is now being joined by the badly defeated & demoralized Dems."

Jill Stein (Green Party Presidential Candidate) has already raised more than $5 million online for the recount in Wisconsin, which may begin some time next week.

Appearing on CNN, Stein dismissed Trump's suggestion that the funds wouldn't be spent on the recount.

"For his information, this is all going into a dedicated and segregated account so that it can only be spent on the recount," she told CNN's Pamela Brown on "Newsroom."

"He may be creating his own facts here as he's been known to do some times in the past," Stein added. "He himself said it was rigged election unless he won it."

Trump said, "The people have spoken and the election is over, and as Hillary Clinton herself said on election night, in addition to her conceding by congratulating me, 'We must accept this result and then look to the future.'"

The Clinton campaign said Saturday it will take part in the recounts, joining with Stein, to ensure the recount is "fair to all sides."

11-29-16

"In addition to winning the Electoral College in a landslide," Trump wrote in a tweet, "I won the popular vote if you deduct the millions of people who voted illegally."

"The president of the United States can't randomly tweet without having somebody check it out," Former House speaker (Republican) Newt Gingrich told USA TODAY's weekly video newsmaker series. "It makes you wonder about whatever else he's doing. It undermines much more than a single tweet."

11-30-16

Jill Stien Green Party Candidate is seeking recounts in three states: Wisconsin, Pennsylvania and Michigan. If the three states were to move into Clinton's column, she would win the Electoral College with 278 electoral votes.

"After a presidential election tarnished by the use of outdated and unreliable machines and accusations of irregularities, people of all political persuasions are asking if our election results are reliable," Stein said Wednesday of the Michigan recount. "We must recount the votes so we can build trust in our election system. We need to verify the vote in this and every election so that Americans can be sure we have a fair, secure and accurate voting system."

  Reince Priebus, the outgoing Republican National
Committee chair, defended Donald Trump's assertion that
"millions" of people had voted illegally during the general
election.

"Face the Nation" host John Dickerson pressed Priebus on
that specific illegal vote claim, asking the incoming White
House chief of staff how he handles the president-elect's
statement "when you know that that's not true."

"I don't know if that's not true, John," Priebus said, saying
that "there are estimates all over the map" on undocumented
immigrants voting in election.

"But you think millions of people voted illegally?" Dickerson
asked.

"I think the president-elect is someone who has pushed the
envelope and caused people to think in this country," he said.
"He's not taking conventional thought -- on every single issue
and has caused people to look at things that maybe they have
taken for granted."

12-04-16

 President-elect Donald Trump sent out a curious tweet. In it,
Trump made a claim, without citing any evidence, that
"millions of people" had voted illegally — and therefore he
was actually also the winner of the popular vote.

On ABC's "This Week" Sunday, host George Stephanopoulos

---

asked Vice President-elect Mike Pence point-blank about the tweet. "That claim is groundless," Stephanopoulos said. "There's no evidence to back it up. Is it responsible for a president-elect to make false statements like that?"

"I think what, you know, what is — what is historic here is that our president-elect won 30 to 50 states, he won more counties than any candidate on our side since Ronald Reagan," Pence said, attempting to pivot back from the tweet. "And the fact that some partisans, who are frustrated with the outcome of the election and disappointed with the outcome of the election, are pointing to the popular vote, I can assure you, if this had been about the popular vote, Donald Trump and I have been campaigning a whole lot more in Illinois and California and New York."

"But can you provide any evidence?" Stephanopoulos asked once more. "Can you provide any evidence to back up that statement?"

Pence: "Well, look, I think he's expressed his opinion on that. And he's entitled to express his opinion on that. And I think the American people — I think the American people find it very refreshing that they have a president who will tell them what's on his mind. And I think the connection that he made in the course..." "... whether it's true or not?" Stephanoupolos asked, as they ran out of time.

"Well, they're going to tell them — ...," Pence said. "He's going to say what he believes to be true and I know that he's always going to speak in that way as president."

The Electoral College exists as a check on the democratic process to prevent an unqualified candidate from making it into the White House.

Lobbist against the Electoral College say Trump is the kind of candidate the Founding Fathers worried about. His character is suspect, according to his critics, as shown by his bizarre tweets, rambling speeches, and constant disregard of facts. Russian hacking might have swayed the election, they add, and Trump's foreign business entanglements seem worrisome.

Hillary Clinton won the popular vote by the widest margin of any losing candidate in US presidential elections history, carrying nearly 2.9 million votes more than President-elect Donald Trump, according to an Associated Press analysis of certified results from all 50 states and the District of Columbia.

TRUMP ZAP! If Trump keeps saying this crazy stuff he might get elected again in 2020!

20 TRUMP SHOULDN'T BE PRESIDENT

"INTERVENTION NEEDED"

09-30-16

Statements written by The Washington Post Editorial Board (09-30-16) 5 weeks before the election:

> You may not approve of everything Mr. Trump has had to say about nuclear weapons, torture or mass deportations, but you doubt he could implement anything too radical. Congress, the courts, the Constitution — these would keep Mr. Trump in check, you think.

> Well, think again. A President Trump could, unilaterally, change this country to its core. By remaking U.S. relations with other nations, he could fundamentally reshape the world, too.

> Could he tear up long-standing international agreements? Round up and expel millions of longtime U.S. residents? Impose giant tariffs? Waterboard terrorist suspects? Yes, yes, yes and yes — all without so much as an if-you-please to Congress. Could he bar the media from covering him? To a large extent, yes. Could he use the government to help his businesses and, as he has threatened, injure those he perceives as enemies? Yes, he could.

> It would be reckless not to consider the damage Mr. Trump might wreak. Some of that damage would

ensue more from who he is than what he does. His racism and disparagement of women could empower extremists who are now on the margins of American politics, while his lies and conspiracy theories could legitimize discourse that until now has been relegated to the fringe. But his scope for action should not be underestimated, either.

TRUMP ZAP! Since Trump is the "Most Powerful Toddler" they had to put a "child proof cap" on the nuclear button!

Trump Holds Up In His Tower after Surprised Win

11-12-16

The New York Times reported:

> "The president-elect is already talking with his advisers about how many nights a week he will actually stay in the official presidential mansion. According to the newspaper he has told them he would like to do what he always has – spend time in New York.
>
> Trump, according to the newspaper, was shocked when he won the election and is trying to come to terms that his life is about to change. The Times noted that during the campaign he often flew hours late at night just to sleep in his own bed in Trump Towers in New York City.
>
> And, the newspaper reported, Trump also enjoys his visiting his golf course in New Jersey and his Mar-a-

Lago estate in South Florida on weekends.

Trump's wife, Melania, is expected to move to
Washington. But the newspaper noted, their 10-year-
old son Barron, is midway through the school year in
New York. It is unclear when Melania and Barron
would officially take up residence in the White House.

11-21-16

New York Mayor Bill de Blasio at a press conference on
Friday said:

"The number one imperative here is safety and
security. We owe that to the president elect, his family
and his team.".
But he added the city will need help with those costs,
particularly police overtime.

"This is a very substantial undertaking. It will take
substantial resources," he said. "We will begin the
conversation with the federal government shortly on
reimbursement for the NYPD for some of the costs that
we are incurring."

"We have never had a situation where a POTUS
(president of the United States) would be here on such
a regular basis," said de Blasio.

"The details of his future plans are unknown, but we
certainly know over these next 65 days [until the
inauguration] he will be here regularly.

The NYPD is up to the challenge and the city of New
York is up to the challenge, I have no doubt about that."

"This makes [previous protection efforts] look quite small obviously," he said. "We'll have to establish a new set of ground rules."

11-14-16

Trump's profits for using his own facilities will far out pace any salary he claims to donate to charity.

The Secret Service is in negotiations with the Trump Organization to take over two vacant floors at Trump Tower.

According to The Post, both the Secret Service and NYPD are planning to run a command post.

Should these negotiations go through, taxpayers would likely be paying the president-elect's corporation to lease the two floors.

The Post reported that a lease deal could cost more than $3 million based on current rates at Trump Tower.

Two of the floors, which are 3,000- to 5,000-square-foot spaces, are currently marketed at $105 per square-foot.

12-14-16

NEW YORK/WASHINGTON (Reuters) - President-elect Donald Trump and some of Silicon Valley's most powerful executives met at his Manhattan tower on Wednesday, a summit convened to smooth over frictions after both sides made no secret of their disdain for each other during the election campaign:

The meeting between tech luminaries, including Apple Inc's Tim Cook, Facebook Inc's Sheryl Sandberg and

Tesla Motors Inc's Elon Musk, took place as Trump has alarmed some U.S. corporations with his rhetoric challenging long-established policy toward China, a main market for Silicon Valley.

"There's nobody like the people in this room, and anything we can do to help this go along we're going to do that for you," Trump told the executives gathered in a conference room on the 25th floor of Trump Tower. "You call my people, you call me, it doesn't make any difference. We have no formal chain of command," he said.

Trump added: "We're going to make fair trade deals. We're going to make it a lot easier for you to trade across borders."

Three of Trump's adult children, Donald Jr., Eric and Ivanka, sat at the head of a large rectangular table as the meeting began. Their attendance may fuel further concern about potential conflicts of interests for Trump, who has said he would hand over control of his business empire to his children while he occupies the White House.

TRUMP ZAP! December 2016 Trump is dreaming of a "white" Christmas!

Racism Escalates, So Does "The Wall"

11-09-16

Droves of disenchanted Americans inundated the immigration website for Canada.

The Immigration and Citizen portal sputtered, repeatedly crashing as Election Day results showed Republican presidential candidate Donald Trump snagging wins in Ohio, Florida and Missouri.

"Shared Services Canada worked through the night and continues to work to resolve the issue to ensure that the website is available for users as soon as possible," the spokesperson said in a statement.

Left-leaning voters have threatened to ditch the United States for their northern neighbor ever since the real estate magnate kicked off his White House bid by disparaging Mexicans, Muslims and women.

11-09-16

Breitbart News Network is expanding its U.S. operations and launching sites in Germany and France, its U.S. editor-in-chief told Reuters.

The right-wing media landscape is shifting in the wake of Trump's campaign to provide a platform for the more radical views that helped fuel the Republican candidate's shock election victory on Tuesday.

Former head Steve Bannon was a leading voice of the so-called Alt-Right movement -- a loose-knit movement of white nationalists, anti-Semites and immigration foes -- it regularly attacks Republican Party elites, publishes anti-immigrant themed stories and promotes political conspiracy theories.

U.S. technology editor Milo Yiannopoulos has faced criticism for comments he has made about Muslims, Black Lives Matter activists and feminists. Social media platform Twitter banned him in July for inciting harassment of the actress Leslie Jones.

11-11-16

 The Southern Poverty Law Center (SPLC), a nonprofit legal advocacy organization specializing in civil rights, investigated the "Trump effect":

After surveying 2,000 K-12 teachers, they found that since the beginning of the campaign, more than half of them noticed "an increase in uncivil political discourse" at their schools.

 Two-thirds of the teachers also said that some of their kids — mostly minorities and immigrants — expressed concern about what might happen to them if Trump became president.

"[Our] study was published during the primary season, but what we heard once school resumed in August and September was that almost everything we had reported on basically continued and got worse," said Maureen Costello, the director of the SPLC's Teaching Tolerance project. "The concern and anxieties of immigrant and Muslim students and the bad behavior and the bullying [was extremely widespread]."

After Donald Trump won the election, a group of white high school students in York, Pennsylvania, celebrated the Republican's victory by marching through the halls of their school chanting "white power" while brandishing a Trump campaign sign. One Hispanic student even claims that her fellow minority classmates were spit on as the hate procession passed again during lunchtime.

"After Tuesday, it was a whole different ballgame. What we are hearing from teachers is that everything we reported is at an extreme," said Maureen Costello, who has been receiving a stream of emails since Wednesday from concerned parents and teachers all across the nation recounting some of the things kids are going through.

"A black girl was spat on because she had the the audacity to argue about Black Lives Matter. An international student was told, 'Take your ass back home, chink.' A gay student was told, 'You better turn straight if you want to survive in America.' A Latino student was told, 'Get ready to build that wall motherfucker.' An Asian student overheard a group of white students say, 'Trump's acceptance speech was pussy to a moderate, I hope he isn't going soft.' And another gay student was followed by white girls as they chanted, 'Trump, Trump, Trump.'"

This week, I corresponded with a high school senior from Queens over email who was harassed on Wednesday morning, as Trump's win was just starting to sink in. "I was on the bus and a group of girls from another school got on," she wrote to me. "They looked around and then looked at me and said, 'Aren't you supposed to be sitting in the back of the bus?

Like, Trump is President.' I never thought something like that would happen to me. I was very shaken up by it." (The girl asked to remain anonymous for fear of being targeted for more bullying.)

Sheri Bauman, a professor at the University of Arizona who studies bullying said:

> "In these cases, it is not that these things didn't happen before, They are just accelerating. They are becoming more cruel, but they feel as though they have license to do it in a way that maybe before they felt they needed to be a little more secretive."

> "We know this bullying doesn't just affect them in the short term, in many cases we see poor psychological adjustment, depression, and anxiety into adulthood," said Bauman. "Bystanders also hear it. Not all marginalized groups are visible. Take someone who might be LGBT, imagine what it is like [to hear this stuff] even if you're not the target. You can develop internalized oppression. And if everyone around you believes you are worthless or expendable or a rapist or a threat, you might begin to believe it."

11-15-16

Joe Coleman, the town recorder in Clay, WV. said that Mayor Beverly Whaling's resigned Tuesday amid fallout from a racist post on Facebook about First Lady Michelle Obama.

Whaling earlier apologized for her response to a post made by Clay County Development Corp. director Pamela Ramsey

Taylor after Republican Donald Trump's election as president.

 Taylor's post said, "It will be refreshing to have a classy, beautiful, dignified First Lady in the White House. I'm tired of seeing an Ape in heels."

Whaling responded: "Just made my day Pam."

Owens Brown, director of the NAACP's West Virginia chapter, is among those calling for the removal of both women. "I feel it's unfortunate that people still have these racist undertones," Brown said. "Unfortunately, this is a reality that we are dealing with in America today. There's no place for these types of attitudes in our state."

11-15-16

 Kansas Secretary of State Kris Kobach is a key member of Trump's transition team, said the immigration advisers were looking at how the Homeland Security Department could move rapidly on border wall construction without approval from Congress by re-appropriating existing funds in the current budget.

To implement Trump's call for "extreme vetting" of some Muslim immigrants, Kobach said the immigration policy group could recommend the reinstatement of a national registry of immigrants and visitors who enter the United States on visas from countries where extremist organizations are active.

Richard Spencer, the president of the National Policy Institute, an arm of the alt-right, spoke at an afternoon news conference:

> "Donald Trump's campaign was the first step towards identity politics in the United States, I do think we have a psychic connection, a deeper connection with Donald Trump, in a way we simply do not have with most Republicans."

> "I think the alt-right, in a way, was too often talking to itself, a head without a body," he said. "The Trump movement was a body without a head."

> "I think, moving forward, the alt-right can, as an intellectual vanguard, complete Trump," he continued.

> Spencer doubled down on his defense of Trump's 2005 comments, recorded by "Access Hollywood," in which the future president-elect could be heard bragging about sexual assault.

> "Yes, women, deep down, do want to be taken by a strong man," Spencer said, though he added he wasn't advocating sexual harassment. "I've looked at a lot of romance novels women read. I've noticed a distinct pattern."

12-12-16

US attorney general Loretta Lynch spoke at a mosque in

Virginia saying:

> "There is a pernicious thread that connects the act of
> violence against a woman wearing a hijab to the assault
> on a transgender man to the tragic deaths of nine
> innocent African-Americans during a Bible study at
> Mother Emanuel AME in Charleston, South Carolina,"
> she said. "There is a thread that links all of those and
> when one of us is threatened all of us are threatened."

The Southern Poverty Law Center has been tracking incidents reported directly to them or published in the media. In the ten days following the election the advocacy group counted 867 hate incidents.

SPLC's president also directly tied these incidents to the election of Donald Trump and the rhetoric he used during the campaign.

01-05-17

Bristol County Massachusetts Sheriff Thomas Hodgson said:

> "That he has proposed to the Trump transition team
> sending "eight to 10" inmates with a guard to start
> work on the massive wall. And, Hodgson noted, he
> was informed by other sheriffs throughout the U.S. that
> they are willing to join in.

> "A lot of the sheriffs across the nation want to use this
> resource," the sheriff said. "This is a chance for us to
> save taxpayers' money. It's long overdue."

> "We need to turn this country around and put law and

order back in place."

Hodgson's proposal is based on Project N.I.C.E., (National Inmates Community Endeavors), a federal prison program designed to aid those needing help after natural disasters.

"Project N.I.C.E. extends beyond rebuilding cities and towns to nationwide projects that have a positive impact on our communities and public safety. Projects like President-elect Donald Trump's border wall," Hodgson said during his swearing-in speech on Wednesday.

The Washington Examiner quotes Jessica Vaughan of the Center for Immigration Studies.

"If any of the inmates working on the wall are criminal aliens from south of the border, they'll be that much closer for deportation."

TRUMP ZAP! Trump uses an "Eco Chamber" to validate his views!

Trump Perfecting his Con-Artist Skills

11-11-16

Trump's transition website is now equipped with the official ".gov" federal web address.

The "Meet the President Elect" section has more than one-quarter of Trump's bio refers to his business properties around the world.

The focus on Trump's individual private properties, from which he draws his income, is a break from the political norms of a candidate transitioning into the White House.

11-18-16

Donald J. Trump has reversed course and agreed to pay $25 million to settle a series of lawsuits stemming from his defunct for-profit education venture, Trump University.

Allegations in the case were highly unpleasant for Mr. Trump: Students paid up to $35,000 in tuition for a programs that, according to the testimony of former Trump University employees, used high-pressure sales tactics and employed unqualified instructors.

"I am pleased that under the terms of this settlement, every victim will receive restitution and that Donald Trump will pay up to $1 million in penalties to the State of New York for violating state education laws," New York attorney general Mr. Schneiderman said in a statement. "The victims of Trump University have waited years for today's result, and I am pleased that their patience — and persistence — will be rewarded by this $25 million settlement."

"It's something I could have settled many times," Mr. Trump said during a debate in February. "I could settle it right now for very little money, but I don't want to do it out of principle."

He added, "The people that took the course all signed — most — many — many signed report cards saying it was fantastic, it was wonderful, it was beautiful."

12-22-16

Trump's son Eric owns a Virginia vineyard called "Trump Vineyard Estates" BuzzFeed reported.

> The Department of Labor petitioned for the winery to bring in six foreign workers using the federal government's temporary work visa program known as H-2.

> Companies owned by Trump or that bear his name have asked for permission from the Department of Labor to bring at least 263 temporary foreign workers to the U.S. since he launched his campaign.

12-26-16

Trump said in a statement Saturday that he has directed his counsel to take the necessary steps to implement the dissolution of the Donald J. Trump Foundation, saying that it operated "at essentially no cost for decades, with 100 percent of the money going to charity."

"The foundation has done enormous good works over the years in contributing millions of dollars to countless worthy groups, including supporting veterans, law enforcement officers and children," he said in a statement.

Trump said he will pursue philanthropic efforts in other ways, but he didn't elaborated on how he'd do so.

IRS regulations prohibit self-dealing by the charity. That's broadly defined as using its money or assets to benefit Trump, his family, his companies or substantial contributors to the foundation.

Whether Trump benefited from the foundation's spending has been the subject of an investigation by New York Attorney General Eric Schneiderman.

Amy Spitalnick, press secretary for Schneiderman's office, said Saturday that the foundation "cannot legally dissolve" until the investigation is complete.

One President at a Time! "Why?"

12-23-16

On sensitive issues of diplomacy and national security, Trump has displayed a continued willingness to pressure and contradict President Barack Obama, eschewing a "one president at a time" policy that Obama insists must govern the peaceful transition of power.

Diplomats at the United Nations were preparing for a vote in the Security Council on a resolution rebuking Israel for its settlement activity in the West Bank and East Jerusalem.

Trump urged Obama to reject the measure, arguing it "puts Israel in a very poor negotiating position and is extremely unfair to all Israelis."

"What I've advised the President-elect is that across the board on foreign policy, you want to make sure that you're doing it in a systematic, deliberate, intentional way," Obama said.

"And since there's only one President at a time, my advice to him has been that before he starts having a lot of interactions with foreign governments other than the usual courtesy calls, that he should want to have his full team in place, that he should want his team to be fully briefed."

Donald Trump tweets toughening up the country's nuclear weapons capabilities, saying the United States must "greatly strengthen and expand" them -- at least until the rest of the world "comes to its senses."

Jason Miller, transition communications director, sent CBS News a statement to specify that the threats the U.S. faces issue from the possibility that terrorist organizations and rogue regimes might obtain nuclear weapons.

"President-elect Trump was referring [in the tweet] to the threat of nuclear proliferation and the critical need to prevent it---particularly to and among terrorist organizations and unstable and rogue regimes," Miller wrote.

"It requires a lot of thought and a lot of study and Twitter, with 140 characters, probably doesn't lend itself to the best discussion of this issue," Nick Burns, the former NATO ambassador, told CBS News.

Trump Still Loves Putin

12-31-16

Obama had promised consequences after U.S. intelligence officials blamed Russia for hacks intended to influence the 2016 election. Officials accused Putin of personally directing the efforts and primarily targeting Democrats.

Washington also put sanctions on two Russian intelligence agencies, the GRU and the FSB, four GRU officers and three companies that Obama said "provided material support to the GRU's cyber operations."

As part of the sanctions, Obama told Russia to close two compounds in the United States that the administration said were used by Russian personnel for "intelligence-related purposes."

A total of 96 Russians are expected to leave the United States including expelled diplomats and their families.

Putin said in a statement, adding that Russia reserved the right to retaliate:

> "We will not expel anyone,"

> "Further steps towards the restoration of Russian-American relations will be built on the basis of the policy which the administration of President D. Trump will carry out," he said.

"Great move on delay (by V. Putin) - I always knew he was very smart!" Trump wrote on Twitter from Florida, where he is on vacation.

01-11-17

Morgan Lewis, a law firm representing President-elect Donald Trump, was named the "Russia Law Firm of the Year" last year by website Chambers and Partners.

"This active Moscow office of an American firm offers top-level advice in regards to the energy sector and also houses very strong banking and M&A teams," Chambers and Partners writes about the award.

The attorney who appeared with Trump at a news conference, Sheri Dillon, specializes in "federal tax controversy matters," according to her bio on the Morgan Lewis website.

01-14-17

Trump's policy towards Russia is the subject of intense interest in Washington amid a Senate inquiry into allegations that the Kremlin ordered a hacking operation against the Democratic Party to help the billionaire politician win the November election:

> Trump told the Wall Street Journal that he would keep sanctions against Russia in place "at least for a period of time".

> "I understand that they would like to meet, and that's absolutely fine with me," Trump said.

> "If you get along and if Russia is really helping us, why would anybody have sanctions if somebody's doing some really great things?" Trump said.

TRUMP ZAP! Trump the "Ugly American" is our President!

21 TRUMP'S CABINET "ADDING ALLIGATORS TO THE SWAMP"

11-15-16

Carson's Business manager and close friend Armstrong Williams said Republican Presidential Candidate Ben Carson won't join the incoming Trump administration and would only serve as an unofficial adviser.

Retired neurosurgeon Ben Carson has told President-elect Donald Trump that he isn't interested in serving as secretary of Health and Human Services.

"Dr. Carson feels he has no government experience, he's never run a federal agency. The last thing he would want to do was take a position that could cripple the presidency" Williams said.

What made Carson think he qualifies to be President but not qualified to be a cabinet member?

TRUMP ZAP! Trump: Meet my black man Carson!

11-17-16

Trump picked retired Lt. Gen. Michael T. Flynn to be National Security Adviser:

> Flynn stunned former colleagues when he traveled to Moscow last year to appear alongside Russian President Vladi-mir Putin at a lavish gala for the Kremlin-run propaganda channel RT, a trip Flynn admitted he was paid to make and defended by saying

he saw no distinction between RT and U.S. news channels such as CNN.

Flynn said he used the trip to press Putin's government to behave more responsibly in international affairs. Former U.S. officials said Flynn, seen dining next to Putin in photos published by Russian propaganda outlets, was used as a prop by the autocratic leader.

Civil rights groups denounced the Flynn selection, saying he has refused to reject Trump's repeated statements supporting the use of waterboarding and other brutal interrogation measures on terrorism suspects. Trump has also advocated killing or capturing innocent relatives of terrorism suspects.

Flynn published an opinion article in which he called for wholesale changes in U.S. policy toward Turkey and the extradition of exiled cleric Fethullah Gulen, who resides in Pennsylvania and has been accused by the Turkish government of fomenting a coup attempt.

Flynn didn't disclose that his consulting firm had been hired for lobbying work by a group with ties to the Turkish government.

Flynn was forced out of his job as director of the Defense Intelligence Agency in 2014 over concerns about his leadership style. After the ouster, he frequently lashed out in public against President Obama and blamed his removal on the administration's discomfort with his hard-line views on radical Islam

11-17-16

Trump's leading contender for Treasury Secretary Steven Mnuchin:

> Former Goldman Sachs Group Inc. partner who later managed hedge funds, assembled OneWest bank in the wake of the 2008 financial crisis.
>
> Mnuchin organized a group of billionaire investors to buy remnants of failed banks including IndyMac. The company was soon profitable. But it and Mnuchin were eventually targeted by protesters over the firm's handling of struggling borrowers. Kevin Stein, deputy director of California Reinvestment Coalition called it a "foreclosure machine" in a statement earlier this week.

11-20-16

Sen. Jeff Sessions (R-Ala.) was picked by Trump to be the 84th attorney general of the United States:

> Sessions was once rejected as a federal judge over allegations he called a black attorney "boy," suggested a white lawyer working for black clients was a race traitor, joked that the only issue he had with the Ku Klux Klan was their drug use, and referred to civil rights groups as "un-American" organizations trying to "force civil rights down the throats of people who were trying to put problems behind them."

Sessions an early Trump supporter who has been playing a major role on the Trump transition team, met with the president-elect in New York on Thursday. In a statement, the Trump team said the president-elect was "unbelievably impressed" with Sessions.

11-23-16

Trump picked Betsy Devos to be Secretary Of Education:

For nearly 30 years, as a philanthropist, activist and Republican fund-raiser, she has pushed to give families taxpayer money in the form of vouchers to attend private and parochial schools, pressed to expand publicly funded but privately run charter schools, and tried to strip teacher unions of their influence.

As a candidate, Mr. Trump proposed steering $20 billion in existing federal money toward vouchers that families could use to help pay for private or parochial schools, perhaps tapping into $15 billion in so-called Title I money that goes to schools that serve the country's poorest children. He called school choice "the civil rights issues of our time."

TRUMP ZAP! Betsy Devos is now "Betsy De Voucher!"

11-28-16

Rep. Tom Price, a Georgia Republican, is President-elect Donald Trump's pick for Secretary of Health and Human Services:

Price has repeatedly introduced legislation to repeal
and replace the ACA (Obamacare) and is one of
hundreds of Republicans who have voted dozens of
times to repeal the federal health care law since it was
enacted in 2010.

Price is conservative. He opposes abortion rights,
receiving a 2016 rating of 0 by Planned Parenthood and
100 percent by National Right to Life. He has voted
against legislation aimed at prohibiting job
discrimination based on sexual orientation; for a
constitutional amendment to define marriage as
between one man and one woman; and against the bill
that would've ended the don't-ask-don't-tell policy
regarding disclosure of sexual orientation in the
military.

12-07-16

Trump has selected Scott Pruitt, the Oklahoma attorney
general to run the Environmental Protection Agency:

> "Scientists continue to disagree about the degree and
> extent of global warming and its connection to the
> actions of mankind," Pruitt wrote in National Review
> earlier this year. "That debate should be encouraged —
> in classrooms, public forums, and the halls of Congress.
> It should not be silenced with threats of prosecution.
> Dissent is not a crime."

> "It is the job of the attorney general to defend the
> interests and well-being of the citizens and state of
> Oklahoma," Mr. Pruitt's office said in a statement in

2014 to The Times. "This includes protecting Oklahoma's economy from the perilous effects of federal overreach by agencies like the E.P.A. The energy sector is a major driver of the Oklahoma economy."

"At a time when climate change is the great environmental threat to the entire planet, it is sad and dangerous that Mr. Trump has nominated Scott Pruitt to lead the E.P.A.," said Senator Bernie Sanders, independent of Vermont, who sits on the committee that must confirm him. "The American people must demand leaders who are willing to transform our energy system away from fossil fuels. I will vigorously oppose this nomination."

12-08-16

President-elect Donald J. Trump chose Andrew F. Puzder, chief executive of the company that franchises the fast-food outlets Hardee's and Carl's Jr. and an outspoken critic of the worker protections enacted by the Obama administration, to be Secretary of Labor:

> Mr. Puzder said that increased automation could be a welcome development because machines were "always polite, they always upsell, they never take a vacation, they never show up late, there's never a slip-and-fall or an age, sex or race discrimination case."

> Mr. Puzder's company, CKE Restaurants, runs advertisements that frequently feature women wearing next to nothing while gesturing suggestively. "I like

our ads," he told the publication Entrepreneur. "I like beautiful women eating burgers in bikinis. I think it's very American."

Richard L. Trumka, president of the A.F.L.-C.I.O., said Mr. Puzder was "a man whose business record is defined by fighting against working people."

As labor secretary, Mr. Puzder would oversee the federal apparatus that investigates violations of minimum wage, overtime and worker safety laws and regulations.

Puzder opposed the Obama administration's efforts to raise the federal minimum wage to $10.10 from $7.25, where it has stood since 2009.

"Andy Puzder has created and boosted the careers of thousands of Americans, and his extensive record fighting for workers makes him the ideal candidate to lead the Department of Labor," Mr. Trump said in a statement.

12-13-16

Trump announced his intention to nominate ExxonMobil chairman and CEO Rex Tillerson to lead the State Department and become the country's top diplomat:

> Steve Coll of the New Yorker said. "ExxonMobil is one of the few American oil companies that has managed to stay in Russia through all kinds of political weather."

> Tillerson developed close ties to state-run oil company Rosneft, NPR's Lucian Kim reports, and had reached

agreements to run development projects with Rosneft in Siberia and the Russian Arctic. Those projects came to a halt when the U.S. imposed economic sanctions following Russia's annexation of Crimea in 2014. But the agreements left him with a good reputation in the country.

"In Kurdistan, during the Obama Administration, Tillerson defied State Department policy and cut an independent oil deal with the Kurdish Regional Government, undermining the national Iraqi government in Baghdad. ExxonMobil did not ask permission. After the fact, Tillerson arranged a conference call with State Department officials and explained his actions, according to my sources, by saying, 'I had to do what was best for my shareholders."

12-13-16

Trump plans to name Rick Perry, the former governor of Texas, to lead the Energy Department:

The department plays the leading role in designing nuclear weapons, thwarting their proliferation, and ensuring the safety and reliability of the nation's aging nuclear arsenal through a constellation of laboratories considered the crown jewels of government science.

Mr. Perry, 66, would bring a different set of credentials. He is the longest-serving governor of Texas — in office from 2000 to 2015 — and before that was the Texas agriculture commissioner. He holds a bachelor's degree in animal science from Texas A&M University.

The last two energy secretaries, Ernest J. Moniz of M.I.T. and Steven Chu of Stanford, brought to the office their doctorates in physics, academic credentials and, in Dr. Chu's case, a Nobel Prize.

In choosing Perry to be secretary of energy, the president-elect is elevating him to a cabinet post that Mr. Perry once said he wanted to eliminate, a proposal that led to one of the most famous gaffes in recent presidential politics.

"Oops," Mr. Perry said in 2011 as he racked his brain during a nationally televised Republican primary debate, trying to remember the three departments he wanted to dismantle. He mentioned the Commerce and Education Departments but could not recall the third: the Energy Department.

01-07-17

Under the 1978 Ethics in Government Act, presidential appointees requiring Senate confirmation must file financial and employment disclosures with the OGE, the director of the federal Office of Government Ethics Walter Shaub, Jr., said:

"As OGE's director, the announced hearing schedule for several nominees who have not completed the ethics review process is of great concern to me," Shaub wrote in a letter to Senate Minority Leader Charles Schumer (D-N.Y.) and Sen. Elizabeth Warren (D-Mass.).

"This schedule has created undue pressure on OGE's staff and agency ethics officials to rush through these important reviews."

"I am not aware of any occasion in the four decades since OGE was established when the Senate held a confirmation hearing before the nominee had completed the ethics review process," said Shaub, who was appointed by President Obama to his position in 2013.

"The Senate and the American people deserve to know that these Cabinet nominees have a plan to avoid any conflicts of interest, that they're working on behalf of the American people and not their own bottom line, and that they plan to fully comply with the law. Senate Republicans should heed the advice of this independent office and stop trying to jam through unvetted nominees," Schumer said.

Trump's Cabinate "Is The Top 1%"

12-09-16

Donald Trump's announced cabinet nominees are worth more than $12 billion:

Wilbur Ross nominated for commerce secretary, the private equity titan with a $2.9 billion net worth.

Betsy DeVos for secretary of education, Her father-in-law Richard DeVos has a net worth of $4.8 billion, thanks mostly to his ownership of direct-seller Amway.

Goldman Sachs Group Inc.'s Gary Cohn is named the president-elect's chief economic policy adviser. Cohn, the firm's chief operating officer and once considered the heir apparent to CEO Lloyd Blankfein. He would walk away from Goldman Sachs with $266 million of stock and awards amassed during more than a quarter century at the investment bank, according to data compiled by Bloomberg.

Andrew Puzder, the CEO of closely held Hardee's and Carl's Jr. parent CKE Restaurants Inc. The opponent of a $15 minimum wage will be nominated for labor secretary.

Linda McMahon, the co-founder of World Wrestling Entertainment Inc., shares a net worth of at least $1.35 billion with her husband, Vince. She's slated to lead the Small Business Administration.

Among the richest members of the administration is Trump himself. The president-elect has a net worth of $3 billion, according to a July assessment by Bloomberg.

"You'd have to go back to Herbert Hoover to see a cabinet that was this reliant on wealthy people," said Robert Dallek, a presidential historian. "But the wealth has changed. Millionaires have become billionaires."

01-05-17

Rex Tillerson, President-elect Donald Trump's choice to become secretary of state, disclosed personal wealth of as much as $400 million, including a Texas cattle and horse ranch.

The newly retired ExxonMobil chief executive's federal financial disclosure filing shows that he directly holds stock in his former employer worth more than $50 million

Tillerson has separately reached a $180 million retirement agreement with ExxonMobil involving additional stock.

Like Trump, Tillerson has refused to provide Congress with his tax returns, promising only "tax return information" upon request.

Tillerson's close personal and business ties to Russia sparked an early backlash from senators, including a handful of key Republicans, who found alarming his acceptance of the Kremlin's Order of Friendship award in 2013 and his recorded opposition to Ukraine-related Russia sanctions in 2014.

TRUMP ZAP! The Trump Administration is like organized crime without the organized!

Trump's White House Advisors, Staff and Ambassadors

11-13-16

The Trump transition team announced that Stephen Bannon would serve as chief strategist and senior counselor to the president:

In Bannon, Trump brought in the head of the most unapologetically pro-Trump conservative media outlet in the country. Basically every time Trump has run into controversy, Breitbart has found a way to defend it. The conservative outlet has morphed into more of a virulently anti-establishment, pro-Trump news outlet than anything else. Critics have taken to calling it "Trumpbart" and the "Trump propaganda arm."

As Bloomberg's Joshua Green reported in a profile of Bannon last year, there began Bannon's alliance with Andrew Breitbart.

"Our vision — Andrew's vision — was always to build a global, center-right, populist, anti-establishment news site," Bannon said.

Green also reported that Andrew Breitbart had "described Bannon, with sincere admiration, as the Leni Riefenstahl of the Tea Party movement."

11-15-16

Power struggles inside Donald Trump's transition team between president-elect's son-in-law, Jared Kushner and loyalists to New Jersey Governor Chris Christie:

As U.S. Attorney for New Jersey, Christie in 2004 prosecuted Kushner's father, Charles, for tax evasion, witness tampering and illegal campaign contributions. A plea agreement led to a two-year prison sentence. Kushner is believed to have been one of the leading voices who kept Christie off Trump's presidential ticket.

11-18-16

Stephen Bannon, whom Donald Trump tapped as his chief strategist in the White House, joined a conservative Facebook group called Vigilant Patriots:

> It claims its goals are defending and upholding the Constitution and preserving "our history and culture."

> It listed nearly 3,600 members, including Stephen Bannon, who apparently joined the group seven years ago.

> It featured racist and extreme material that includes posts urging a military coup against President Barack Obama, featuring an image of the president dressed as an SS officer, celebrating the Confederate flag, highlighting a photoshopped picture of Obama with watermelons, praising a police officer who called Obama a "F*cking Nigger," and calling for Obama to be "executed as a traitor."

12-16-16

Donald Trump has picked Fox News analyst Monica Crowley to join his national security council as senior director of strategic communications:

> She once claimed that concerns over Obama's birthplace are in nature "legitimate" because the President's "un-American" policies signal he is "not one of us."

> "And yet, this guy is campaigning as black and painting anybody who dares to criticize him as a

racist," Crowley said at the time. "I mean that is — it is the biggest con I think I've ever seen."

Crowley frequently uses her Twitter account to share stories from the "alt-right" Breitbart news site, which has been accused of propagating racism and anti-Semitism.

12-17-16

 Donald Trump's pick for the next U.S. Ambassador to Israel is David Friedman:

Friedman is an Orthodox Jewish lawyer who advised Trump during the campaign. A close friend and confidant of Trump, he specialized in bankruptcy law and represented Trump in his investments in Atlantic City casinos.

Friedman opposes a two-state solution to the Israeli-Palestinian conflict, actively supports Israeli settlements and advocates for Israel's annexation of the West Bank, maintaining that the occupied Palestinian Territories are not occupied

.

Friedman also wants to move the U.S. embassy from Tel Aviv to Jerusalem, thus recognizing Jerusalem as Israel's capital, a disputed city of which both Israelis and Palestinians claim ownership. Jerusalem is home to the Israeli legislature, the Knesset, and the Israeli Prime Minister's office.

Palestinian chief negotiator Saeb Erekat "I look David Friedman and Trump in the eye and tell them -- if you were to take these steps of moving the embassy and annexing settlements in the West Bank, you are sending this region down the path of something that I call chaos, lawlessness and extremism." These moves, Erekat said, would "destroy" the peace process.

The United Nations considers Israeli settlements illegal under international law. For its part, the Obama administration has routinely "strongly condemned" Israeli plans to build a new Jewish settlement in the West Bank and that such actions undermine the ability to achieve a two-state solution.

Friedman, as the president of the American Friends of Bet El Institutions, associated with the Jewish settlement of Bet El, has consistently and actively supported the construction of new settlements. Friedman, already a frequent visitor, also owns property in Jerusalem.

12-21-16

Trump picks Billionaire Carl Icahn as Special Advisor on Regulation:

"I am proud to serve President-elect Trump as a special advisor on regulatory reform. Under President Obama, America's business owners have been crippled by over $1 trillion in new regulations and over 750 billion hours dealing with paperwork," Icahn said in a statement. "It's time to break free of excessive regulation and let our entrepreneurs do what they do best: create jobs and support communities. President-elect Trump is serious about helping American families, and regulatory reform will be a critical component of making America work again."

01-04-17

 Former Apprentice contestant and reality TV star Omarosa Manigault will serve as assistant to the president and director of communications for the Office of Public Liaison. Omarosa served as Trump campaign's director of African American outreach.

TRUMP ZAP! "All The President's Thugs!"

22 TRUMP'S ADMINISTRATION "BULL IN A CHINA CLOSET"

11-19-16

Trump Tower was a hive of scurrying courtiers, from a prime minister, media mogul and nonagenarian diplomat to senators, congressmen and businessmen.

One by one they came, walking by the marble walls, the cascading waterfall, the ogling tourists and the eager cameras, into the shiny lifts and up to the 26th floor to kiss the ring of the new king.

"I am Thomas Cromwell in the court of the Tudors," Steve Bannon, Trump's chief strategist, told the Hollywood Reporter, likening himself to Henry VIII's righthand man and master manipulator (who, in a fact he may have overlooked, was ultimately executed for treason).

Bannon did not propose historical roles for Reince Priebus, chief of staff, or Jared Kushner, an intimate adviser married to Trump's daughter, but they are his rivals for Trump's attention.

Shaun Bowler, associate dean of political science at the University of California, Riverside, likened the plot to Hilary Mantel's historical novel Wolf Hall.

"Her account of people tiptoeing around a character like Henry VIII strikes me as providing lots of insight into what life for advisers will be like inside the White House from now on," he said.

"What we probably can say is that – whatever the actual pattern of influence – we can be pretty sure that at least one of them will end up leaving after a blow-up."

12-14-16

 Donald Trump's transition into the White House has the lowest approval rating of any incoming president dating back to 1992, according to a Gallup poll.

The billionaire has taken dozens of meetings inside Trump Tower with government officials, business leaders and celebrities, including rapper Kanye West and former Baltimore Ravens linebacker Ray Lewis, as reporters have staked out in the lobby taking note of notable figures who come in and out.

He's tweeted commentary about prospective Cabinet members and the "great meetings" he's scheduled, hailed nominees at thank-you rallies across the country and led a true reality TV-style secretary of state search.

12-18-16

 Trump's transition team and the NSC conflict:

The top level officials in the National Security Council (NSC) are political appointees who have to submit resignations and leave in a normal transition.

>	The rest of the 400 NSC staff are career civil servants on secondment from other departments.

>	An unusual number of these more junior officials are now looking to depart.

Many are concerned by a proliferation of reports about the incoming national security adviser, Michael Flynn. On Wednesday the Washington Post reported that Flynn had improperly shared classified information with foreign military officers.

On the same day, CNN reported that the former Defense Intelligence Agency chief had this week deleted a tweet he had sent out a few days before the election that linked to a fake news story suggesting Hillary Clinton took part in crimes against children.

12-28-16

Donald Trump accused President Barack Obama of making "many inflammatory statements and roadblocks" during the President-elect's transition to the White House:

> "Doing my best to disregard the many inflammatory President O statements and roadblocks. Thought it was going to be a smooth transition - NOT!" Trump tweeted.

> Obama said in an interview published this week that he could have beaten Trump in the 2016 election if he were eligible to run a third time.

"I am confident in this vision because I'm confident that if I had run again and articulated it, I think I could've mobilized a majority of the American people to rally behind it," Obama told his former senior adviser David Axelrod in an interview for the "The Axe Files" podcast, produced by the University of Chicago Institute of Politics and CNN.

01-09-17

On 9 January 2017, Gizmodo published an article reporting:

"Between the Trump transition team's infighting, incompetence, and high-profile resignations, any decisions that signaled even a modicum of stability for the country would come as a relief at this point. Unfortunately, the nascent Trump Administration isn't inclined to calm anyone's nerves."

"According to an official within the Department of Energy, this past Friday, the President-elect's team instructed the head of the National Nuclear Security Administration and his deputy to clean out their desks when Trump takes office on January 20th."

"The NNSA is the $12 billion-a-year agency that "maintains and enhances the safety, security, and effectiveness of the U.S. nuclear weapons stockpile."

01-17-17

According to a new CNN/ORC Poll:

Following a tumultuous transition period, approval ratings for Trump's handling of the transition are more than 20 points below those for any of his three most recent predecessors. Obama took the oath in 2009 with an 84% approval rating, 67% approved of Clinton's transition as of late December 1992 and 61% approved of George W. Bush's transition just before he took office in January 2001.

Trump's wobbly handling of the presidential transition has left most Americans with growing doubts that the President-elect will be able to handle the job. About 53% say Trump's statements and actions since Election Day have made them less confident in his ability to handle the presidency.

01-27-17

The new White House residents clean house:

Two senior administration officials said Thursday that the Trump administration told four top State Department management officials that their services were no longer needed as part of an effort to "clean house" at Foggy Bottom.

Patrick Kennedy, who served for nine years as the undersecretary for management, Assistant Secretaries for Administration and Consular Affairs Joyce Anne Barr and Michele Bond, and Ambassador Gentry Smith, director of the Office for Foreign Missions, were sent letters by the White House that their service was no longer required, the sources told CNN.

"Any implication that that these four people quit is

wrong," one senior State Department official said. "These people are loyal to the secretary, the President and to the State Department. There is just not any attempt here to dis the President. People are not quitting and running away in disgust. This is the White House cleaning house."

TRUMP ZAP! Trump runs his White House like a business, like a Waffle House at 2 A.M.

Kellyanne Conway said, "Don't Believe What's Coming out of His Mouth."

11-24-16

Fareed Zakaria (Washington Post Opinion) describes some off Trump's flip-flops:

Before: "Donald Trump wants to kill Iran deal:

After: 'I hadn't focused so much on the benefits of the deal,' Trump said."

Before: "'We haven't been bombing the s--- out of ISIS,' says Trump:

After: The president-elect described a phone conversation with President Obama in which he learned that the United States and its coalition partners have conducted more than 16,000 airstrikes on the Islamic State.

'That's a lot,' said Trump, noting that in Syria, the Obama administration had been focused on defeating the Islamic State and not on deposing President Bashar al-Assad. 'They have been doing what I suggested all along,' he noted proudly."

Before: "Trumpcare will be a 'terrific' improvement on Obamacare "no mandate."

After:The Trump administration plans to propose a health-care bill that will require insurance companies to enroll people with preexisting conditions. In return, the companies will gain millions of new customers, since people will now face a mandate to buy health insurance or else face a $10,000 fine — much higher than under Obamacare.

'I figured out, like with houses or cars, insurance can't work unless we're all in,' explained the president-elect."

Before: "Trump plans to deport all illegal aliens:

After: "Trump plans to limit deportations: The Trump administration is going to proceed slowly and carefully with the deportation of undocumented workers. 'If we deport millions of these people, industries such as construction and agriculture would collapse and we would have a big recession. How does that help the American worker?' asked Trump."

01-09-17

Kellyanne Conway said the press should take Trump's word for it when he says he did not mock a reporter with a disability at a November 2015 rally. Trump appeared to mock New York Times reporter Serge Kovaleski, who suffers from a congenital condition that restricts his mobility, by spastically moving his arms on stage.

Amid a back and forth on CNN's "New Day," anchor Chris Cuomo suggested that Trump was not deserving of the benefit of the doubt relating to the Kovaleski episode "because he's making a disgusting gesture on video." Conway interjected to finish the host's sentence, that the gestures were "not about that reporter, and that's just a fact." Cuomo argued that Trump's explanation was unbelievable because he had made "a gesture that is so keenly tuned to what Serge's vulnerability is."

"You have to listen to what the president-elect has said about that. Why don't you believe him? Why is everything taken at face value?" she asked anchor Chris Cuomo. "You can't give him the benefit of the doubt on this and he's telling you what was in his heart? You always want to go by what's come out of his mouth rather than look at what's in his heart."

"No Press Allowed, I'm On the Toilet Tweeting"

11-16-16

Trump Ditches His Press Pool Again, Violating Media Protocol. It is setting up a dangerous precedent for press coverage of his administration:

> While documenting something like a dinner might seem trivial, the pool travels with the president because there's always a possibility something newsworthy

might happen in relation to him — and as the White House Correspondents Association, which oversees the White House Press Corps, has said, Americans need to know about his "whereabouts and well-being in the event of a national crisis." President Ronald Reagan's traveling pool documented an assassination attempt on the president in 1981, for example, and President John F. Kennedy's press pool had special access that helped them cover his assassination in 1963.

Reporters traveling with Trump were not allowed to travel on the same plane, and the campaign sometimes failed to inform them when he was leaving for events. He even mocked them for being late to a rally.

11-19-16

Hillary Clinton, the press, refugees, fellow Republicans — the list of Donald Trump's Twitter targets is long, with no signs of letup now that he's less than two months away from inauguration day. We can now add a cultural phenomenon to the extensive list of perceived enemies: the cast of the Broadway smash Hamilton.

The president-elect demanded an apology Saturday from the cast of the Tony Award-winning play for their treatment of Vice President-elect Mike Pence, who cast members directly addressed Friday evening. Although readying for a day of meetings concerning administration appointments, Trump found time to defend "our wonderful future V.P. Mike Pence" from alleged harassment with tweets barely distinguishable from a parody Twitter account.

Trump focus on TV ratings:

The Saturday Night Live skit went on to skewer Trump's comments to television executives and anchors about using photos of him with a double chin, his dinner with Mitt Romney and his chief strategist Steve Bannon, who they painted as the Grim Reaper.

"Just tried watching Saturday Night Live - unwatchable! Totally biased, not funny and the Baldwin impersonation just can't get any worse. Sad," Trump wrote in a tweet before the episode had concluded.

Alec Baldwin wasted no time hitting back at Trump.

"Release your tax returns and I'll stop," he tweeted.

01-06-17

Trump mocked successor Arnold Schwarzenegger for getting lower ratings than he did in his last season of the NBC reality Celebrity Apprentice:

"Wow, the ratings are in and Arnold Schwarzenegger got "swamped" (or destroyed) by comparison to the ratings machine, DJT. So much for him being a movie star-and that was season 1 compared to season 14. Now compare him to my season 1. But who cares, he supported Kasich & Hillary."

The former California governor issued a grown-up response: "There's nothing more important than the people's work."

As in, get back to it, please, Donald.

Schwarzenegger said "I wish you the best of luck and I hope you'll work for ALL of the American people as aggressively as you worked for your ratings."

01-09-17

Meryl Streep called out Donald Trump when she accepted her award at the Golden Globe Awards, about the president-elect once mocked the disability of a reporter who displeased him:

Streep said "There was one performance this year that stunned me. It sank its hooks in my heart. Not because it was good. There was nothing good about it. But it was effective and it did its job. It made its intended audience laugh and show their teeth. It was that moment when the person asking to sit in the most respected seat in our country imitated a disabled reporter, someone he outranked in privilege, power, and the capacity to fight back."

"Meryl Streep, one of the most over-rated actresses in Hollywood, doesn't know me but attacked last night at the Golden Globes. Hillary flunky who lost big" Trump tweeted.

"Look, I don't like Tweeting. I have other things I could be doing," Trump told Fox News host Ainsley Earhardt in an interview taped Tuesday and broadcast on Wednesday morning's "Fox & Friends." "But I get very dishonest media, very dishonest press. And it's my only way that I can counteract."

TRUMP ZAP! The only part of Trump's tweets that aren't lies . . . .

Trump's War on the Intelligence Agencies

12-08-16

What Ben Cardin of Maryland and Dianne Feinstein of California (Top Democrats on the Foreign Relations Committees) wrote in an op-ed published Thursday by USA TODAY:

> "Indeed, we find it particularly troubling that President-elect Trump has mostly declined to take the daily intelligence briefing. Presidents and presidents-elect going back decades have begun their day this way — understanding national security threats and opportunities, asking probing questions, and making tough decisions," they wrote.

> In an interview on "Face the Nation" Sunday, former CIA Director Leon Panetta told host John Dickerson that "one of the concerns I have right now is that this president is not getting his intelligence briefings."

On the same show, Mr. Trump's incoming chief of staff, Reince Priebus, said the intelligence briefings for the president-elect are "happening quite frequently" and he thought "those are just going to ramp up as we get closer to January 20."

Even during the campaign, there were reports that Trump was at odds with what intelligence officials briefing him. Rep. Michael McCaul, R-Texas the chairman of the House Homeland Security Committee, said in late October that he told Mr. Trump that Russia was trying to influence the U.S. election through hacking, but he said Mr. Trump rejected that information.

01-01-17

What Trump said about Russia Hacks:

"I just want them to be sure, because it's a pretty serious charge, and I want them to be sure," Trump said of assessments that Russia, and possibly its president Vladimir Putin, was involved in the campaign of cyber-attacks and attempted interference in the electoral process.

"And I know a lot about hacking. And hacking is a very hard thing to prove," Trump said. "So it could be somebody else. And I also know things that other people don't know, and so they cannot be sure of the situation."

What Trump said about cyber-security:

"If you have something really important, write it out and have it delivered by courier, the old fashioned way because I'll tell you what, no computer is safe," Trump said.

"I have a boy who's ten years old; he can do anything with a computer. You want something to really go without detection, write it out and have it sent by courier," Trump said.

Trump said in a statement after the sanctions were announced by Obama that "it's time for our country to move on to bigger and better things" but that he would meet with U.S. intelligence officials next week to be briefed on the claims against Russia.

Trump said "Hopefully we're going to have great relationships with many countries, it includes Russia and it includes China."

01-17-17

Trump tweeted the CIA was akin to Nazi Germany when it came to leaks about the intelligence report (dossier) written by Christopher Steele, a former British spy hired to conduct opposition research on Trump.

"I think it's the right and, indeed, the responsibility of the president of the United States to challenge the conclusions of the intelligence community," Outgoing CIA Director John Brennan said in response. But he made it clear that it crosses a line to accuse these agencies of leaks.

"Tell the families of those 117 CIA officers who are forever memorialized on our wall of honor that their loved ones who gave their lives were akin to Nazis," he said. "Tell the CIA officers who are serving in harm's way right now and their families who are worried about them that they are akin to Nazi Germany. I found that to be very repugnant."

He specified that it was the FBI's responsibility to investigate links between Trump and Russia, not the CIA's.

"There was an interest on the part of the bureau to make sure that the president-elect was aware of and informed of" the dossier, he said. "The feeling was wanting to make sure that given the very salacious nature of it, the president-elect was at least aware of it so he could take it into account and do what needs to be done."

23 "CONFLICT OF INTEREST" "ANTI-NEPOTISM" "SHOW
   ME THE LAW"

11-14-16

 CBS News reported that the "Trump team" has asked the White House to explore the possibility of the "Trump Team" be designated as national security advisers, which technically would include Trump's offspring — Ivanka, Eric and Donald Jr..

The State Department website says, "Eligibility will be granted only where facts and circumstances indicate access to classified information is clearly consistent with the national security interests of the United States. Access to classified information will be terminated when an individual no longer has need for access."

Ivanka Trump has said she intends to stay in Trump's business empire where she is executive vice president of development and acquisitions. Her husband also is a real-estate investor and publisher of the New York Observer.

Donald Trump Jr. and Eric Trump also are executive vice presidents at the Trump Organization.

Nepotism "rules" prevent them from being hired to work in the White House if the President follows "rules."

11-18-16

The Trumps opened the hotel in the Old Post Office pavilion, a 117-year-old property the company leases from the federal government. Officials at the General Services Administration, the landlord, have consulted the Office of Government Ethics about how to handle such conflicts, but the measures preventing other federal employees from profiting from their positions "do not apply to the president."

Statements about conflict of interest with Trump ownership of Trump International Hotel in Washington D C:

> "The place was packed," said Lynn Van Fleit, founder of the nonprofit Diplomacy Matters Institute, which organizes programs for foreign diplomats and government officials. She said much of the discussion among Washington-based diplomats is over "how are we going to build ties with the new administration."

> "Why wouldn't I stay at his hotel blocks from the White House, so I can tell the new president, 'I love your new hotel!' Isn't it rude to come to his city and say, 'I am staying at your competitor?' " said one Asian diplomat.

> Arturo Sarukhan, a former Mexican ambassador to the United States said, "The temptation and the inclination will certainly be there … some might think it's the right way to engage, to be able to tell the next president … 'Oh, I stayed at your hotel.' If I were still in government, I would discourage it, among other reasons because it can be questioned and looked at in a very poor light, as though you are trying to buy influence via a hotel bill."

More than a dozen watchdog organizations penned a letter to Trump on Thursday, urging him to create a true blind trust or liquidate the assets. (Under a blind trust, an independent trustee with no familial ties would manage the properties.)

"Failure to follow this course of action will create conflicts of interest of unprecedented magnitude," groups including Common Cause wrote.

"Consequently, there is no current legal requirement that would compel the President to relinquish financial interests because of a conflict of interest," an analysis produced last month by the Congressional Research Service at the Library of Congress said.

11-20-16

At least 111 Trump companies have done business in 18 countries and territories across South America, Asia and the Middle East, a Washington Post analysis of Trump financial filings shows.

Trump has refused calls to sell or give his business interests to an independent manager or "blind trust," a long-held presidential tradition designed to combat conflicts of interest. Now, policy and ethics experts are scrambling to assess the potential dangers of public rule by a leader with a vast web of private business deals.

Many modern presidents and major nominees — including Ronald Reagan, both Bushes, Bill Clinton and Mitt Romney — have nevertheless committed to selling or divesting their interests into a blind trust run by an independent overseer with unassailable control.

Donald Trump has a lot of potential conflicts of interest as president – but there's "no law" that specifically requires a commander in chief to remove themselves from all of their business interests.

Most government officials must follow strict conflict-of-interest regulations designed to block public servants from making decisions in their own private interest. But presidents are largely exempt from those rules for fear they could impede on their wide-ranging constitutional duties.

Trump's global business interests also make him vulnerable to legal risks, including a passage in the Constitution, known as the emoluments clause that forbids government officials from receiving gifts from a foreign government.

A payment from a foreign official or state-owned company to a Trump hotel or other branded company could potentially violate that clause, constitutional experts said.

A group of ethics advisers, including former chief White House ethics lawyers during Democratic and Republican administrations, wrote Trump a letter Thursday urging him to sequester his business in a genuine blind trust or commit to a "clear firewall" between his Oval Office and his family.

"You were elected to the presidency with a promise to eliminate improper business influence in Washington," they wrote. "There is no way to square your campaign commitments to the American people — and your even higher, ethical duties as their president — with the rampant, inescapable conflicts that will engulf your presidency if you maintain connections with the Trump Organization."

TRUMP ZAP! Trump calls China Thailand because that's
where they make his ties.

12-06-16

Palm Beach Post business reporter Jeff Ostrowski writes after
reviewing newly released data from the U.S. Labor
Department that President-elect Donald Trump recently won
approval to hire 64 foreign workers at his Mar-a-Lago Club
through the federal government's H-2B visa program.

"It's very, very hard to get people," Trump said. "Other hotels
do the exact same thing."

01-02-17

Trump's name appeared in the credits of the show Celebrity
Apprentice as "Executive Producer Donald J. Trump,"
according to a CNBC employee

.

Variety also reported that Trump remains a credited
executive producer.

"I have NOTHING to do with The Apprentice except for the
fact that I conceived it with Mark B & have a big stake in it.
Will devote ZERO TIME!" Trump tweeted.

01-12-17

President-elect Donald Trump at his first formal press
conference on January 11, 2017 invited an attorney, Sherri
Dillon, to the podium and gestured at a nearby table stacked
high with file folders, saying, "these papers are just some of
the many documents that I've signed turning over complete
and total control to my sons."

"So this is all — just so you understand, these papers — because I'm not sure that was explained properly — but these papers are all just a piece of the many, many companies that are being put into trust to be run by my two sons that I hope at the end of eight years, I'll come back and say, oh, you did a good job. Otherwise, if they do a bad job, I'll say, "You're fired" said Trump.

Despite their being so prominently displayed, however, reporters were not allowed to touch or examine the documents. According to CNN:

Many on social media pointed out that the displayed folders and documents appeared to be untouched, unlabeled, and, in some cases, empty.

 Filmmaker Amy Berg even claimed, "based on her own experience, that the paper documents in some of the folders, to the extent they were visible, were blank."

The Independent, a British online newspaper, made the same observation, "While the majority of the sheets were hidden, some of them were visible – and there was no sign of page numbers or the sticky notes that lawyers tend to use to mark places in large documents. The paper itself also appeared to be the wrong size, printed on A4 rather than legal size sheets, and appears to have fallen like fresh sheets of paper. And the folders themselves were also entirely blank, despite Mr. Trump suggesting that each of them related to a different business that Mr. Trump was moving himself away from."

The left-leaning BipartisanReport.com said, "A dramatic stunt, meant to showcase how much work it is for Trump to transfer his businesses to his sons, turned out to be fake. The documents inside the folders were blank, and simply for show."

TRUMP ZAP! Trump is our first "Part time President!"

The Fake News Continues, "Spicer Stressed Out"

11-17-16

 Paul Horner, the 38-year-old impresario of a Facebook fake-news empire, has made his living off viral news hoaxes for several years.

In March, Donald Trump's son Eric and his then-campaign manager, Corey Lewandowski, even tweeted links to one of Horner's faux-articles. His stories have also appeared as news on Google.

Horner said "I didn't think it was possible for him to get elected president. I thought I was messing with the campaign, maybe I wasn't messing them up as much as I wanted — but I never thought he'd actually get elected. I didn't even think about it. In hindsight, everyone should've seen this coming — everyone assumed Hillary [Clinton] would just get in. But she didn't, and Trump is president."

"This whole Google AdSense thing is pretty scary. And all this Facebook stuff. I make most of my money from AdSense — like, you wouldn't believe how much money I make from it. Right now I make like $10,000 a month from AdSense" said

Horner.

"Facebook and AdSense make a lot of money from [advertising on fake news sites] for them to just get rid of it. They'd lose a lot of money" Horner said.

11-22-16

 Representatives from CNN, NBC, ABC and other networks assembled at Mr Trump's gilded residence believing they were there to learn about the access they would be granted to the billionaire business magnate after he is sworn into the White House.

Instead, members were rebuked for their reporting and branded "liars", according to an account given by an unnamed source to the New York Post.

"Trump started with [CNN chief] Jeff Zucker and said 'I hate your network, everyone at CNN is a liar and you should be ashamed,' " the source was quoted as telling the New York Post.

"The meeting was a total disaster. The TV execs and anchors went in there thinking they would be discussing the access they would get to the Trump administration, but instead they got a Trump-style dressing down," the Post reported.

11-24-16

Russia's increasingly sophisticated propaganda machinery — including thousands of botnets, teams of paid human "trolls," and networks of websites and social-media accounts — echoed and amplified right-wing sites across the Internet as they portrayed Clinton as a criminal hiding potentially fatal health problems and preparing to hand control of the nation to a shadowy cabal of global financiers.

The sophistication of the Russian tactics may complicate efforts by Facebook and Google to crack down on "fake news," as they have vowed to do after widespread complaints about the problem.

12-05-16

A popular pizza restaurant in Washington D.C. called Comet Ping Pong was subject of social media in the days before the election after fake news stories circulated claiming that then-Democratic presidential nominee Hillary Clinton and her campaign chief were running a child sex ring from the restaurant's backrooms.

28-year-old Edgar Maddison Welch, of Salisbury, N.C., was arrested Sunday after he walked into Comet Ping Pong carrying an assault rifle and fired one or more shots, D.C. police said.

The man told police he had come to the restaurant to "self-investigate" a false election-related conspiracy theory involving Hillary Clinton that spread online during her presidential campaign.

Police said all occupants had fled when Welch began shooting.

Even Michael Flynn, a retired general whom President-elect Donald Trump has tapped to advise him on national security, shared stories about another anti-Clinton conspiracy theory involving pedophilia. None of them were true.

01-15-17

President-elect Donald Trump's team is reportedly considering evicting the press corps from the White House.

Instead, the press corps may work out of the White House Conference Center, near Lafayette Square, or in the Old Executive Office Building, next door to the White House, Esquire reported.

"There has been no decision," said Sean Spicer, Trump's incoming White House press secretary, adding "there has been some discussion about how to do it."

01-23-17

In an interview with "Meet the Press" on Sunday, the counselor to President Trump Kellyanne Conway defended Press Secretary Sean Spicer's inaccurate claim that the 2017 inauguration was "the largest ever" by explaining that he was offering "alternative facts." The Twitter-sphere went to town playing with that rationale.

12-09-16

"It is the assessment of the intelligence community that Russia's goal here was to favor one candidate over the other, to help Trump get elected," said a senior U.S. official briefed on an intelligence presentation made to U.S. senators. "That's the consensus view."

In September, during a secret briefing for congressional leaders, Senate Majority Leader Mitch McConnell (R-Ky.) voiced doubts about the veracity of the intelligence, according to officials present.

"I don't believe they interfered" in the election, Trump told Time magazine this week. The hacking, he said, "could be Russia. And it could be China. And it could be some guy in his home in New Jersey."

"I'll be the first one to come out and point at Russia if there's clear evidence, but there is no clear evidence — even now," said Rep. Devin Nunes (R-Calif.), the chairman of the House Intelligence Committee and a member of the Trump transition team. "There's a lot of innuendo, lots of circumstantial evidence, that's it."

According to several officials, McConnell raised doubts about the underlying intelligence and made clear to the administration that he would consider any effort by the White House to challenge the Russians publicly an act of partisan politics.

"We may have crossed into a new threshold, and it is

incumbent upon us to take stock of that, to review, to conduct some after-action, to understand what has happened and to impart some lessons learned," Obama's counterterrorism and homeland security adviser, Lisa Monaco, told reporters at a breakfast hosted by the Christian Science Monitor.

12-16-16

What Obama said about Russia interfering in our election:

> "Not much happens in Russia without Vladimir Putin … This is a pretty hierarchical operation. Last time I checked, there's not a lot of debate and democratic deliberation, particularly when it comes to policies directed at the United States."

> "Over a third of Republican voters approve of Vladimir Putin, the former head of the KGB … Ronald Reagan would roll over in his grave."

> "The Russians can't change us or significantly weaken us … They are a smaller country, they are a weaker country, their economy doesn't produce anything that anyone wants to buy except oil and gas and arms. They don't innovate. But they can impact us if we lose track of who we are. They can impact us if we abandon our values."

12-29-16

Obama slaps sanctions on Russia, expels intelligence agents over election hacks.

"All Americans should be alarmed by Russia's actions," Mr. Obama said in a statement. "These data theft and disclosure activities could only have been directed by the highest levels of the Russian government. Moreover, our diplomats have experienced an unacceptable level of harassment in Moscow by Russian security services and police over the last year. Such activities have consequences."

The president's executive order sanctioned nine entities and individuals: the GRU and the FSB, two Russian intelligence services; and four individual officers of the GRU. In addition, the Treasury designated two Russians for using cyber-enabled means to cause misappropriation of funds and personal identifying information.

The State Department is also shutting down two Russian compounds, in Maryland and New York, used by Russian personnel for intelligence gathering, and declared the 35 Russian intelligence operatives as "persona non grata." The personnel and their families, from the Russian Embassy in Washington and the Russian Consulate in San Francisco, were given 72 hours to leave the U.S.

Mr. Trump said that "it's time for our country to move on to bigger and better things."

01-05-17

U.S. officials said that American intelligence agencies intercepted communications in the aftermath of the election in which Russian officials congratulated themselves on the outcome.

According to the report from the Washington Post, the Russians weren't just happy about Trump's victory – they were congratulating themselves for making it happen.

Declassified version of a long-awaited intelligence report from the Office of the Director of National Intelligence on Russian involvement in the election was released.

In "Key Judgments," the report says, "We assess Russian President Vladimir Putin ordered an influence campaign in 2016 aimed at the U.S. presidential election. Russia's goals were to undermine public faith in the U.S. democratic process, denigrate Secretary Clinton, and harm her electability and potential presidency. We further assess Putin and the Russian Government developed a clear preference for President-elect Trump."

The report says that the Russian government tried to help Trump "by discrediting Secretary Clinton." It says that of the three agencies that prepared the report, the CIA, the FBI have "high confidence" in this judgment, while the NSA "has moderate confidence."

The report also says that the Russian hacking campaign targeted or compromised "elements of multiple U.S. state or local electoral boards," but not systems involved in vote tallying.

The 25-page report called "Assessing Russian Activities and Intentions in Recent U.S. Elections," offers the public a flavor of what officials say is a much more detailed dossier of still-secret evidence that led all 17 American intelligence agencies to conclude with high confidence that the Russians — not the

Chinese or a 400-pound hacker in his bedroom, as Trump famously put it — were behind an unprecedented cyber intrusion that some lawmakers have called an act of war.

The report said "We assess Moscow will apply lessons learned from its Putin-ordered campaign aimed at the U.S. presidential election to future influence efforts worldwide, including against U.S. allies and their election processes."

Earlier in the day, the New York Times published a Trump interview in which he complained that the media attention focused on the hacking amounted to an unfair "political witch hunt" perpetrated by people who can't accept that he won the election.

01-13-17

The Senate Select Committee on Intelligence said, "It will conduct a bipartisan inquiry into possible Russian intelligence agencies."

"We believe that it is critical to have a full understanding of the scope of Russian intelligence activities impacting the United States," committee chairman Sen. Richard Burr and vice chairman Sen. Mark Warner said in a statement.

The inquiry will include "any intelligence regarding links between Russia and individuals associated with political campaigns," the committee said.

The Senate committee plans to, "interview senior officials of both the outgoing and incoming administrations including the issuance of subpoenas if necessary to compel testimony."

The Dossier and "The Golden Shower Gate"

01-12-17

BuzzFeed published a 35-page document (Dossier) produced by Christopher Steele, a former British foreign intelligence official, that outlined the allegations of compromising behavior by Trump and alleged links between him and people in Russia.

What Trump said at a New York news conference about the Dossier being released:

> "I think it was disgraceful, disgraceful that the intelligence agencies allowed any information that turned out to be so false and fake out. I think it's a disgrace, and I say that ... that's something that Nazi Germany would have done and did do,"

> Trump said, without offering evidence, that the news he had been briefed on the memo "was released by maybe the (U.S.) intelligence agencies. Who knows? But maybe the intelligence agencies which would be a tremendous blot on their record if they in fact did that."

01-17-17

Vladimir Putin told reporters at the Kremlin that he doesn't believe Donald Trump hired prostitutes when he visited Russia back in 2013 and that the allegations made against the president-elect are "obvious fabrications."

"When Trump came to Moscow, he was not a political figure, we were not even aware of his political ambitions ... Does somebody think that our secret services are chasing every American billionaire? Of course not," said Putin.

Putin went on to dismiss the lengthy dossier published last week, calling those who disseminated the allegations as "worse than prostitutes."

Putin said, "he had no reason either to criticize him, or to defend [Trump] and that the allegations are "nonsense" and fake news. I find it hard to imagine he ran to a hotel to meet our girls of "low social responsibility"... though they are, of course, also the best in the world."

TRUMP ZAP! "Golden Gate" A hotel in Moscow with memory foam mattresses!

25 THE INAUGURATION

12-14-16

Donald Trump's President-elect team is struggling so hard to book A-list performers for his inaugural festivities.

Two talent bookers, who spoke on the condition of anonymity, said they were approached by members of Trump's Presidential Inaugural Committee in recent weeks with offers of cash or even plush diplomatic posts in exchange for locking in singers.

One anonymous booker said, "He was "shocked" at the proposal … Never in a million years have I heard something so crazy … That was the moment I almost dropped the phone."

"It's a bad policy to offer ambassadorships to unqualified, inexperienced individuals, no matter who is president," spokeswoman Jenn Topper said.

 "The public deserves an opportunity to vet the people who will be at the forefront of our diplomatic relations, and this alleged backroom dealing is alarming," One veteran inaugural organizer told The Wrap.

12-14-16

D.C. Public Schools spokeswoman said she was not aware of any band in the district that had applied to participate in President-elect Donald Trump's inaugural parade Jan. 20.

An Arizona company that organizes band trips for schools

across the country has seen lower interest than usual in this inaugural parade.

"We didn't get the response that we got the last time, with Obama. Some groups responded, but with some groups it was crickets … We're seeing a little less enthusiasm to be a part of this event." Music Celebrations International marketing director Luke Wiscombe said.

Local universities also did not apply. University of Maryland, College Park, which played in 2013, did not apply. Neither did Bowie State University or University of the District of Columbia.

The Lesbian and Gay Band Association, which included the D.C. group Different Drummers, also opted to skip Trump's inaugural parade. The association played in Obama's second inaugural parade but did not to apply this year because of political and safety concerns.

12-27-16

 Some Rockettes (famed chorus line dancers) were reduced to tears and reacted with fear after learning they'd be dancing for Donald Trump at his inaugural next month.

"If I had to lose my job over this, I would … It's too important, And I think the rest of the performing arts community would happily stand behind me." one hoofer going with the pseudonym "Mary" told Marie Claire magazine

Mary recalled one of her fellow dancers crying throughout a 90-minute show on Thursday, three days before Christmas.

"She felt she was being forced to perform for this monster," Mary said.

Another dancer told her co-workers in an email: "I wouldn't feel comfortable standing near a man like that in our costumes."

01-13-17

Virginia-based Don's Johns calls itself the Washington area's top provider of portable toilet rentals. But the name apparently strikes too close to home for inaugural organizers.

Workers have placed blue tape over the company name on dozens of portable restrooms installed near the Capitol for the inauguration.

Robert Weghorst, chief operating officer for Don's Johns, said "We don't know why it's being done. We didn't tell someone to do it ... We're proud to have our name on the units."

01-19-17

The "Queer Dance Party" was organized by the groups Werk for Peace and #J20Disrupt.

Bearing rainbow flags and blasting Beyoncé tunes, about 200 protesters marched and shimmied toward Vice President-elect Mike Pence's temporary home in northwest Washington, D.C. on Wednesday night to send a message of unity.

"Dance is so integral to the queer community as a form of self-expression and a form of asserting our power and our beauty and our love for one another. The idea is to leave a mark that Mike Pence will never forget" Firas Nasr, a 23-year-old protest organizer from Virginia, told the Washington Post.

01-20-17

More than 60 Democrats won't go to Trump's inauguration.

Civil rights icon John Lewis Lewis' announcement that he wouldn't attend the inauguration sparked a response from the president-elect, which prompted other House Democrats to follow suit.

Lewis said "I don't see this president-elect as a legitimate president … I think the Russians participated in helping this man get elected."

That's when Trump tweeted that Lewis was "all talk" and suggested he pay more attention to his "crime infested" district.

Rep. Terri Sewell (Alabama) said in a statement that she wouldn't attend because of the "blatant disrespect shown by President-elect Trump towards American civil rights icon, my colleague, friend and mentor, the Honorable John Lewis."

Rep. Raúl Grijalva (Arizona) said "My absence is not motivated by disrespect for the office, or motivated by disrespect for the government that we have in this great democracy … but as an individual act – yes, of defiance – at the disrespect shown to millions and millions of Americans by this incoming administration."

Rep. Jared Huffman (California) said "I do accept the election results and support the peaceful transfer of power, but it is abundantly clear to me that with Donald Trump as our President, the United States is entering a dark and very dangerous political chapter … I will do everything I can to limit the damage and the duration of this chapter, and I believe we can get through it."

California is the state with the largest congressional delegation and the most members avoiding the inauguration.

01-20-17

What CNN anchor Jake Tapper had to say about Trump's inauguration Speech:

"I think it's fair to say this is one of the most radical inaugural speeches we've ever heard. It was purely populist, it talked about the forgotten people, it attacked Washington while standing inside the center of Washington. He's surrounded by Washington insiders. There's nothing really particularly conservative about this Republican president's speech, it was pure populism. And in fact, it looked at the United States and the role of the United States in a way that departs greatly from what we've heard from his predecessors on the stage."

01-20-17

Following the traditional luncheon with members of Congress at the Capitol, Trump and his wife and new first lady, Melania, rode down Pennsylvania Avenue at the head of the inaugural parade, ending at the White House.

The parade itself drew a smaller than expected crowd, with entire stands along the route empty. The inaugural festivities were similarly more lightly attended than previous ones, with plenty of empty spaces on stretches of the Mall that had been packed for previous inaugurations.

Just a few blocks to the north, meanwhile, protesters opposing Trump gathered by the thousands.

01-20-17

Trump Inauguration Day Protests in Washington D.C.

At least 217 people have been arrested and charged with rioting from this morning's incident. Three of the six injured officers suffered head injuries from flying objects, according to the Metropolitan Police Department.

Thousands of protesters fanned out across downtown Washington in the morning, including some who tried to block security checkpoints to the inauguration festivities.

Dramatic video published on social media showed men and women using signs and sticks to shatter glass at a Starbucks and a bank. Police then attempted to chase down the suspected vandals.

After the inauguration, protesters started a fire on the street, burning what appeared to be garbage and a plastic newspaper stand.

Outside the International Spy Museum, protesters in Russian-style hats ridiculed Trump's praise of Russian President Vladimir Putin, marching with signs calling Trump "Putin's puppet" and "Kremlin employee of the month," the AP reported.

The capital's interim police chief, Peter Newsham, said in a Periscope video posted on Twitter earlier today that the problems were caused by one group, "and it's a very, very small percentage of the number of folks that came here to peacefully assemble in our city."

"Pussy Hats" Record Protest at D.C. Women's March (up to 1,000,000)

01-03-17

The Pussyhat Project, which launched over Thanksgiving, is the brainchild of two friends and recreational knitters screenwriter Krista Suh and architect Jayna Zweiman.

The women were devastated by the election results and looking for ways to channel their grief. With Kat Coyle, owner of their neighborhood knitting shop, they designed a "pussy power hat" pattern — an extremely simple hat that knitters, crocheters and sewers of all levels can whip up for themselves or for other marchers.

It's not just about making a strong visual statement on the day of the march, or offering up a symbolic rebuke of Trump's infamous "grab them by the pussy" comment, though that's definitely a factor. It's also about giving people who aren't able to march for physical, financial or other logistical barriers a concrete way to take part.

"For me, a lot of the magic lies in saying, 'Hey women of the country, you might not think you're politically active, but you're already community organizing in your knitting groups and women's groups, you just don't call it that, ... the Pussyhat Project calls it that, which is where a lot of the power comes from ... We hope these hats will become a symbol long after the march" said Suh.

01-22-17

AP reports Trump protests around the world:

> Many of the women came wearing pink, pointy-eared "pussyhats" to mock the new president. Plenty of men joined in, too, contributing to surprising numbers everywhere from New York, Philadelphia, Chicago and Los Angeles to Mexico City, Paris, Berlin, London, Prague and Sydney.

> "Welcome to your first day, we will not go away!" marchers in Washington chanted.

> "We want a leader, not a creepy tweeter," some marchers chanted in Washington.

> The Washington rally alone attracted over 500,000 people according to city officials — apparently more than Trump's inauguration drew on Friday.

> It was easily one of the biggest demonstrations in the city's history, and as night fell, not a single arrest was reported.

> "We march today for the moral core of this nation, against which our new president is waging a war, ... our dignity, our character, our rights have all been under attack, and a platform of hate and division

assumed power yesterday. But the president is not America. ... We are America, and we are here to stay." actress America Ferrera told the Washington crowd.

The hand-knit "pussyhats" worn by many women served as a message of female empowerment, inspired by Trump's crude boast about grabbing women's genitals. They "ain't for grabbing," actress Ashley Judd told the Washington crowd.

Around the world, women brandished signs with slogans such as "Women won't back down" and "Less fear more love." They decried Trump's stand on such issues as abortion, health care, diversity and climate change. And they branded him a sexist, a bully, a bigot and more.

In Chicago, organizers canceled the March portion of their event for safety reasons because of an overflow crowd that reached an estimated 250,000. People made their way through the streets on their own anyway.

 In New York, well over 100,000 marched past Trump's home at glittering Trump Tower on Fifth Avenue. More than 100,000 also gathered on Boston Common, and a similar number demonstrated in Los Angeles.

All told, more than 600 "sister marches" were planned worldwide. Crowd estimates from police and organizers around the globe added up to well over a million.

"I feel very optimistic even though it's a miserable

moment," said Madeline Schwartzman of New York City, who brought her twin 13-year-old daughters to the Washington rally. "I feel the power."

Tens of thousands of protesters squeezed into London's Trafalgar Square. In Paris, thousands rallied in the Eiffel Tower neighborhood in a joyful atmosphere, singing and carrying posters reading "We have our eyes on you Mr. Trump" and "With our sisters in Washington." Hundreds gathered in Prague's Wenceslas Square in freezing weather, mockingly waving portraits of Trump and Russia's Vladimir Putin.

TRUMP ZAP! Trump's Presidential Library will have to have an "Adult-Section!"

"Ego Maniac" Thank You Tours

11-17-16

 Washington (CNN) President-elect Donald Trump will host a new round of rallies in the coming weeks to celebrate his 2016 election win, according to one of his top aides.

George Gigicos, the head of the Trump advance team, asked Trump's former campaign manager, Kellyanne Conway (who was behind him) when the "the victory tour" would be happening.

She came forward to reporters and said, "'Thank you tour.' It's not a 'victory tour,'" to which Gigicos repeated, "Thank you tour.""Thank America tour," Conway said.

Gigicos said the tour would be happening in "the next couple of weeks -- after Thanksgiving" and would focus on "the swing states we flipped over."

12-01-16

 At a rally in Ohio billed as the beginning of a "thank-you tour," Trump repeatedly pledged to unite the country and "find common ground." But his rhetoric, almost word for word, matched the raucous and incendiary rallies of his campaign.

"I'm going to discuss our action plan to make America great again, … Although we did have a lot of fun fighting Hillary, right?" said Trump.

"Hey, in the great state of Ohio, we didn't have the upper echelon of politician either, did we?" Trump said, a mocking reference to Kasich, who refused to support Trump and was a vocal critic.

Trump bragged that world leaders have joined in celebrating his victory in phone calls to him.

"They all tell me, they sat in their magnificent rooms in wonderment, … One of them told me, 'I truly respect the United States again because of what happened.'"

"Now that you have put me in this position, even if you don't help me one bit, I'm going to get it done, believe me, … Don't worry about it. It would be easier if you helped, but that's all right. Don't worry, I'll get it done." Said Trump.

12-17-16

Trump's thank-you tour in Orlando, Florida.

Trump said:

> "So we are going to start using our head. We are going
> to do things right and try to patch that up and try to
> help people. We'll build safe zones," Trump told his
> supporters. "We are going to build safe zones in Syria.
> We are going to build safe zones. And we are going to
> get the Gulf States to pay for the safe zones, and we'll
> try on help people. We are going to try, and we are
> going to get it done."

> "Four weeks ago, just prior to, you people were vicious,
> violent, screaming, 'We want the wall,' screaming
> 'Prison, prison, lock her up!' You were going crazy. I
> mean, you were nasty and mean and vicious, and you
> wanted to win, right?" Trump said at the Central
> Florida Fairgrounds complex. "But now it's much
> different. Now you're laid back, you're cool, you're
> mellow, right? You're basking in the glory of victory."

01-25-17

 Never straying far from his business roots, Mr. Trump has
already submitted an application to trademark the slogan he
plans to use for his 2020 re-election run: "Keep America
Great."

Records from the United States Patent and Trademark Office
show that the president applied on Wednesday (Jan 18) —
before he was even sworn into office — to trademark the
phrase, both with and without an exclamation point.

26 TRUMP AND THE REPUBLICAN'S PRIORITIES

Repealing "Obamacare" and Creating "Richcare"

11-10-16

More than 100,000 people signed up for coverage under the Affordable Care Act on Wednesday, the highest since Open Enrollment began Nov. 1, according to the Obama administration.

Health and Human Services Secretary Sylvia Burwell announced in a tweet that a record number of people have enrolled and selected a health plan.

The high volume of sign-ups occurred right after Election Day, as Donald Trump has pledged to repeal Obamacare when he's President.

11-21-16

In June Speaker of the House Paul Ryan has released the "fullest" outline of Republican's healthcare plan.

Ryan said:

> "Well, here it is, a real plan, in black and white, right here. We are officially putting it on the table."

> "Don't force people to buy insurance," Ryan told the crowd.

> "Make insurance companies compete for our business."

> "And, yes," he added, "we're going to help you buy insurance."

Paul Howard, director of health policy at the conservative Manhattan Institute said.

> A major aim of his overhaul is to move people to insurance policies that carry high deductibles. To pay those deductibles and other health care costs, people would have tax-free health savings accounts. The individual, government or employer could contribute to such an account. That could keep premium costs down for young, healthy people.
>
> "Most of the care that most people need for most of their adult lives can be very inexpensive," said Howard.
>
> So rather than spending a lot of money on premiums for insurance they don't need, people could "save" that money for when they do get sick. Howard says people could start young and save for major health problems over time.
>
> "By the time you're 40, ideally, you would have built up a health savings plan that would be partly funded by government sources, plus your own sources, a significant nest egg," he says.

Sabrina Corlette, a professor at the Georgetown Center for Health Policy Reform said:

> "You could be denied a policy because you have diabetes, and the next time you could get coverage again would be when you turn 65 and become eligible for Medicare."
>
> "The effect of it could be to lock a lot of people out who

have pre-existing conditions."

"What Paul Ryan has called for is a much skimpier set of protections so that tax credit buys you a lot less than it would have under the ACA. A key feature of Obamacare is that it spreads the cost of insurance across generations. So healthy young people subsidize older sicker people who use more health care. Ryan's plan would change that," Corlette said.

01-03-17

Senate Republicans took the first official step toward repealing President Barack Obama's signature healthcare law Tuesday afternoon, filing a budget resolution that puts the wheels of overhauling the Affordable Care Act into motion.

Broad legislation to repeal and replace Obamacare would require 60 votes in the Senate, and Republicans don't control enough seats to make that happen or to squash a filibuster by the Democrats.

Republican lawmakers are expected to use the budget process, which is limited to provisions that affect federal revenues and spending and requires only a simple majority to pass.

It would enable Congress to repeal the Obamacare mandates that individuals have coverage and that companies with 50 or more employees provide workers with affordable insurance.

Also, it can do away with the federal subsidies, eliminate funding for Medicaid expansion and cancel a multitude of Obamacare-related taxes.

GOP Sen. Lamar Alexander, the chairman of the Senate
Health Committee, has gone as far as to say that it would be a
mistake to repeal Obamacare before Republicans craft a
replacement.

01-05-17

 Leighton Ku, director of the Center for Health Policy
Research and professor at the Milken Institute School of Public
Health at George Washington University was the lead author
of a report done on repealing Obamacare.

> Up to 3 million jobs in the health sector and other areas
> would be lost if certain key provisions of the
> Affordable Care Act are repealed by Congress, the
> report says.
>
> At the same time, ending those provisions could lead to
> a whopping $1.5 trillion reduction in gross state
> product from 2019 through 2023, according to the
> study.
>
> Repealing key parts of the ACA could trigger massive
> job losses and a slump in consumer and business
> spending that would affect all sectors of state
> economies.

"The immediate and most visible effect of ACA repeal would
be the loss of coverage and access to care for millions of
people who have gained insurance because of the law," said
Sara Collins, vice president for health-care coverage and
access at the Commonwealth Fund.

"This study points to even larger potential economic effects

that would be detrimental to the health and well-being of
millions more," Collins said.

01-17-17

What the Congressional Budget Office report says about
repealing Obamacare (ACA):

> The number of people who are uninsured would
> increase by 18 million in the first new plan year
> following enactment of the bill. Later, after the
> elimination of the ACA's expansion of Medicaid
> eligibility and of subsidies for insurance purchased
> through the ACA marketplaces, that number would
> increase to 27 million, and then to 32 million in 2026.

01-20-17

Within hours of taking the oath of office, President Donald
Trump on Friday night signed an executive order that stated
that the administration's official policy is to "seek the prompt
repeal" of the Affordable Care Act -- but at the same time
emphasized that it must continue to uphold the law.

The order stressed that agencies can "waive, defer, grant
exemptions from or delay implementation of any provision or
requirement" of Obamacare that imposes a burden to States
"to the maximum extent permitted by law."

The order does not change the law, but could have a
significant impact nonetheless.

01-28-17

What was said at the Republican policy retreat in

Philadelphia about repealing Obamacare (behind closed doors):

"We'd better be sure that we're prepared to live with the market we've created" with repeal, said Rep. Tom McClintock (R-Calif.), according to a tape recording of the session which was provided to the Post and other news outlets.

"That's going to be called Trumpcare. Republicans will own that lock, stock and barrel, and we'll be judged in the election less than two years away."

The Anti-environment President

12-05-16

What Al Gore said after Trump win:

> "My message would be that despair is just another form of denial. There is no time to despair. We don't have time to lick our wounds, to hope for a different election outcome. We have to win this struggle and we will win it; the only question is how fast we win. But more damaged is baked into the climate system every day, so it's a race against time."

> Gore said that he hoped Obama and Clinton will join in the effort to call for action to combat dangerous climate change.

Trump, who has called climate change a hoax, has pledged to withdraw the US from the Paris climate accord, dismantle the Clean Power Plan, slash renewable energy funding and somehow prop up the ailing US coal industry.

12-05-16

Activists have spent months protesting plans to route the $3.8 billion Dakota Access Pipeline beneath a lake near the Standing Rock Sioux reservation, saying the project poses a threat to water resources and sacred Native American sites.

President Barack Obama denied a permit for the pipeline last year.

U.S. President-elect Donald Trump on Thursday said for the first time that he supports the completion of a pipeline project near a North Dakota Indian reservation despite media reports that Trump owns a stake in Energy Transfer Partners, the company building the pipeline.

12-13-16

The Washington Post reported:

> Worried that government climate data might disappear under the incoming Trump administration, scientists are beginning to preserve current material on private servers.
>
> The effort includes a "guerrilla archiving" event in Toronto, and the collaboration of scientists and database experts to compile an online site for storage of scientific data.
>
> "Something that seemed a little paranoid to me before all of a sudden seems potentially realistic, or at least something you'd want to hedge against," environmental researcher Nick Santos of the University

of California at Davis told the Post.

Michael Halpern, deputy director of the Center for Science and Democracy at the advocacy group, Union of Concerned Scientists, charged that Trump has appointed a "band of climate conspiracy theorists" to run transition efforts at various agencies, as well as nominees to lead them.

TRUMP ZAP! Usually the President ages fast, with Trump the people are aging fast.

Republicans Stole Supreme Court Seat

11-14-16

What a Slate article said about the stolen Supreme Court seat:

> "The seat that became vacant when Antonin Scalia died earlier this year was blocked by the Republican Party for 9 months for reasons that were transparently false from the outset."

> "At first the senators obstructed the president's pick of moderate Merrick Garland because they claimed Obama was a "lame-duck president" with only a year remaining in his term, and the "people" should be allowed, for the first time in history, to decide for themselves."

> "Later, the reasons for obstruction changed when Senate Republicans began to run on the promise to block any nominees put forward by a Democratic president. Virtually all of those senators won their seats back on the strength of that pledge."

"The only proper response from progressives today must be that Donald Trump is a lame-duck president with only FOUR YEARS left in his term, and we must let the people decide the next justice for the Supreme Court."

"Less fatuously, it must be to obstruct the nomination and seating of any Trump nominee to fill Scalia's seat. We will lose. But that's not the point now.

"Democrats need to repeat Ted Cruz's lie that EIGHT justices will suffice. If Democrats can muster the energy to fight about nothing else, it should be this, because even if you believe the election was fair or fair enough, the loss of this Supreme Court seat was not. That seat is Merrick Garland's."

11-16-16

Feinstein (D-Calif.) ranking member of the Senate Judiciary Committee said:

"After the unprecedented and disrespectful treatment of Merrick Garland — a moderate judge who should have been quickly confirmed — the committee will pay very close attention to proposed nominees to ensure the fundamental constitutional rights of Americans are protected."

"When President-elect Trump is willing to support responsible policies and nominees, I'll hear him out, but this committee has a vital role to protect the Constitution and scrutinize policies, senior officials and judges very carefully, and that's what we intend to do, we simply won't stand aside and watch the tremendous successes achieved over the past eight years be swept away or allow our nation's most vulnerable populations to be targeted."

12-25-16

The New York Times' Christmas Day editorial tags Senate Republicans for "stealing" a seat on the Supreme Court that should have been filled by President Barack Obama.

The Times accuses Republicans of impugning the institutional integrity of the court by a hyper-partisan charade, arguing the justices derive their legitimacy from their separation from the two political branches of government.

"Mr. McConnell and his allies took a torch to that idea — an outrageous gambit that, to nearly everyone's shock, has paid off,"… "But while Republicans may be celebrating now, the damage they have inflicted on the confirmation process, and on the court as an institution, may be irreversible." Said the Times.

TRUMP ZAP! Trump's "First 100 Days" is like a to-do list on Satan's Refrigerator!

11-16-16

Senate Democratic Leader-elect Chuck Schumer of New York said, "Bernie Sanders the Vermont independent will be the chair of "outreach" for Senate Democrats next Congress."

Senate Historical Office said, "He will be the first independent to hold a party leadership position since the modern leadership structure began in the early 20th Century."

"Real change doesn't take place on Capitol Hill," Sanders said in a statement. "It takes place in grassroots America. It takes place when millions of working people, young people and senior citizens come together to demand that our government works for all of us and not just the 1 percent. When the people lead, the leaders follow."

The former presidential candidate will also serve as the top-ranking minority member of the Senate Budget Committee. He said that he will work to ensure the budget "represents the needs of working families and a shrinking middle class, not billionaires."

Sanders said, "He aims to use new leadership role to expand Democrats' grassroots' efforts."

"I was named today part of the leadership, I think my title is to head of outreach efforts and that is something that I take very seriously,"... "so I think again whether it's the Supreme Court, the fight against bigotry, the fight for climate change our job is to bring millions of people together."

"The Democratic Party has got to make it very clear that it is the party of working people in 50 states in this country, not just in New York and California,"… "We've got a lot of work to do," Said Sanders.

Sanders also said, "In almost every instance, we got a strong majority of young people voting for the agenda that I brought forth,"… "My role in the future is to make certain that that agenda that has so much support becomes the agenda of the Democratic Party."

Sanders won more than 13 million votes and 22 states, and raising millions from about 2.5 million donors mostly through small-dollar contributions online in the Democratic Primary.

11-17-16

Sen. Bernie Sanders, I-Vt. told reporters at a Christian Science Monitor breakfast:

> "Mr. Trump campaigned as a populist, campaigned as somebody who is anti-establishment, and I have zero doubt that he received the support of many working class people all across the country because of some of the positions that he took."

> "During the campaign Trump said a lot, and we will find out soon enough about whether what he said was sincere ... our job is to hold him accountable and we intend to do that."

> And, Sanders added, that if Trump keeps his campaign promises and "has the guts" to stand up to corporate America and fight to stop countries from moving

overseas, "he will have an ally with me."

Sanders was also very clear on where he disagreed with Trump, saying, "there are places where there can be no compromise — racism, homophobia, sexism, Islamophobia."

11-18-16

Any efforts by a Trump administration to weaken consumer protection or climate change policies, for example, could lead to conflict between the states and the federal government, attorney general offices in Maryland, Virginia, Washington, Massachusetts, and New York told Reuters. In some instances, that could see them asking a federal judge to block federal action nationwide.

"I view my role as being on the first line of defense against a Trump administration if it chooses to act in an unconstitutional fashion," said Bob Ferguson, the Democratic attorney general of Washington State.

Michael Kelly, a spokesman for Virginia's attorney general, Mark Herring, said that if a Trump administration "crosses the line and pursues actions that are illegal or violate the Constitution, Attorney General Herring will be ready to stand up and defend the rights of Virginians."

"The President-elect has made a number of promises that, if implemented, would violate the Constitution or Massachusetts law," Massachusetts Attorney General Maura Healey said in a statement.

"If the incoming administration chooses to try to act in ways that are unconstitutional, my office will take action to protect the rights and liberties of our residents and our state," Healey said.

Amy Spitalnick, a spokeswoman for New York Attorney General Eric Schneiderman said, "His office will continue to fight to protect New Yorkers' public health, property, and environment, and to lead the coalition of states defending the Clean Power Plan."

On consumer protection, states can both challenge any Trump efforts to loosen regulations and ramp up their own enforcement efforts, said Doug Gansler, a Democrat who served as Maryland's attorney general from 2007 to 2015.

Gansler also said, "If the federal government abdicates that responsibility, the more aggressive and progressive state attorneys general will fill that vacuum."

12-23-16

The UN Security Council passed a resolution 14-0 condemning the construction of Israeli settlements in east Jerusalem and the West Bank. The resolution called continuing construction in the Palestinian territory a "flagrant violation" of international law, and it called on Israel to halt all settlement activities in order to salvage a two-state solution.

The U.S. abstained from the vote, in a departure from past U.S. diplomatic practice of vetoing such a resolution in support of Israel.

U.S. Ambassador to the UN Samantha Power also warned that settlements make it harder to negotiate a separate Palestinian state, which the administration believes is crucial to a lasting peace, CBS News' Margaret Brennan reports.

"The United States has been sending a message that the settlements must stop, privately and publicly, for nearly five decades," Power said.

Trump has vowed to move the U.S. Embassy from Tel Aviv to Jerusalem, potentially putting the U.S. at odds with the Palestinians and almost the entire remainder of the international community.

Trump's pick for ambassador to Israel, Jewish-American lawyer David Friedman, is a donor and vocal supporter of the settlements.

12-30-16

30 mayors from around the country are asking President Obama to tighten immigration protections before leaving office, making it harder for President-elect Donald Trump to undo them.

A group called Cities for Action, sent Obama a letter asking him to offer early renewals to immigrants who have a protected status under his Deferred Action for Childhood Arrivals program.

The program allows young immigrants who were brought to the country illegally as children — or so-called "dreamers" — to remain in the United States without threat of deportation and work legally.

The mayors said Obama should allow them to apply early, before he leaves office, to get their status renewed, and put extra privacy protections in place to make sure their participation in the program isn't used to go after them later.

"We have benefited from President Obama's actions to protect vulnerable immigrants during his time in office. In the wake of the election, many of our residents are uncertain about the future. That's why I am standing with my fellow mayors to thank the President for his leadership and call on him to take additional, lawful steps to help immigrants before leaving office," said, NYC Mayor De Blasio.

"We must stand up against practices that demonize someone based on their faith, race, background or sexual orientation," said, Chicago Mayor Rahm Emanuel.

Boston Mayor Marty Walsh added, his city "is a place of inclusion, a city of compassion, a welcoming, diverse city. We'll stay that way and I hope the federal government will support us in that."

01-12-17

Assemblyman Kevin Kiley has asked the California Attorney General's office to investigate whether legislative Democrats ran afoul of the law by retaining former U.S. Attorney Eric Holder and his law firm, Covington & Burling, for $25,000 per month to do a job that can be performed by state employees.

Mr. Holder was hired last week by the California legislature, which is controlled by Democrats, as outside counsel to provide advice on "our efforts to resist any attempts to roll back the progress California has made" on issues such as CLIMATE CHANGE TO IMMIGRATION.

TRUMP ZAP! Watching Trump is like watching a snake swallow democracy!

NOTES

P13 Diagnostic And Statistical Manual Of Mental Disorders (DSM-IV-TR) American Psychiatric Association

P15 Hunter Walker, "Donald Trump reportedly paid actors $50 to cheer for him at his 2016 presidential announcement," Business Insider, June 17, 2016.

Lyrics to Goldfinger (From Metrolyrics)

P17 Adam Taylor, "Is Vladimir Putin hiding a $200 billion fortune? (And if so, does it matter?) The Washington Post, February 20, 2015.

Glenn Kessler, "No, Putin did not call Donald Trump' a genius. The Washington Post, May 3, 2016.

P18 Jeremy Diamond, CNN POLITICS, December 22, 2015.

Pamela Engel, "Donald Trump just mocked Marco Rubio's supposedly big ears at a rally", Buisness Insider, February 26, 2016.

P19 Sophie Tatum, Rubio on Trump: "He's not gonna make America great, he's gonna make America orange" CNN, February 29, 2016.

P20Tierney Mcafee, "Having trouble stomaching the 2016 election? Wait'll sink your teeth into the latest squabble." People, april 26 2016.

Jenna Johnson, "Donald Trump gets called out for calling Elizabeth Warren 'Pocahontas'" The Washington Post May 26, 2016.

P21 Gabriel Sherman, "Donald Trump's Alliance With the National Enquirer" New York Magazine October 30, 2015.

P22 Tal Kopan, "Sen. Lindsey Graham did not mince words Thursday about choosing between Donald Trump or Sen. Ted Cruze, comparing it to a choice between poision or being shot." CNN POLITICS January 21, 2016.

Sean Sullivan, "Rubio labels Trump a 'con artist,' Trump responds with 'Mr. Meltdown': Debate fight spills onto the campaign trail" The Washington Post February 26, 2016.

P23 Logan Mar, "The images are worth a thousand words: Trump shares an unflattering photo of Ted Cruz's wife" Buisness Insider March 24, 2016.

Nina Strochlic, "The Dumbest Stuff Donald Trump Has Ever Said" The Daily Beast June 30, 2015.

P25 Daniel Chaitin, "Robert Reich: Trump is a 'bully' who 'deserves to be condemned' Washington Examiner March 13, 2016.

Rosalind S. Helderman and Tom Hamburger, "Trump has profited from foreign labor he says is killing U.S. jobs" The Washington Post March 13, 2016.

P26 Joe Crowe, "Michael Hayden: Trump Bigger Threat to National Security Than Hillary" NewsMax March 31, 2016.

Jeremy Diamond, "Abortion and 10 other Donald Trump flip-flops" CNN Politics April 1, 2016.

P27 Bob Woodward and Robert Costa, "In a revealing interview, Trump predicts a 'massive recession' but intends to eliminate the national debt in 8 years." The Washington Post April 2, 2016.

P28 Gideon Resnick, "Trump's Get Rich Seminar Partnered with Couple Prosecuted for Fraud" The daily Beast April 07, 2016.

Alan Rappeport, "That Judge Attacked by Donald Trump? He's Faced a Lot Worse" The new York Times June 3, 2016.

P29 Asawin Suebsaeng, "You Have to Treat 'Em like Shit': Before Megyn Kelly, Trump Dumped Wine on a Female Reporter. Attacking women for doing their jobs is nothing new for The Donald. In fact, it's his M.O." The Daily Beast August 8, 2015.

Chris Kahn, "Half of U.S. women have 'very unfavorable' view of Trump: poll." Reuters March 17 2016.

P30 Alan Rappeport, "Donald Trump Keeps Playing 'Woman's Card' Against Hillary Clinton." The New York Times April 27, 2016.

P31 Thomas B. Edsall, "What Donald Trump Understands About Republicans" The New York Times September 2, 2015.

P32 Allan Smith, "Ted Cruz wants police empowered to 'patrol and secure Muslim neighborhoods' after Brussels attacks". Buisness Insider March 3, 2016.

Tessa Berenson @tcberenson, "Donald Trump Celebrates Cinco de Mayo with a Taco Bowl: 'I Love Hispanics!'". Time May 5, 2016.

Elahe Izadi, "Secret Service to investigate after Trump's ex-butler calls for Obama to be killed". The Washington Post May 12, 2016.

P33 Milo Yiannopoulos, "Why Equality And Diversity Departments Should Only Hire Rich, Straight White Men". Brietbart December 29, 2015.

MST, "Donald Trump, supporters shred New York paper for 'mindless zombies' cover February 10, 2016" EXAMINER.COM February 10, 2016.

Tim Mak, "Donald Trump's Trolls Unleash Hell on Veterans"The Daily Beast February 16, 2016.

P34 David Weigel, Ted Cruz Says He Has Asked the Pentagon for Answers on Jade Helm 15. Bloomberg May 2, 2016.

P35 Teddy Schleifer, "Trump disavows robo-call from David Duke" CNN POLITICS August 29, 2016.

Allegra Kirkland, "New White Supremacist PAC Robocalls: 'Don't Vote For A Cuban,' Vote Trump!" TPM February 24, 2016.

P36 Casey Quinlan, "Trump Plays Dumb On David Duke's History Of White Supremacy. Here's Proof He's Lying." Think Progress February 28, 2016.

P37 "White nationalist robocalls on behalf of Trump in Wisconsin" Fox News Radio April 4, 2016.

Josh Harkinson, "Trump Selects a White Nationalist Leader as a Delegate in California. Meet William Johnson, head of the American Freedom Party." Mother Jones May 10, 2016.

P38 Michael Scherer, "Exclusive: Donald Trump Says He Might Have Supported Japanese Internment." Time December 8, 2015.

Dan Good, "Students in Indiana, Iowa taunt Latinos with Trump-themed insults during basketball games — including 'Build a wall!' chant. Indiana Students Held Trump Cutout, Chanted 'build the Wall'" New York Daily News February 29, 2016.

P39 Aaron Rupar, "Trump Tries To Have It Both Ways On Muslim Ban, Now Says It's 'Just A Suggestion'" Thinkprogress May 11. 2016.

P40 Deputy Politics Editor, "Jimmy Carter: Trump tapped a reservoir 'of inherent racism' Yahoo News May 24, 2016.

Todd C. Frankel, "Why the CDC still isn't researching gun violence, despite the ban being lifted two years ago
Fear and funding shortfalls remain at the CDC, even though the agency was ordered to resume firearm studies after Newtown shooting." The Washington Post January 14, 2015.

P41 Tim Devaney, "Gun lobby pushes to loosen restrictions on silencers" The Hill October 25, 2015.

P42 Reuters, "Donald Trump: I could shoot people on Fifth Ave. and wouldn't lose voters" Newsday January 23, 2016.

Katherine Faulders, "Secret Service Will Not Allow Guns at GOP Convention Despite Petition for Open Carry" ABC News March 28, 2016.

P43 Camerson Joseph, "NRA endorses Donald Trump, to nobody's surprise; candidate takes aim at Hillary Clinton in gun-group convention speech." New York daily News May 21, 2016.

  Jennifer Steinhauer, "Senate Rejects 4 Measures to Control Gun Sales." The New York Times June 20, 2016.

P44 Kyle Mantyla, "Franklin Graham To Save America With Right-Wing 'Prayer Rallies' In All 50 States Before 2016 Election" Right Wing Watch May 12, 2015.

P45 Elizabeth Bruenig, "How Trump Is Romancing the Christian Right. Evangelical leaders have lost control of their flocks." New Republic January 29, 2016.

  "Donald Trump easily won the Nevada Republican caucuses on Tuesday, finishing more than 20 points ahead of Florida Sen. Marco Rubio and cementing his status as the frontrunner for the 2016 GOP presidential nomination." Yahoo Politics February 24, 2016.

  Jason Torchinsky, "God Tells Truck Driver to Strand Bernie Sanders Supporter On Side Of Road "JALOPNIK.COM May 6, 2016.

P46 Brianna Gurciullo, "Billionaire oil tycoon Harold Hamm endorses Trump" Politico April 22, 2016.

P47 Alex Isenstadt, "T. Boone Pickens to host event for pro-Trump super PAC" Politico May 11, 2016.

Peter Feiden, "Readers shine a spotlight on Sheldon Adelson's Trump endorsement" The Washington Post May 17, 2016.

P48 Nolan D. McCaskill, "Mexican president compares Trump to Hitler, Mussolini" Politico March 7, 2016.

Michael Crowley, "Trump fails to impress foreign-policy experts. A speech aimed at boosting his credibility got low marks from across the spectrum." Politico April 27, 2016.

P50 Nick Corasaniti, "Donald Trump Assails U.S. Chamber of Commerce over Trade" The New York Times June 29, 2016.

P51 Maggie Haberman, "Donald Trump, Revoking a Vow, Says He Won't Support Another G.O.P. Nominee" New York Times First Draft March 29, 2016.

Adam Shaw, "Cruz and Kasich join forces against Trump -- but will it work?" Fox News Politics April 25, 2016.

P52 Patrick Temple-West and Jake Sherman, "Boehner backs Paul Ryan for president" March 16, 2016.

Carrie Dann, "Former Speaker Boehner Calls Cruz 'Lucifer in the Flesh'" NBC News Politics April 28, 2016.

P53 Jennifer Stienhauer and Alexander Burnsmay, "Paul Ryan Says He Is 'Not Ready' to Endorse Donald Trump" The New York Times May 5, 2016.

Sean Sullivan, "Sarah Palin says Paul Ryan will soon be 'Cantored'" The Washington Post May 8, 2016.

P54 Paul Kane, "Paul Ryan endorses Donald Trump" The Washington Post June 2, 2016.

P55 Dr. Fienman, "The Political Establishment "Rebellion" in Full Swing in Summer of 2015" The Progressive Professor September 10, 2015.

Robert Reich, "Robert Reich: The establishment is dying The rise of figures like Bernie Sanders and Donald Trump isn't the cause; it's the symptom" Salon February 24, 2016.

Alicia Parlapiano and Gregor Aish, "G.O.P. Delegate System Rigged" The New York Times April 23, 2016.

P56 Alexander Burns, Maggie Haberman and Jonathan Martin, "GOP failing at blocking Trump.Feverish fight to stop candidate could be too late" Times Union February 27, 2016.

Curt Mills, "McConnell on Trump: 'We'll drop him like a hot rock" Washington Examiner February 27,2016.

Adam Edelman, "GOP presidential front-runner Donald Trump is less popular than Nickelback, traffic jams, lice" New York Daily News May 10, 2016.

P57 Dylan Byers, "National Review, conservative thinkers stand against Trump" CNN Politics January 22, 2016.

Alan Rappeport and Jonathan martin, "In an extraordinary public rebuke of Donald J. Trump's campaign, Mitt Romney and John McCain, the last two Republican presidential nominees, denounced Mr. Trump in forceful terms on Thursday and warned that his election could put the United States and even its democratic political system in peril." The New York Times March 3, 2016.

P58 Joan E. Solsman, "GOP and Tech Leaders Hold Secret Meeting to Stop Trump" Yahoo News (The Wrap) March 8, 2016.

P59 Tierney Mcafee@tierneymcafee, "Lindsey Graham Begrudgingly Endorses Ted Cruz for President – But Says He 'Would Not Be My First Choice" People March 18, 2016.

P60 Eric Bradner and Jim Acosta, "Mitt Romney ends recruiting efforts for an independent candidate" CNN Politics May 19, 2016.

  Paige Lavender, "Lindsey Graham Wants Republicans To Unendorse Donald Trump." "If anybody was looking for an off-ramp, this is probably it." Huffington Post June 7, 2016.

P61 Al Tompkins, "Sun Sentinel picks none of the above for Florida primary" POYNTER March 8, 2016.

P62 Kelly Riddell, "N.Y. Daily News shows its true (blue) colors" The Washington Times June 4, 2016.

  Alan Rapport, "Donald Trump Breaks with Recent History" The New York Times May 11, 2016.

P64 Richard F. Miniter, "Wall Street Journal columnist wants teach Republican voters a lesson by defeating Trump" American Thinker May 30, 2016.

  Todd Beamon, "Mitch McConnell: I Fear a 'Goldwater' Scale Loss with Trump" Newsmax June 2, 2016.

P66 Reuters, "Man charged with assaulting protester at Trump rally in North Carolina" Yahoo March 3, 2016.

Geoff Ziezulewicz, Bill Ruthhart and Rick Pearson Contact Reporters, "Chicago Tribune March 3, 2016.

P67 PTI, "Donald Trump 'trafficking in hate and fear': Hillary Clinton" The Economic News March 14, 2016.

P68 Jason Silverstein, "Donald Trump might pay legal fees for man who punched and threatened to kill North Carolina protester." Daily News March 14, 2016.

Donovan Slack, "Ben Carson warns violence at Trump events could escalate" USA Today March 14, 2016.

P69 AP Andrew Welsh-Huggins, "Feds charge Ohio man who tried to rush Trump stage." Yahoo News March 15, 2016.

P70 Larry Celona and Amanda Woods, "Envelope with white powder, threatening note sent to Trump's son." New York Post March 18, 2016.

Caitlin Dickson, "Anti-Trump movement escalates with large protests in Arizona" Yahoo Politics March 19, 2016.

P71 AP Brennan Linsley, "A protester is taunted as he is removed from a Donald Trump rally in Albuquerque" May 25, 2016.

Richard Marosi and Debbi Baker, "Trump praises police for handling 'thugs' in San Diego; 35 arrested" Los Angeles Time May 28, 2016.

P72 Los Angeles Times staff and wire reports, "'Disgusted' police condemn violent protesters at Donald Trump rally in San Jose" Los Angeles Times June 11, 2016.

P74 Steven Shepard, "Trump's poll ratings in a historic hole with most voters viewing him as 'strongly unfavorable,' his image is harder to repair than Hillary's."Politico June 17, 2016.

P75 Asawin Suebsaeng, "Trump Slut-Shames Alicia Machado, Urges People to Watch Nonexistent 'Sex Tape'.The GOP presidential nominee woke up Friday and continued to rail against the 'disgusting' former Miss Universe, whom he has repeatedly attacked for her weight." The Daily Beast September 30, 2016.

   Garance Burke, "AP: 'Apprentice' Cast and Crew Say Trump Was Lewd and Sexist." ABC News October 3, 2016.

P76 Penn Bullock, "Transcript: Donald Trump's Taped Comments About Women." The New York Times October 8, 2016.

P77 Laura Bassett, "Donald Trump: Sure, Call My Daughter A 'Piece Of Ass' He even objectifies Ivanka.The Huffington Post October 8, 2016.

P78 Stephanie Petit, "Teen Beauty Queens Say Donald Trump Walked in on Them Changing When They Were as Young as 15" Peoplepolitics October 13, 2016.

P79 Hallie Jackson and Alex Johnson, "Miss USA Contestant Details Unwanted Encounters with Trump" NBC News October 13, 2016.

P80 Mark Hensch, "Trump: Boycott issue of People magazine with assault allegations" The Hill October 14, 2016.

P81Karen Tumulty, "Woman says Trump reached under her skirt and groped her in early 1990s" The Washington Post October 14, 2016.

P82 Ale Russian, "Trump Boasted of Avoiding STDs While Dating: 'Vaginas Are Landmines … It Was My Personal Vietnam" Peoplepolitics October 15, 2016.

P84 Kyung Lah and Jack Hannah, "Republicans for Hillary?" CNN Politics May 31, 2016.

P85 Ed Mazza, "Hell Freezes Over? Glenn Beck Says Electing Hillary Clinton Could Be A 'Moral, Ethical Choice'
"If one helps to elect an immoral man to the highest office, then one is merely validating his immorality, lewdness and depravity." Huffington post October 11, 2016.

P86 Ines De La Cuetara, "Mitt Romney Loyalists Weigh Trump Support After Utah Retreat" ABC News June 13, 2016.

P87 James Wilkinson, "We have one goal - anyone but Trump': Republican delegates push for 'conscience clause' in last-ditch bid to block Donald Trump" Daily mail.com June 17, 2016.

P88 Daniel Halper, "George Will leaves Republican Party because of Trump" New York Post June 26, 2016.

P89 Oliver Darcy, "George W. Bush reportedly 'worried' he could be 'the last Republican president" Buisness Insider July 19, 2016.

Bret Stephens, "To the Go-Along Republicans. Memo to Paul Ryan: Trump's problem is his character, not his 'ideas.'" The Wall Street Journal August 8, 2016.

P90 Igor Bobic, "Richard Hanna Becomes First Republican Congressman to Say He'll Vote for Hillary Clinton.
Donald Trump "is unfit to serve our party and cannot lead this country," he says." Huffington Post August 2, 2016.

P91 Michael J. Morell, "I Ran the C.I.A. Now I'm Endorsing Hillary Clinton." The New York Times August 5, 2016.

P92 Susan Collins, "GOP senator Susan Collins: Why I cannot support Trump" The Washington Post August 8, 2016.

P93 David E. Sanger and Maggie Haberman, "50 G.O.P. Officials Warn Donald Trump Would Put Nation's Security 'at Risk'" The New York Times August 8, 2016.

 P94 Richard J. Cross III, "GOP speechwriter may vote for Hillary Clinton" The Baltimore Sun August 17, 2016.

P95 Kyle Cheney, "Anti-Trump Republicans to launch swing-state ad buy" Politico August 27, 2016.

P96 Kevin Liptak, Manu Raju and Deirdre Walsh, "Paul Ryan said he won't defend Donald Trump" CNN Politics October 11, 2016.

   Stephen Collinson, Eugene Scott and Eric Bradner, "Donald Trump: 'The shackles have been taken off me' CNN Politics October 11, 2016.

P97 Leigh Ann Caldwell, "Major GOP Donors Are Asking Trump for Their Money Back" NBC News October 12, 2016.

P99 Matt Fuller, "Republicans Threaten Lawsuits over TV Ads Linking Them to Donald Trump, Saying a candidate supports Trump is basically defamation, they argue." Huffington Post October 25, 2016.

P100 Jacob Davidson, "Donald Trump Piñatas Are a Hit in Mexico" Money June 30, 2016.

David E. Sanger and Maggie Haberman, "Donald Trump Sets Conditions for Defending NATO Allies against Attack" The New York Times July 20, 2016.

P101 Sam Stien, "It Appears Donald Trump Doesn't Know About The Crimea Annexation Or Doesn't Care. "He's not going into Ukraine," he says of Putin. Spoiler alert: He's already there." The Huffington Post July 31, 2016.

P103 AP Brian Slodysko, "Pence's unflappability could help Trump stay cool" Indystar July 12, 2016.

Rachel Dicker Associate Editor, Social Media July 14, 2016, "Who Is Mike Pence?Here are 11 things you should know about Trump's likely VP pick." U.S. News November 28, 2016.

P105 Celena Chong @CelenaChong, "Mike Pence, Donald Trump's VP pick: 'Smoking doesn't kill' CNBC July 15, 2016.

Jason Silverstien and Adam Eldelman, "What you need to know about Indiana Gov. Mike Pence, Donald Trump's reported running mate. Trump officially picks Indiana Gov. Mike Pence as running mate." New York Daily News July 16, 2016.

P106 Rebecca Shabad, "Mike Pence in 1999 op-ed: Disney's "Mulan" is liberal propaganda" CBS News July 18, 2016.

P107 Gavin Newsom, "Mike Pence — Conversion Therapy True Believer — Adds More Hate to Donald Trump's GOP Fire" The Daily Beast July 20, 2016.

P108 Jonathan Capehart, "Guess how many African American delegates are going to be at the Republican convention" The Washington Post June 6, 2016.

Alex Isenstadt, "Hardly anybody wants to speak at Trump's convention. POLITICO reached out to more than 50 prominent Republicans. Few said they plan to attend the convention in Cleveland, let alone speak." Politico June 27, 2016.

P109 Jeremy W. Peters, "Emerging Republican Platform Goes Far to the Right" The New York Times July 12, 2016.

P110 Istacker, "Donald Trump called into Fox News during the RNC and competed with his own convention" July 18, 2016.

P111 AP, "Colo., Iowa delegates walk out of convention" Associated Press, July 18, 2016.

P112 Alexandra Jaffe, "Melania Trump Republican Convention Speech Bears Striking Similarities to Michelle Obama Address" NBC News July 19, 2016.

P113 Stephen Dinan, "Imam's closing prayer marred by Trump supporter's 'No Islam' chant" The Washington Times July 19, 2016.

Clyde Hughes, "Queen: GOP Convention Used 'Champions' Against Wishes" Newsmax July 20, 2016.

P115 Theodore Schleifer and Stephen Collinson, "Defiant Ted Cruz stands by refusal to endorse Trump after being booed during convention speech" CNN Politics July 22, 2016.

P117 Sam Frizell, "Hillary Clinton Chooses Tim Kaine as Her Running Mate" Time July 22, 2016.

P117 Sarah Burris, "Elizabeth Warren rips Trump to shreds in Democratic National Convention speech" Rawstory July 25, 2016.

P119 Sandra Sobieraj Westfall and Kathy Ehrich Dowd, "Bernie Sanders Supports Hillary Clinton in DNC Speech Amid Controversy: 'I Am Proud to Stand with Her' People July 25, 2016.

Emily Ngo emily.ngo@newsday.com," Michael Bloomberg on Trump: 'I know a con when I see one' Newsday July 27, 2016.

P121 Mike DeBonis, "Even one of Donald Trump's most ardent Capitol Hill backers is exasperated" The Washington Post June 17, 2016.

P122 Stephen Collinson, "Paul Ryan defends support of Donald Trump" CNN Politics July 12, 2016.

Allison Takeda, "Jeb Bush's Son George P. Bush Urges Republicans to Vote for Donald Trump" US Magazine.com August 8, 2016.

Oliver Darcy, "TED CRUZ: 'I will vote for the Republican nominee, Donald Trump' Buisness Insider September 23, 2016.

P124 Marc Torrence (Patch National Staff), "You can get the baby out of here," he said from the podium. Ashburn Patch August 2, 2016.

Rebecca Morin, "Trump portrays Clinton as mentally unfit for the White House." Politico August 6, 2016.

P125 Cris D' Angelo, "Trump to Dying People: Stick Around Long Enough to Vote For Me "I say kiddingly, but I mean it." The Huffington Post October 6, 2016.

Paul Blumenthal, "Donald Trump Dismantles Teleprompters At North Carolina Rally, The shackles really are off.The Huffington Post October 14, 2016.

P126 Michael Finnegan, "Scorching TV ad targets Trump for mocking reporter's disability" Los Angeles Times June 6, 2016.

P127 Todd Beamon, "Trump: Orlando Shootings Might Have Been Different If Patrons Had Guns" Newsmax June 17, 2016.

P128 John Santucci and Candace Smith, "Donald Trump Says Receiving a Purple Heart as a Gift Is 'Much Easier'" ABC News August 2, 2016.

P129 Tami Luhby and Jim Sciutto, "Secret Service spoke to Trump campaign about 2nd Amendment comment" CNN Politics August 11, 2016.

Eric Thayer/Reuters, "Trump to Supporters: Obama Is 'Founder of ISIS'" The Daily Beast August 11, 2016.

Candace Smith and John Santucci, "Donald Trump Says Hillary Clinton Could Shoot Somebody, Not Be Prosecuted" ABC News September 9, 2016.

P130 Editorial Board, "Mr. Trump's fake charity" The Washington Post July 3, 2016.

P131 David A. Fahenthold Washington Post, "Despite grand shows of generosity, little proof of Trump's big giving" Chicago Tribune October 29, 2016.

P132 Elizabeth Preza, "The 5 Biggest Lies in Donald Trump's Hillary Attack Speech" Alternet June 22, 2016.

P134 Steven T. Dennis, Bloomberg News, "Trump's minimum-wage reversal is latest headache for Republicans" Arcamax July 27, 2016.

P135 Fareed Zakaria, "The unbearable stench of Trump's B.S." The Washington Post August 4, 2016.

P136 The Fixer, "Pence Laughs at Trump's Claim to 95% of Black Support" The Daily beast August 22, 2016.

P137 Abby Phillip and Sean Sullivan, "New questions about Trump's doctor's note create opening for Clinton to fire back on health rumors" The Washington Post August 29, 2016.

P138 Leonard E. Burman, "Donald Trump's tax proposals could double the trade deficit" Tax Policy Center August 29, 2016.

James West, "Former Models for Donald Trump's Agency Say They Violated Immigration Rules And Work Illegally, It's Like Modern-day Slavery" Mother Jones August 30, 2016.

P139 Jeva Lange, "Trump could save a lot of donor money if he stopped paying himself" The Week September 1, 2016.

P140 Kelly Weill, "All they wanted was to hawk some merchandise and money for airfare, but the lawyer for three patriotic girls say all they got was broken promises." The Daily Beast August 6, 2016.

Adam Eldeman New York Daily News, "It was a million dollar shot until it wasn't." The Washington Post September 20, 2016.

P141 Sean Sullivan, "Trump says he ended birther talk to 'get on with the campaign'" The Washington Post September 21, 2016.

P142 Kurt Eichenwald, "How Donald Trump Ditched U.S. Steel Workers in Favor of China" Newsweek October 3, 2016.

P143 Scott Detrow, "Hillary Clinton: Donald Trump 'Temperamentally Unfit' For White House" NPR Politics June 2, 2016.

P144 Bill Hoffman, "Clinton Fires Back on 'Radical Islam': Deeds Matter More Than Words" Newsmax June 13, 2016.

Nolan D. Mccaskill, "Clinton, Warren team up to trash Trump. Warren calls Trump a man 'who wants it all for himself' while Clinton blasts him for controversies he has sparked." Politico June 27, 2016.

P146 Associated Press, "Donald Trump now calls his opponent Hillary 'Rotten' Clinton" New York Post July 25, 2016.

Hannah Fraser-Chanpong, "Hillary Clinton rips into Donald Trump's speech on the economy" CBS News August 8, 2016.

P147 Jennifer Rubin, "Hillary skewers Trump on racism" The Washington Post August 25, 2016.

P148 Elizabeth Landers, "Kaine: Trump 'pushing' KKK values" CNN Politics August 26, 2016.

Daily News Bin, "Lock him up: Donald Trump is once again calling for Hillary Clinton's assassination" The Daily News Bin September 16, 2016.

P149 Brian Stelter, "Buzzfeed terminates contract and refuses to take Trump ads" CNN Politics June 6, 2016.

P150 Allen Smith, "A newspaper that hasn't endorsed a Democrat for president in 7 decades shreds Trump as 'not qualified'" Business Insider Politics September 6, 2016.

P151 Paige Lavender, "After Backing Republicans For Almost A Century, Cincinnati Enquirer Endorses Hillary Clinton" Huffington Post Politics, September 23, 2016.

P152 Daniel Marans, "The paper made a positive case for her candidacy, rather than focus on Donald Trump's flaws." The Huffington Post September 24, 2016.

Reena Flores, "Former GOP Sen. John Warner endorses Hillary Clinton" CBS News September 28, 2016.

P153 Melissa Chan, "Conservative Arizona Newspaper Endorses Hillary Clinton: 'This Year Is Different'" Time Politics September 28, 2016.

The Editorial Board, "USA TODAY's Editorial Board: Trump is 'unfit for the presidency'" USA Today September 30, 2016.

P154 Emily Tate Politics Intern, "After 148 Years, The San Diego Union-Tribune Endorses A Democrat For President. The editorial board fears that Donald Trump could be America's Hugo Chávez." The Huffington Post September 30, 2016.

P155 The editors of The Atlantic, "For the third time since The Atlantic's founding, the editors endorse a candidate for president. The case for Hillary Clinton." The Atlantic.com/magazine nov. issue, October 7, 2016.

P156 Hrafnkell Haraldsson, "For the First Time Ever, Foreign Policy Magazine Endorses a Candidate: Hillary Clinton" Politicus USA October 10, 2016.

P157 Kim Bellware, "Variety Magazine Goes To Bat For Hillary Clinton In First-Ever Presidential Endorsement. The entertainment industry magazine broke with a 111-year-old tradition on Tuesday." Variety November 1, 2016.

P158 Brian Tashman, "Anti-LGBT Pastor Steven Anderson Applauds Orlando Massacre: 'There's Fifty Less Pedophiles In The World'" Right Wing Watch June 13, 2016.

David Francis, "Newt Gingrich Wants to Deport Muslims Who Believe in Sharia. Seriously." Yahoo News July 15, 2016.

P159 Teddy Schleifer, "Trump disavows robo-call from David Duke" CNN Politics August 29, 2016.

Pema Levy, "Alt-Right Movement Presents Its Vision for an All-White Society With Trump Paving the Way. In a bizarre press conference, these white nationalists hailed the GOP nominee's style." Mother Jones September 9, 2016.

P161 Josh Harkinson, "Trump Campaign CEO Was a Big Promoter of Anti-Muslim Extremists. Before Trump hired him in August, Stephen Bannon hosted a daily radio show where many of his guests demonized Islam." Mother Jones September 15, 2016.

P163 Sean Sullivan, "With Skittles tweet, Donald Trump Jr. draws another round of condemnation" The Washington Post September 20, 2016.

"Omarosa Manigault: 'Every Critic, Every Detractor, Will Have to Bow Down To President Trump'. "It is the ultimate revenge to become the most powerful man in the universe." The Huffington Post September 22, 2016.

P164 Reena Flores, "Donald Trump campaign chair in Ohio County resigns over Obama racism remark" CBS News September 24, 2016.

P165 Peter Holley, "An Indiana parade featured a 'disgusting' float showing Donald Trump executing Hillary Clinton" The Washington post October 4, 2016.

P166 Katie Reilly @katiemacreilly, "White Powder at Clinton Campaign Headquarters Found 'Non-Hazardous'" Time October 22, 2016.

Amanda Sakuma, "KKK Paper 'The Crusader' Backs Trump; Campaign Rejects It." NBC News November 2, 2016.

P167 Abigal Tracy, "Rent at Trump Tower Surged after Donald Trump stop self-funding his campaign. A new report shows many of the G.O.P. nominee's campaign expenditures are boosting his own businesses." Vanity Fair August 23, 2016.

Betsy Woodruff and Gideon Resnick, "Donald Trump Mega-Donors Robert and Rebekah Mercer Take Aim at John McCain. The father-daughter duo gives big to an Arizona insurgent who says the former POW 'is directly responsible for the rise of ISIS' and might want to blow up her car, too." The Daily Beast August 24, 2016.

P168 Shane Goldmacher, "Trump shatters GOP records with small donors. 'He's the Republican Obama,' one operative says as Trump monetizes his Republican supporters." Politico September 19, 2016.

Chris Cillizza, "It's already too late for Donald Trump to save his campaign by writing a big check." The Washington Post October 28, 2016.

P169 Adam Edelman, "Donald Trump hires Breitbart News exec Stephen Bannon to lead campaign, promotes pollster Kellyanne Conway in epic shake-up amid plummeting poll numbers." Daily News August 17, 2016.

P170 Sam Lavine, "Paul Manafort Resigns As Head Of Trump Campaign. The latest shakeup in the Trump campaign comes amid reports of Manafort's work with pro-Russian forces in Ukraine." Huffington Post August 19, 2016.

P171 Robert N. Costa, "Trump enlists veteran operative David Bossie as deputy campaign manager." The Washington Post September 1, 2016.

P172 John Santucci and Candace Smith, "Roger Ailes Advising Trump on Debates, But No Formal Campaign Role, Sources Say." ABC News August 16, 2016.

P173 Thomson Reuters, "Trump vows to hit Clinton harder in next U.S. presidential debate." AOL.News September 27, 2016.

P174 Mathew Ingram, "Why Donald Trump's Lies During the Presidential Debate Don't Matter." Fortune September 27, 2016.

P175 Steven A. Holmes, "Reality Check: Trump's debate excuses." CNN Politics September 28, 2016.

P176 Patrick Healy and Matt Flegenheimer, "Hillary Clinton Piles Up Research in Bid to Needle Donald Trump at First Debate." The New York Times September 29, 2016.

Irin Carmon, "Poll: After Debate, Women Think Less of Trump and Better of Clinton." NBC News September 29, 2016.

P177 CBS NEWS N.Y., "Clinton Vs. Trump: Second Presidential Debate Is Coming To A Theater Near You" CH 02 CBS N.Y. October 6, 2016.

P177 Susan Wright, "Battleground State Republicans Have A Message For Trump: GO AWAY" Redstate August 5, 2016.

Tamar Hallerman, "AJC poll: Georgians have more confidence in Hillary Clinton on immigration" AJC.COM August 8, 2016.

P179 Louis Nelson, "Trump lawyer on polls showing him losing: 'Says who?'" Politico August 17, 2016.

P179 Dan Balz and Scott Clement, "A new 50-state poll shows exactly why Clinton holds the advantage over Trump" The Washington Post September 16, 2016.

P180 Sandy Fitzgerald, "NBC News/Survey Monkey Poll: Clinton Holds 6-Point Lead Over Trump" Newsmax October 4, 2016.

P182 David M. Jackson, "Trump's 'African-American' says he isn't a supporter" USA Today June 6, 2016.

David A. Graham, "What Steve King Doesn't Understand About Harriet Tubman. Despite the Iowa Republican's effort to block her, putting Tubman on the $20 bill isn't about political correctness — it's about historical correctness." June 22, 2016.

P183 Mollie Reilly, "Rush Limbaugh: Black Lives Matter Is A 'Terrorist Group'. He also accused Democrats of "seeking to benefit" from police violence. The Huffington Post July 8, 2016.

Denis Slattery, "Donald Trump predicts he'll win 95% of the black vote when he's re-elected in 2020: 'What the hell do you have to lose?'" Daily News August 19, 2016.

P184 Jessy Byrnes, "Trump: 'Hillary Clinton is a bigot'" The Hill August 24, 2016.

P185 The Hill Staff, "Trump's popularity with African-American voters polling at zero" The Hill August 29, 2016.

Michael Barbaro, Maggie Haberman and Yamiche Alcindor, "Donald Trump Embraces Wider Use of Stop-and-Frisk by Police' The New York Times September 21, 2016.

P186 Ron Dicker, "Civil Rights Museum Rejects Donald Trump's VIP Visit Request. Co-founder says Trump team was "bullying us to use the museum in their manner." The Huffington Post September 26, 2016.

MJ Lee and Dan Merica, "Clinton: 'My worries are not the same as black grandmothers'" CNN Politics October 2, 2016.

P187 Jose A. DelRea, "Trump blames Obama for Orlando shooting, blasts Clinton on immigration" Chicago Tribune June 13, 2016.

P188 Michael A. Memoli, "Obama says Trump is 'unfit to serve,' and Trump threatens to walk away from leading Republicans." Los Angeles Times August 2, 2016.

P190 Jennifer Agiesta, "Can a rising Obama help Hillary Clinton?" CNN Politics August 4, 2016.

Edward-Issaac Dovere, "Obama, Holder to lead post-Trump redistricting campaign. The former attorney general heads up a new Democratic effort to challenge the GOP's supremacy in state legislatures and the U.S. House." Politico October 17, 2016.

P191 Christi Parsons, "Obama's campaign mission: Protect his legacy, pummel Republicans — oh, and elect Hillary Clinton." L.A. Times October 24, 2016.

P193 Douglas Guilbeault and Samuel Woolley, "How Twitter Bots Are Shaping the Election. Between the first two presidential debates, a third of pro-Trump tweets and nearly a fifth of pro-Clinton tweets came from automated accounts." Atlantic November 1, 2016.

P195 Craig Silverman and Lawence Alexander, "How Teens In The Balkans Are Duping Trump Supporters With Fake News. BuzzFeed News identified more than 100 pro-Trump websites being run from a single town in the former Yugoslav Republic of Macedonia." Buzzfeed November 3, 2016.

P197 Tal Kopan, "Russian hackers stole Dems' Trump files, firm says" CNN Politics June 14, 2016.

P198 Shane Harris and Nancy A. Youssef, "FBI Suspects Russia Hacked DNC; U.S. Officials Say It Was to Elect Donald Trump" Daily Beast July 25, 2016.

P200 Noah Bierman and Tracy Wilkinson, "Donald Trump invites Russia to hack into Clinton's emails, an extraordinary step for a presidential nominee." The los Angeles Times July 27, 2016.

P202 Mark Hensch, "Trump: I'm 'being sarcastic' about Russia and Clinton's emails" The Hill July 28, 2016.

Reuters in GOA, "Putin dismisses US threat of retaliation over alleged hacking. Russian president says US warnings show Washington is using cyber-attacks as a political tool after Joe Biden says 'we are sending a message' to Putin" The Guardian October 16, 2016.

P203 MJ Lee and Dan Merica, "Clinton campaign wages new war against James Comey." CNN Politics October 30, 2016.

P205 David Corn, "A Veteran Spy Has Given the FBI Information Alleging a Russian Operation to Cultivate Donald Trump" Mother Jones October 31, 2016.

P206 Spencer Ackerman, "'The FBI is Trumpland': anti-Clinton atmosphere spurred leaking, sources say. Highly unfavorable view of Hillary Clinton intensified after James Comey's decision not to recommend an indictment over her use of a private email server. FBI director: new Clinton emails do not show criminal wrongdoing." The Guardian November 4, 2016.

P207 Emily Schultheis, "FBI director to Congress: Still no charges recommended after latest Clinton emails reviewed." CBS News November 6, 2016.

P209 Erin Corbett, "WATCH: Woman at Pence rally calls for 'revolution' if Hillary is elected" Rawstory October 11, 2016.

P210 Allan Smith and Andy Kiersz, "Clinton maintains a huge lead" Buisness Insider October 20, 2016.

Alex Isenstadt, "Panicking GOP makes major last-minute Senate investment. 'We're going to go out guns blazing,' Mitch McConnell ally says." Politico October 25, 2016.

P211 Anthony Salvanto and Kabir Khanna, "Early voting update – an analysis of North Carolina and Florida" CBS News October 26, 2016.

Ben Kamisar, "Trump calls on early Clinton voters to change their ballots" The Hill November 1, 2016.

P212 Mark Berman and William Wan, "Democrats sue Trump, Republicans in four states and allege 'campaign of vigilante voter intimidation'" The Washington Post November 1, 2016.

P213 Derek Hawkins, "No, you can't text your vote. But these ads tell Hillary Clinton supporters to do just that." The news and Observer November 4, 2016.

P214 Nolan D. Mccaskill, "Trump rushed off stage by Secret Service at Reno rally. An unidentified individual yelled 'gun,' but none was found on a man escorted from the crowd, the Secret Service said. Politico November 5, 2016.

P215 Ariane de Vogue, "Democrats falling short on pre-emptive poll-watching lawsuits." CNN Politics November 6, 2016.

P216 CBS News, "Trump campaign's Denver office vandalized twice in same day." November 6, 2016.

   Alexandra King, "Fareed Zakaria: Trump is a cancer on American democracy" Washington Post November 7, 2016.

P221 Christopher Mele and Annie Correal, "'Not Our President': Protests Spread After Donald Trump's Election." The New York Times November 9, 2016.

P222 Rebecca Kheel, "ACLU to Trump: 'See you in court'" The Hill November 9, 2016.

P223 Benjamin Siegel, Donald Trump Tells Protesters 'Don't Be Afraid,' Calls for Hate Crimes to Stop." ABC News November 13, 2016.

P224 Madison Park, Ralph Ellis, Khushbu Shah and Azadeh Ansari, "Anti-Trump protests move through fifth day." CNN November 14, 2016.

P224 Antonio Jose' Viema, "Manhattan Buildings to Drop 'Trump' Name After Petition by Residents." NBC News November 15, 2016.

P225 Mike McPhate, "California Today: Some Opt to Pass on Thanksgiving Politics." The New York Times November 23, 2016.

Teddy Schleifer, "John Lewis: Trump is not a 'legitimate' president." January 14, 2017.

P226 Jason Devaney, "Michael Moore Leads Celebrity Protest Against Trump in NYC." Newsmax January 20, 2017.

P227 Nicholas Hautman, "Who Won the Popular Vote: Donald Trump or Hillary Clinton?" US Weekly November 16, 2016.

P228 Matt Flegenheimer and Michael Barbaro, "Donald Trump Is Elected President in Stunning Repudiation of the Establishment." The New York Times November 9, 2016.

P229 Agency France, "Exploding the 'uneducated white men' myth of Trump's rise to power." Rawstory November 10, 2016.

P231 Nico Lang, "The real reason black voters didn't turn out for Hillary Clinton — and how to fix it.GOP voter suppression efforts are the key to combatting a changing demographic that trends blue." Salon November 10, 2016.

P233 Martin Pengelly, "Hillary Clinton blames Comey letters for election defeat, reports say." The Guardian November 13, 2016.

P234 Fareed Zakaria, "Fareed's Take; The Election of Donald Trump: How it Happened?; The Trump Presidency: U.S. Against the World; Discussion of Iraq Fighting; How Did So Many People Wrongly Predict a Clinton Victory?. Aired 10-11a ET." CNN Transcripts November 13, 2016.

P235 Dan Merica, "Hillary Clinton calls fake news 'an epidemic' with real world consequences." CNN Politics December 9, 2016.

P236 Marc Schulman, "Why The Electoral College" History Central, No Date.

P237 Tom Liddy, "Donald Trump Says Electoral College 'Genius' After Calling It 'Disaster'" ABC News November 15, 2016.

P238 Eugene Scott, "Donald Trump blasts recount as 'ridiculous' and 'a scam'" CNN Politics November 28, 2016.

P239 Susan Page, "Gingrich calls Trump tweet about vote fraud a big mistake." USA Today November 29, 2016.

Emily Schultheis, "Trump campaign objects to Michigan recount: Here's what you need to know." CBS News November 30, 2016.

P240 Reena Flores, "Citing no evidence, Priebus defends Trump's claim on millions of illegal voters." CBS News December 4, 2016.

Amy B. Wang, "Watch Mike Pence try to defend Trump's false claim that 'millions' voted illegally" The Washington Post December 4, 2016.

P242 Steven Porter, "Clinton wins US popular vote by widest margin of any losing presidential candidate.Despite Donald Trump's comfortable win in the Electoral College, which voted on Monday, Hillary Clinton won the popular vote by nearly 2.9 million votes, according to an Associated Press analysis. The Christian Science Monitor December 22, 2016.

P243 The Washington Post Editorial Board, "The clear and present danger of Donald Trump" September 30, 2016.

P244 Jeffrey Rodack, "Trump Not Expected To Live In White House Full Time" Newsmax November 12, 2016.

P245 Chris Isidore, Shimon Prokupecz and David Shortell, "Protecting Donald Trump costs New York City more than $1 million a day" CNN Money November 21, 2016.

P246 Brooke Seipel, "Secret Service in talks to rent space in Trump Tower: report" November 24, 2016.

   Gina Cherelus and Dustin Volz, "Trump Meets With Silicon Valley Tech Titans At His Manhattan Tower.Attendees included Apple Inc's Tim Cook, Facebook Inc's Sheryl Sandberg and Tesla Motors Inc's Elon Musk." Huffington Post Politics December 14, 2016.

P248 Nicole Hensley, "Canadian immigration website crashes as American voters watch Election Day results." Daily News November 9, 2016.

   Emily Flitter, New York "Reuters" November 9, 2016.

 P249 Erica Fuse, "How the 'Trump Effect' Is Making School Hell for Minority Students." Vice November 11, 2016.

P251 Associated Press, "Mayor of West Virginia town resigns after response to racist post about Michelle Obama, official says." L.A. Times November 15, 2016.

P252 Mica Rosenberg and Julia Edwards, "Immigration hardliner says Trump team preparing plans for wall, mulling Muslim registry." Reuters November 15, 2016.

P253 Katie Glueck, "Alt-right celebrates Trump's election at D.C. meeting." Politico November 19, 2016.

   Mazin Sidahmed, "Loretta Lynch: 'a pernicious thread' links rise in hate crimes after US election." The Guardian December 12, 2016.

 P254 Jeffrey Rodack, "Massachusetts Sheriff Offers Inmates to Build Trump's Border Wall." News Max January 5, 2017.

P255 Amanda Sakuma, "Donald Trump '.gov' Transition Website Plugs Firm's Properties" CBS News November 11, 2016.

P256 Steve Eder, "Donald Trump Agrees to Pay $25 Million in Trump University Settlement." The New York Times November 18, 2016.

P257 Jennifer Calfas, "Trump vineyard asks to have more foreign workers: report." MSN News December 22, 2016.

   Vivian Salama, "Not So Fast: Trump Foundation Can't Close While Still Under Investigation." TPM December 26, 2016.

P258 Kevin Liptak, "One President at a time? For Trump, no qualms in contradicting Obama." CNN Politics December 23, 2016.

P259 Reena Flores, "Donald Trump tweets on expanding U.S. nuclear capabilities." CBS News December 22, 2016.

Richard Cowan and Polina Devitt, "Trump praises Putin for holding back in U.S.-Russia spy dispute." Reuters December 31, 2016.

P260 Sophie Tatum, "Law firm representing Trump won Russia award in 2016." CNN Politics January 11, 2017.

P261 Martin Farrer, "Donald Trump suggests he may drop Russia sanctions if Moscow 'is helpful'" The guardian January 14, 2017.

P262 Doug Mataconis, "Ben Carson Forgoes Cabinet Position Because He Believes He Lacks Experience." Outside The Beltway November 15, 2016.

Greg Miller, "Trump's pick for national security adviser brings experience and controversy." The Washington Post November 17, 2016.

P264 Dakin Campbell, "Mnuchin's Bank Accused of Redlining Black, Latino Home Buyers." Bloomberg November 17, 2016.

Ryan J. Relly, "Jeff Sessions Was Deemed Too Racist To Be A Federal Judge. He'll Now Be Trump's Attorney General. He once joked that he only took issue with the KKK's drug use and referred to civil rights groups as "un-American." The Huffington Post November 20, 2016.

P265 Kate Zernike, "Betsy DeVos, Trump's Education Pick, Has Steered Money From Public Schools." The New York Times November 23, 2016.

Joe Neel, "Trump Chooses Rep. Tom Price, An Obamacare Foe, To Run HHS." NPR November 28, 2016.

P266 Coral Davenport and Eric Lipton, "Trump Picks Scott Pruitt, Climate Change Denialist, to Lead E.P.A." The New York Times December 7, 2016.

P267 Noam Scheiber, "Trump's Labor Pick, Andrew Puzder, Is Critic of Minimum Wage Increases" December 8, 2016.

P268 Christopher Dean Hopkins, "What We Know About Rex Tillerson, Trump's Pick For Secretary Of State." NPR December 13, 2016.

P269 Coral Davenport, "Rick Perry, Ex-Governor of Texas, Is Trump's Pick as Energy Secretary." The New York Times December 13, 2016.

P270 Max Greenwood, "Ethics office accuses GOP of rushing Trump Cabinet confirmations." The Hill January 7, 2017.

P271 Bloomberg News, "Team Trump's wealth tops $12 billion as Goldman Sachs' Cohn to be tapped." The Denver Post December 9, 2016.

P272 Anne Gearan, "Trump's secretary of state nominee reveals personal wealth of up to $400 million." The Washington Post January 5, 2017.

P273 Aaron Blake, "It's official: The chief of Breitbart News is headed to the West Wing." The Washington Post November 13, 2016.

 P274 Jennifer J. Jacobs, "Trump Transition Slows as Kushner Said to Oust Christie Allies." Bloomberg Politics November 15, 2016.

P275 David Corn and AJ Vicens, "Here's Evidence Steve Bannon Joined a Facebook Group That Posts Racist Rants and Obama Death Threats." Mother Jones November 18, 2016.

    Chris Sommerfeldt, "Donald Trump appoints Fox News' Monica Crowley to his national security team." Daily News December 16, 2016.

P276 Elizabeth Mclaughlin, "Donald Trump's Pick for US Ambassador to Israel Signals Changes in US Policy." ABC News December 17, 2016.

P277 Jacob Pramuk, "Trump Names Billionaire Carl Icahn as Special Advisor on Regulation, Vows to Shred Obama Rules." NBC News December 21, 2016.

 P278 Us Weekly Staff, "Omarosa Manigault Officially Joins Donald Trump's White House Staff." US Weekly January 4, 2017.

P279 David Smith, "Bannon, Kushner and Priebus: rivals for power at the heart of Trump's team." The Guardian November 19, 2016.

P280 Nolan D. Mccaskill, "Poll: Trump's transition has lowest approval rating in decades." Politico December 14, 2016.

Julian Borger, "White House faces exodus of foreign policy experts ahead of Trump's arrival." The Guardian December 18, 2016.

P281 Eugene Scott, "Trump: 'NOT' a smooth transition after Obama 'roadblocks'" CNN Politics December 28, 2016.

P282 Kim LaCapria, "Did Donald Trump Fire the People in Charge of Maintaining the U.S. Nuclear Arsenal? A report that President-elect Trump had fired the keepers of America's nuclear arsenal caused predictable concern on social media." Snopes.com January 9, 2017.

Jennifer Agiesta, "CNN/ORC Poll: Confidence drops in Trump transition" CNN Politics January 17, 2017.

P283 Elise Labott, "Trump administration asks top State Department officials to leave." CNN Politics January 27, 2017

P284 Fareed Zakaria, "Here's hoping Trump flip-flops even more" The Washington Post Opinion November 24, 2016.

P285 Louis Nelson, "Conway: Judge Trump by what's in his heart, not what comes out of his mouth." Politico January 9, 2017.

P286 Marina Fang, "Trump Ditches His Press Pool Again, Violating Media Protocol. It is setting up a dangerous precedent for press coverage of his administration. Huffington Post November 16, 2016.

P287 Nicholas Loffredo, "Trump's Latest Twitter Target" Newsweek November 19, 2016.

P288 Cara Kelly, "Trump responds immediately to 'Saturday Night Live' skit mocking his tweets." USA Today December 4, 2016.

Jayme Deerwester, "Schwarzenegger tells Trump to get back to work after 'Apprentice' tweet." USA Today January 6, 2017.

P289 David M. Jackson, "Trump responds: Meryl Streep 'a Hillary flunky' (and 'overrated') USA Today 01-09-17.

P290 Louis Nelson, "Trump: I don't like tweeting" Politico January 18, 2017.

Rebecca Shabad, "Trump has declined many intelligence briefings offered to him according to Senate aide." CBS News December 8, 2016.

P291 Phil Helsel, "Trump Says of U.S. Intel: 'I Want Them to Be Sure' About Russia Hacks." NBC News January 1, 2017.

P292 Willa Frej, "CIA Director: Donald Trump's Nazi Germany Comments Are 'Repugnant'. "Tell the families of those 117 CIA officers who are forever memorialized on our wall of honor that their loved ones who gave their lives were akin to." Huffington Post January 17, 2017.

P294 Marcy Kreiter, "Who Gets Top Secret Clearances? Trump Wants His Kids — Donald Jr., Ivanka, Eric — To Have Them." International Business Times November 14, 2016.

Jonathan O'Connell and Mary Jordan, "For foreign diplomats, Trump hotel is place to be." The Washington Post November 18, 2016

P296 Drew Harwell and Anu Narayanswamy, "A scramble to assess the dangers of President-elect Donald Trump's global business empire." The Washington post November 20, 2016.

P298 George Bennett, "Donald Trump gets approval for 64 foreign workers at Mar-a-Lago." Palmbeachpost.com December 6, 2016.

Jennifer Calfas, "Trump's executive producer credit appears in 'Apprentice' premiere." The Hill January 2, 2017.

David Emery, "Reporters weren't allowed to examine stacks of files presented at a press conference by Donald Trump as evidence he was turning his businesses over to his sons." Snopes.com January 12, 2017.

P300 Caitlin Dewey, "Facebook fake-news writer: 'I think Donald Trump is in the White House because of me'" The Washington Post November 17, 2016.

P301 Heather Saul, "Donald Trump gathers media at Trump Tower for 'dressing-down', reportedly tells them: 'We're in a room of liars'" Independent November 22, 2016.

Craig Timberg, "Russian propaganda effort helped spread 'fake news' during election, experts say." The Washington Post November 24, 2016.

P305 Faiz Siddiqui and Susan Svrluga, "N.C. man told police he went to D.C. pizzeria with gun to investigate conspiracy theory." The Washington Post December 5, 2016.

P303 Rebecca Savransky, "Trump team considers evicting press from White House: report." The Hill January 15, 2017.

Emily Tess Katz, "Kellyanne Conway's "alternative facts" comment sparks internet memes." CBS News January 23, 2017.

P304 Adam Entous, Ellen Nakashima and Greg Miller, "Secret CIA assessment says Russia was trying to help Trump win White House." The Washington Post December 9, 2016.

P305 Olivier Knox, "Obama says Reagan 'would roll over in his grave' over GOP fondness for Putin." Yahoo News December 16, 2016.

Dave Boyer, "Obama slaps sanctions on Russia, expels intelligence agents over election hacks." The Washington Times December 29, 2016.

P306 Sean Colarossi, "U.S. Intelligence Report Finds That Top Russian Officials Rejoiced After Trump's Win." Politicususa January 5, 2017.

P307 Ken Dilanian, "Report: Putin, Russia Tried to Help Trump By 'Discrediting' Clinton." NBC News January 6, 2017.

P308 Phil Helsel, "Senate Intelligence Committee to Probe Russian Intel Activities." January 13, 2017.

P309 Reuters, "Trump accuses US spy agencies of Nazi practices over 'phony' Russia dossier." CNBC Reuters January 12, 2017.

Marketwatch, "Russia undoubtedly has the world's best prostitutes, says Vladimir Putin." Marketwatch January 17, 2017.

P311 Itay Hod, "Insiders: Trump Team Dangled Ambassadorships to Lure A-List Inauguration Singers (Exclusive)" The Wrap December 14, 2016.

NBC, "DC-Area Marching Bands Opt to Sit Out Trump's Inaugural Parade. The band at D.C.'s Howard University, which marched in Obama's first inaugural parade, also did not apply to march in Trump's parade." CH4 NBC Washington D.C. December 14, 2016.

P312 David K. Li, "Some Rockettes say they're still being forced to dance for Trump." New York Post December 27, 2016.

P313 AP, "Name of Inauguration Day port-a-potties sparks cover-up." CBS News January 13, 2017.

Stephanie Petit, "'Queer Dance Party' Kicks Off Inaugural with Protest Outside VP-Elect Mike Pence's DC Home." People January 19, 2017.

P314 Steph Solis and Eliza Collins, "More than 60 Democrats are not attending the Trump inauguration." USA Today January 20, 2017.

P315 Maxwell Tani, "'One of the most radical speeches ever given by a president': Jake Tapper reacts to Trump's inauguration speech." Buisness Insider January 20, 2017.

Huff Post, "President Donald Trump Looks At America, Sees Carnage. Light crowds, gloomy weather and protests welcome the new president to the White House." Huffington Post January 20, 2017.

P316 <u>Michael Edison Hayden</u>, "At Least 217 Arrested, Limo Torched Amid Trump Inauguration Day Protests in Washington." ABC News January 20, 2017.

P317 Catherine Pearson, "Thousands Are Knitting 'Pussy Hats' For The Women's March On Washington." Huffington Post January 3, 2017.

P318 Nancy Benac and Ben Nuckols, "Defiant women to Trump: Your agenda won't go unchallenged." AP Politics January 22, 2017.

P320 Daniella Diaz, "Trump team set to do 'Thank America tour'CNN Politics November 17, 2016.

P321 Marina Fang, "Trump 'Thank-You Tour' Revives His Campaign Rallies' Scariest Hits. He told some lies and attacked the media — pretty much like he did before he won the election."The Huffington Post December 1, 2016.

   Katherine Faulders and Paola Chavez, "Trump: Post-Election, Florida Supporters Have Gone From 'Mean and Vicious' to 'Cool and Mellow'" ABC News December 17, 2016.

 P322 Today, "Trump trademarks 2020 campaign slogan: 'Keep America Great'" Today January 25, 2017.

P323 Julia Zorthian, "Record Number of People Sign Up for Obamacare After Donald Trump Elected President." Time November 10, 2016.

   Alison Kodjak, "If Republicans Repeal Obamacare, Ryan Has Replacement Blueprint." NPR November 21, 2016.

P325 M.J. Lee, "Senate Republicans take first step to repeal Obamacare." January 3, 2017.

P326 Dan Mangan, "Obamacare repeal costs: 3 million jobs gone, $1.5 trillion in lost gross state product." CNBC January 5, 2017.

P327 CBO, "How Repealing Portions of the Affordable Care Act Would Affect Health Insurance Coverage and Premiums." Congressional Budget Office January 17, 2017.

Mj Lee and Tami Luhby, "Trump issues executive order to start rolling back Obamacare. CNN Politics January 20, 2017.

Solange Reyner, "Behind Closed-Doors Meeting, GOP Airs Concerns Over Obamacare." Newsmax January 28, 2017.

P328 Oliver Milman, "Al Gore: climate change threat leaves 'no time to despair' over Trump victory." The Guardian December 5, 2016.

P329 Valerie Volcovici, "Trump supports completion of Dakota Access Pipeline." Reuters December 5, 2016.

Cathy Burke, "Scientists Scramble to Save Climate Data Before Trump Takes Office." Newsmax December 13, 2016.

P330 Dahlia Lithwick, "Republicans Stole the Supreme Court Democrats, don't let them get away with it." Slate November 14, 2016.

P331 Mike DeBonis, "Sen. Dianne Feinstein will lead Democrats as they take on Trump's Supreme Court nominees." The Washington Post November 16, 2016.

P332 Kevin Daley, "NYT Says GOP Stole Supreme Court Seat From Obama." The Daily Caller December 25, 2016.

P333 Nicole Gaudiano, "Senate Democrats tap Bernie Sanders to lead outreach." USA Today November 16, 2016.

P334 Jessica Taylor, "Sanders: Trump 'Will Have An Ally With Me' If He Stands Up To Corporate America." NPR November 17, 2016.

P335 Lawrence Hurley, "'First line of defense': Democratic states vow to fight Trump in court." Reuters November 18, 2016.

P336 Julia Boccagno, "UN Security Council votes 14-0 to condemn Israeli settlement construction." CBS News December 23, 2016.

P337 Erin Durkin, "De Blasio, 30 other mayors ask Obama to tighten immigration protections before Trump takes over." Daily News December 30, 2016.

P338 Valerie Richardson, "Hiring Eric Holder to fight Donald Trump violates state constitution, California Republican says." The Washington Times January 12, 2017.

"Trump Zaps:" The Late Show with Stephen Colbert, The Tonight Show Starring Jimmy Fallon, Saturday Night Live, The President Show, Last Week Tonight with John Oliver, and Our Cartoon President.